THE
PROJECTIONIST

The Story of Ernest Gébler

Carlo Gébler

NEW ISLAND

THE PROJECTIONIST: THE STORY OF ERNEST GÉBLER

First published in 2015
by
New Island Books,
16 Priory Hall Office Park,
Stillorgan,
County Dublin,
Republic of Ireland.

www.newisland.ie

PRINT ISBN: 978-1-84840-457-1
EPUB ISBN: 978-1-84840-458-8
MOBI ISBN: 978-1-84840-459-5

Typeset by JVR Creative India
Cover design by Anna Morrison
Printed by ScandBook AB

LOTTERY FUNDED

Supported by the Arts Council of Northern Ireland.

10 9 8 7 6 5 4 3 2 1

22nd June '19

For my mother

&

For Anne, With
my warmest wishes,

from a forgetful

Carlo Gébler

(With apologies!)

'There is properly no history; only biography.'

– Ralph Waldo Emerson

Projection. *Psychoanalysis.* The unconscious process or fact of projecting one's fears, feelings, desires or fantasies on to other persons, things or situations, in order to avoid recognizing them as one's own and so as to justify one's behaviour.

– O.E.D.

Contents

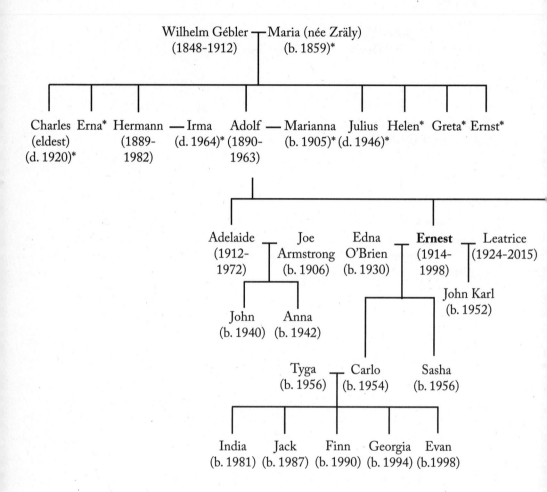

* denotes where birth or death date is unknown.
Every effort has been made to ensure that the family tree is as complete as possible, but the unavailability of certain genealogical records in Ireland has made some omissions of birth and death dates unavoidable.

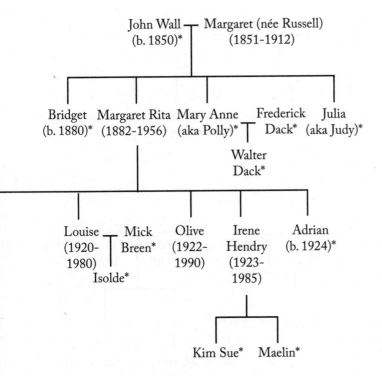

John Wall (b. 1850)* ── Margaret (née Russell) (1851-1912)

Bridget (b. 1880)* Margaret Rita (1882-1956) Mary Anne (aka Polly)* Frederick Dack* Julia (aka Judy)*

Walter Dack*

Louise (1920-1980) ── Mick Breen* Olive (1922-1990) Irene Hendry (1923-1985) Adrian (b. 1924)*

Isolde*

Kim Sue* Maelin*

GÉBLER
FAMILY
TREE

Chronology

1848 Wilhelm Gébler born in western Bohemia (Austria-Hungary).

1850 John Wall born in County Wicklow.

1851 Margaret Wall (née Russell) born County Tipperary.

1859 Maria Gébler (née Zräly) born in northern Bohemia (Austria-Hungary).

1880 Margaret Wall gives birth to Bridget ('Bee').

1882 Margaret Wall gives birth to Margaret ('Rita').

1889 Hermann Gébler born in Bohemia.

1890 Adolf Gébler born in Bohemia.

1905 Marianna Gébler (née Blaschitz) born in Pellau, Austria.

1906 Adolf graduates from the Prague Conservatory and begins work in the Algiers Opera House.
    Joe Armstrong born in Little Mary Street, Dublin.

1907 Rita works as a model at the Irish International Exhibition, Dublin.

1908	Adolf arrives in Dublin, plays at the first night of *The Merry Widow*, and meets Rita. She takes him to her family home, 26 Marguerite Road, Glasnevin.
1911	Adolf performs with the Dublin Orchestral Society at the Antient Concert Rooms, Dublin. The UK census lists him as a boarder at 26 Marguerite Road.
1912	Adolf and Rita marry at St Columba's Church, Dublin. The newly married couple start their life together at 119 Royse Terrace, Phibsborough Road. Wilhelm Gébler dies in Westphalia, Germany. Margaret Wall (Rita's mother) dies in Dublin.
1913	Birth of Rita's and Adolf's first child, Adelaide ('Ada') Armstrong (née Gébler).
1914	Adolf begins working at The Bohemian Theatre, Phibsborough (a cinema). Adolf is arrested and sent first to County Tipperary and then to Oldcastle Aliens' Camp in County Meath. Ernest Gébler born.
1915–1916	Rita and children move to 43 Botanic Avenue, Glasnevin.
1916	Charles Gébler (Adolf's revered older brother) enlists in the French Army.
1917	Charles Gébler wounded on the Western Front and found to have TB.
1918	Adolf transferred to Knockaloe Aliens' Camp, Isle of Man.
1919	Rita Gébler registers with Dublin Metropolitan Police as an Austrian citizen. Adolf signs an 'Undertaking of

Neutrality' in order to return to Dublin, where he meets his son, Ernest, for the first time.

1920   Charles Gébler dies in France.
Mary Louise Breen (née Gébler) is born in Londonderry.
The Géblers move to Germany. Adolf plays with the Berlin State Opera Orchestra while Rita and the children live in Düsseldorf.

1922   The Irish Public Record Office in the Four Courts, Dublin is destroyed. The Gébler family leave Germany and return to Ireland.
Olive Davies (née Gébler) born (probably at 43 Botanic Avenue).
The Géblers move to Sea View Cottage, Rosslare, County Wexford.

1923   Iris (Irene) Hendry (née Gébler) born in Rosslare, County Wexford.
The family move to Church Villa, Tramore, County Waterford, where they are joined by Adolf's elder brother, Hermann.

1924   Adrian Gébler born Tramore, County Waterford.
Leatrice Gilbert, Ernest's future first wife, born in California, USA.

1925   Adolf starts work at the Scala Cinema, Wolverhampton, England, as an accompanist. He later moves to Agricultural Hall Cinema, Snow Hill, Wolverhampton.
Rita and children (Adelaide, Ernest, Louise, Olive, Irene and Adrian) move to England. Adolf secures a council house on the Low Hill Estate, and later buys a house on Old Fallings Road, Bushbury, Wolverhampton. Adolf names the house 'Villa Bohème'.

1928	Ernest Gébler, aged thirteen, begins an apprenticeship as a trainee projectionist at the Agricultural Hall Cinema.
1929	Wolverhampton's first 'talkie', *The Singing Fool*, opens at the Agricultural Hall Cinema.
	Adolf loses Villa Bohème and returns with his family to live on the Low Hill Estate. He takes a grocer's shop and goes bankrupt.
1931–1932	Adolf and Rita, along with Adelaide, Louise, Olive, Irene and Adrian, return to Dublin and live temporarily in Drumcondra.
	Ernest remains in Wolverhampton and continues his apprenticeship, lodging with his aunt Judy and her husband, Frederick Dack, at the Rose & Crown public house in Walsall.
	In Dublin, Adolf plays with the 2RN Orchestra but fails to secure a permanent position there. He becomes bandmaster at the Irish Transport & General Workers' Union.
1932	Gaumont Palace Cinema opens on the Agricultural Hall Cinema site. Ernest resumes his apprenticeship.
1933	Ernest is sacked by the management at Gaumont Palace Cinema, returns to Ireland and rejoins the family, who are now back living at 43 Botanic Avenue.
1934	Adolf and family are allocated a corporation house, 2 Offaly Road, Cabra, Dublin.
	Adolf takes Ernest to meet Hilton Edwards and Micheál Mac Liammóir, proprietors of the Dublin Gate Theatre, beginning Ernest's long association with the Gate.
	Ernest secures a position as projectionist at the Camden Cinema, Dublin.

1936   Adolf buys 3 Cabra Grove, Dublin on a long lease.
        Adelaide meets Joe Armstrong. They move to Bray,
        County Wicklow, and start to live together.

1938   Following an argument with Adolf, Ernest leaves 3
        Cabra Grove and moves to the outskirts of Dublin.

1940   Adelaide's son, John Armstrong, is born in Bray.

1942   Adelaide's daughter and second child, Ann, is born
        in Bray.
        On his way to visit his sister and her new baby, Ernest
        meets Rudolf Jones (born 1917), who publishes
        under the pseudonym 'John Ross'.

1946   The Irish state issues Hermann Gébler a Certificate
        of Naturalization, and he becomes an Irish Citizen.
        Irma, who has been working in Frankfurt, Germany
        since Hermann left for Ireland in 1923, joins her
        husband in Ireland.
        Sampson Low, Marston & Company publish Ernest's
        first novel, *He Had My Heart Scalded*.
        Ernest resigns from the Camden Cinema.
        Marianna moves to Dublin to work, where she meets
        Adolf.

1947   Ernest is issued with an Irish passport and a visa to
        enter the UK.
        Ernest travels to London where he joins Micheál
        Mac Liammóir's niece, Sally Travers, whom he had
        known at the Gate. They live together at 2 Palace
        Gardens Terrace, Notting Hill Gate, and later at 51
        Colet Gardens, Hammersmith, London.

1948   Olive marries Max Davies.

1949   The Abbey Theatre rejects Ernest's play *She Sits Smiling*.

She Sits Smiling is broadcast on the BBC Home Service. Ernest returns to Dublin for a holiday, leaving Sally Travers in London.

1950   In early January, instead of returning to London and Sally, Ernest decides to stay in Dublin with Leatrice Gilbert, who is sick. Later, Ernest and Leatrice move to a cottage at Ballinabrocky, Glendalough, County Wicklow.

Rita leaves 3 Cabra Grove and Adolf, and moves in with her married daughter Olive Davies. Marianna moves into 3 Cabra Grove to work as Adolf's housekeeper.

Ernest's novel *The Plymouth Adventure* is published in New York.

In the autumn Ernest and Leatrice travel to New York separately. On 12 December Ernest and Leatrice marry.

1951   Irene marries Jim Hendry in London.

Ernest buys Lake Park, Roundwood, County Wicklow at auction, and shortly thereafter Ernest and Leatrice move in.

John Karl Gébler (later known as John Fountain) born at Lake Park in July.

1952   Ernest, Leatrice and John Karl set sail for America. In March, Ernest, Leatrice and John Karl enter the US at San Pedro, California. In mid May, Ernest, having agreed to sell Lake Park and wind up his affairs in Ireland, leaves the US and returns to Ireland.

Leatrice writes to Ernest in June informing him that John Karl is not his son and that she plans to divorce him.

Leatrice is granted a divorce from Ernest by a court in the USA in October. She marries John

Fountain on 10 November. On 14 November the film *The Plymouth Adventure*, based on Ernest's novel and starring Spencer Tracy, opens in the US.

Ernest meets Edna O'Brien.

1954   Ernest and Edna marry in July, and Carlo Gébler is born in August.

1956   Ernest sells Lake Park and buys 29 Garville Avenue, Dublin.

Sasha Gébler is born.

In October Rita returns from her daughter Louise Breen's, where she has been living, to 3 Cabra Grove, where she is nursed by Adolf and Marianna.

Rita dies in December. Louise, encouraged by Adelaide, alleges that Rita has died of unnatural causes. A post-mortem on Rita's body follows. Adolf and Marianna are interrogated by the police.

1957   A public inquest concludes that Rita was not poisoned by her husband and his housekeeper as was alleged but died of natural causes.

Adolf and Marianna marry in April.

A dramatization of *The Plymouth Adventure* is broadcast on the BBC Home Service.

Adolf and Marianna emigrate to the US in December.

1958   Adolf and Marianna arrive in San Francisco in January.

A Week in the Country by Ernest Gébler is published.

Ernest, Edna, Carlo and Sasha move from 29 Garville Ave to 257 Cannon Hill Lane, Morden, London, SW20.

1960   *The Country Girls* by Edna O'Brien is published.

1961 *The Love Investigator* by Ernest Gébler is published.

1962 *The Lonely Girl* (renamed *The Girl with Green Eyes*) by Edna O'Brien is published.
Edna O'Brien is obliged to quit the matrimonial home in September.

1963 Irma Gébler (Hermann's wife), dies in Waterford.
Adolf Gébler dies in San Francisco, USA in July.
Edna O'Brien buys 9 Deodar Road, Putney, after which Carlo and Sasha divide their time between their parents' houses.

1964 Edna O'Brien buys 87 Deodar Road, Putney.
Ernest and Phyllis 'Jane' Innot meet and begin a relationship.

1965 *August is a Wicked Month* by Edna O'Brien is published.
Edna O'Brien is granted full custody of her sons.

1966 Ernest's TV play *Why Aren't You Famous?* is broadcast in February and repeated in August.
Ernest's TV play *Where Shall I Find What Will Change My Life?* is broadcast.

1967 Ernest's TV play *Call Me Daddy* is broadcast.
Ernest is granted a decree nisi.

1968 *Call Me Daddy* wins the 1968 American Academy of Arts and Science Award, the Emmy, for the Best Entertainment Programme in the International Division.
Ernest's TV play *Women Can Be Monsters* is broadcast in November.

1969 Peter Sellers agrees to star in *Hoffman*, the film version of *Call Me Daddy*. Ernest is offered £21,000 for the

Hoffman rights and the script. *Shall I Eat You Now?*, his novelization of *Call Me Daddy*, is published in the UK and in the US.

Hoffman is filmed in September. Ernest is banned from the set.

1970   Ernest sells 257 Cannon Hill Lane in January.
Ernest and Jane arrive in Dublin in March, intending to settle in Ireland.
Ernest buys *Cnoc Aluin* (92 Coliemore Road, Dalkey) in April. He and Jane move into the house in May.

1972   Adelaide Armstrong dies.

1975   Ernest's stage play *A Cry For Help* is produced on the Peacock Stage at the Abbey Theatre.

1977   Ernest buys 5 Leslie Avenue, Dalkey, at auction.

1980   Louise Breen dies.

1982   Hermann dies in Waterford, aged ninety-three.

1983   Jane moves out of the bedroom she shared with Ernest.

1985   Ernest finishes his last novel, *Not The End Of The World*. It is rejected by the London agent, Christine Green, and Doubleday in New York.
Irene Hendry dies in New Zealand.

1986   Sally Travers dies in London. Jane leaves Ernest, goes to England and takes a job in a school in Highgate, London. Ernest commences work on his 'Autobiog'.

1987   Jane returns to Ernest in Dublin.

1989   Ernest agrees to marry Jane. On 5 May, Jane suffers a brain haemorrhage in the garden of *Cnoc Aluin*, dying on the following day.

1991   Ernest enters the Grove Nursing Home and *Cnoc Aluin* is sold.

1995   John Fountain (née John Karl Gébler) visits Ireland and meets Ernest, whom he has not seen since 1952. He subsequently changes his surname back to Gébler and moves to Ireland.

1998   Ernest dies.

2000   *Father & I* by Carlo Gébler is published.

2015   Leatrice Gilbert Fountain dies.

A Note

This is an unauthorized life. Readers should bear in mind that had the subject (my father) been given a choice he would never have allowed the writer (his estranged son) to tell his story.

Many of the characters in this story either spelt their names in different ways or had several names. For clarity's sake I've opted for one preferred name and used this throughout. Some names have also been changed. This is the limit of my inventions, and otherwise I've only included what I believe to be true. Of course I'm sure that inaccuracies and even lies must have slipped in without my realizing. How could they not?

The *O.E.D.* describes a story as 'A recital of events that have or are alleged to have happened.'

What follows is just that. It is a recital of the events of my father's life that have or are alleged to have happened.

1.

Beginnings

I'm fortunate that a photograph of my Gébler forebears has come down to me. It's black and white. It was taken, I'd guess, in 1908 or 1909. I don't know where. A studio in Prague perhaps, or a provincial Bohemian or south German town. Whatever the location, the setting is unmistakably middle European, high bourgeois. On the floor in front of clan Gébler there's a hideous fur rug (of the kind you might see in a 1960s' German porno, a couple writhing atop it, a fire burning merrily behind, the firelight reflecting off their oiled limbs). On either side of the Géblers there are fussy tables with doilies and flowers. Behind them are heavy drapes and a kitsch landscape (add a naked nymph and it too could be in a porno).

There are ten in the picture – my two paternal great-grandparents and their eight children: going from left to right they are Helen, Julius, Adolf, Gretel (or Greta), Hermann, Ernst, Charles and the eldest, Erna – and they are posed in two semicircles. In the one at the rear stand the four hulking older Gébler men: Julius, Adolf (my grandfather), Hermann and Charles. They're all in suits and collars and ties, though my grandfather, in evidence of his theatrical leanings, also sports a brocade waistcoat. The other thing that strikes is the posture adopted by Charles (the second eldest, a violinist, a pianist, and I think a medical doctor): he has his arms crossed, and he stands slightly apart from everyone else. He looks semi-detached.

In a semicircle in front of the hulking sons are the other family members, seated. These are the three Gébler daughters (two, like Romanov princesses, wear white summer dresses and sport matching white bows in their hair, while the third is in sombre black), the baby, Ernst (his head shaved, he looks like a manikin), and the parents of the eight children the picture features. My great-grandfather looks like a middle European patriarch as supplied by Central Casting: he has a big head and a white beard. His wife, my great-grandmother, wears a white blouse and (I think) a locket around her neck, the sober dress of a sober *hausfrau*. She also looks older than her husband, when actually she's younger. She looks sad too, like she's been through the mangle.

The faces that look back at me from this photograph all seem familiar. It's partly that I see the Gébler family look (big noses and high foreheads) in these faces (though perhaps I see this because I want to and not because it's actually there), and partly because these faces remind me of the faces that look back at me from the photographs taken by that great contemporary documenter of everyday German life, August Sander (1876–1964). But then that's hardly surprising: these Géblers were just the sort of solid, provincial, resolute and absolutely rooted people Sander photographed.

My father's grandfather, Wilhelm Gébler (he of Central Casting), was born on 2 May 1848 in Schluckenau, a town located inside a little hook of Bohemia (then Austria-Hungary) that pokes up provocatively into Saxony. His ancestors were Armenians who settled in German speaking Bohemia, which later become Sudetenland before reverting to Czechoslovakia.

My father's grandmother and Wilhelm's wife (she of the sad face) was Maria Gébler, née Zräly. She was born on 21 May 1859 in Königinhof in eastern Bohemia, also in Austria-Hungary. The Zrälys were teachers and professors and Slav patriots, and did not like the Germans or Austrians. Severin Zräly, a relative of Maria's, hacked off his firing fingers so he would not have to serve in the Austro-Hungarian Army. He pretended it was an accident, but he was found out, put in a fortress for several years, and afterwards emigrated to the US, where he got into shipping and made a fortune. Maria asserted her Czech identity more gently by insisting that the Czech feminine of her married name, Géblerova, was used in all communications. As a person, she was supposedly not melancholy (as she seems to be in the family portrait) so much as chilly, even severe. Of course, this may have just been how mothers were at the time, and in this she was not alone. Ultimately, I do not know.

II

According to some reports, Wilhelm was a gynaecologist, and according to others he was a tax collector or an accountant. He probably lived and worked in Teplice-Šanov in western Bohemia, close to Germany, and at some stage he acquired part-ownership of a musical instrument factory in Markneukirchen, a German town just over the border in Saxony, where something like 80 per cent of the world's instruments were made by 1900. According to family lore, Wilhelm won his share in a game of cards.

The factory made woodwind instruments (oboes, flutes, clarinets), and most of the factory's output was sold either in Germany or Austria-Hungary. Because their market was so German, and he was now an entrepreneur with manufacturing interests, Wilhelm reconfigured his half-Czech family as a wholly German one, and insisted that everyone embrace German language and culture. Perhaps this was why Maria Géblerova looked so sad when her photograph was taken: it was a sacrifice to renounce her Slav identity. As part of this process my father's father, who was born on 2 April 1890 and who was named Adolphe or sometimes Adolphus, became Adolfe, and finally Adolf.

At first he didn't mind. He was young. He was flexible. His father was right, he thought. He saw that this embrace of things German was good for business. He saw how the factory prospered, and as it prospered he saw how wealth was generated, and as wealth was generated he saw that the family's place within the bourgeoisie was secured and enhanced.

As Adolf grew older, however, his acquiescence was challenged by his elder brother, the outlier in the group photo. Charles was a Slav nationalist, and believed in an independent Czech state where Czech was the state language. He also believed that the Géblers were the worst sort of Czechs because they forfeited their ethnicity and linguistic identity for social and material advantage. The rewards of the switch to German were huge, but according to Charles these did not compensate for what was lost. As he had it, to surrender one's authentic Czech nature and assume German identity was a terrible mistake.

As he grew older, Adolf, who worshipped Charles, began to adopt his elder brother's beliefs as his own, and inevitably his identifying with the Czech cause entailed an amount of anti-German sentiment. This was why, later, when Adolf was in Ireland, whenever someone assumed he was German (hearing him speak in his appalling heavily accented English, this was an easy assumption to make), he always threw back at them the same mangled corrective: 'No German, no! Czech ... Bohemia ... Bohemia ... Czech.' But this was in the future.

III

Adolf was sent to the Prague Conservatory in his teens, a school for the musically gifted that offered a rounded, and by contemporary standards, exemplary, education. At the conservatory, as well as his French and Italian and general education lessons, plus his composing, arranging, music theory and conducting classes, it was compulsory to study and master three instruments. Most students opted for three complementary instruments – violin, viola and cello were a typical combination. Adolf, however, opted for clarinet, piano and violin, which was much harder because the instruments were not complementary. He also played in the conservatory's orchestra and other ensembles.

Adolf graduated in 1906 when he was sixteen, although typically students didn't graduate until they were seventeen at the earliest, with a high commendation for his clarinet technique and high grades in composition and music theory. In recognition of his son's precocity and talent, Wilhelm gave him a gold pocket watch of the kind that's worn with a chain in a waistcoat pocket. It was a Hunter with a glass porthole in the lid, which allowed the time to be read without releasing the cover. In time this watch would assume heirloom status.

With his qualification he secured work as a clarinettist on a production of Puccini's *Tosca* in Algiers, and travelled to the North African city, then under French control. Two things so impressed him that he never forgot them. One was the reek of coffee in the hot streets. The other was the girls he saw everywhere, plump, shy, olive-skinned, their eyes large, dark and alluring. This North African port city was very different to the places he knew, Bohemia and Prague, and it was thrilling.

Rehearsals began in the Algiers Opera House in Place Bresson. He attended and he was diligent, but he did not experience the emotional power of the music. It didn't touch him.

Then came the first night. During the scene in Act 2 when Tosca, in Scarpia's apartment, hears her lover, Caravadossi, being tortured in the nearby cell, quite unexpectedly Adolf began to cry, and he had to play on with tears running down his face. Fortunately, he knew the music off by heart.

Later in the run, his emotions now mastered, it was the glittering women up on the stage that engaged him. In performances, during those bars when he didn't play, he didn't rest his eyes like the other orchestral players on the score as he waited for his cue: he rested them on the women on stage instead. Their beauty amazed him, though he knew that their allure was mostly the product of lighting and make-up. He never approached or spoke to any of them, however, although as a member of the company he might have. He did not think he was attractive, and never would, which was perhaps why he settled for what he got.

IV

The next part of Adolf's life was complex and elusive, but there is one bright thread that can be got hold of, and that is Franz Lehár's *The Merry*

Widow, a heady, even saucy, opera about middle-aged love that in the years before the outbreak of the First World War was all the rage in Europe.

The Merry Widow had been running in Daly's Theatre, London, since 1907, with Lily Elsie in the role of the widow, Sonia Sadoya, which was the idea of Daly's manager, George Edwardes. The role made Lily Elsie a star, and was her greatest success. Edward VII came to see her four times.

Sometime in 1908, Edwardes agreed to bring the production, with Lily Elsie in the widow role, to the Gaiety Theatre in Dublin during Horse Show Week. A genius at marketing, he warned the Gaiety's management to issue their usherettes with smelling salts for the duration of the run in order to revive the numerous women who, he predicted, ravished by Lehár's music, would faint and need reviving.

Adolf was contracted to play first clarinet during the Gaiety run. Whether he'd had any part in the London performances isn't clear, but the Gaiety job is a fact. But then (the best laid plans, et cetera) he had an accident in Paris. The door of a railway carriage got closed on his right hand, crushing the tip of his index finger. Without a functioning right forefinger he could not play the clarinet. The injury also affected his ability to play the piano. For a musician, it was a disaster.

Adolf went to a doctor. The medic washed his forefinger in disinfectant, but that was all. The doctor thought, though he didn't know for sure, that the bone tip might be splintered. He wouldn't undertake to fix the finger, and advised his patient to seek specialist help.

Adolf's people in Bohemia sent him money.

He returned home.

His father, Wilhelm, took his son to a specialist. This doctor said that he could get the bone to reattach and grow back with a regime that included daily massages and simple hydrotherapy – immersion of the injured finger in hot and cold water – and that it would be painful. Adolf agreed to the treatment – what alternative did he have? The work to restore his finger began.

2.

Adolf's Arrival, Dublin

I

There was a dress rehearsal of *The Merry Widow* in the Gaiety Theatre in Dublin on Monday 23 August 1908. Adolf wasn't at it because he missed his train connection (Paris again), and it was not until Tuesday 24 August, the day *The Merry Widow* opened, that he got to Liverpool Docks, from where he would catch the boat to Ireland. He was not worried that he had missed the dress rehearsal – the confidence of youth, perhaps – plus he knew his part, and his sight-reading was exemplary. What worried him was his finger, which was not yet completely right.

He boarded the Dublin packet. He had two suitcases: one held his boiled shirts and evening dress, the other his two clarinets. The vessel cast off and steamed out onto the Irish Sea. A few months earlier he may never have heard of Dublin, but because he was heading there he had decided to read up on this city. He had brought along a clipping from a German newspaper, and he read it as the vessel lurched westwards. The article comprehensively described Dublin's history, from its foundation in the ninth century by Vikings, through its incorporation into the English Crown as the Pale, its centuries as the most faithful of English settlements in Ireland, right up to the present, when it was known as the United Kingdom's second city.

The packet entered Dublin Bay. He took himself to the prow to get a look at where he was headed. He saw a thin green slip of land, and behind that he saw mountains, dark, lovely and graceful. Something in his psyche shifted. He was not to know it at the time, but a love affair had just begun.

II

The packet tied up in the harbour of Kingstown – as Dun Laoghaire was then known. He had to get to the theatre before the curtain went up. He hurried down the gangplank, along the pier and into the Kingstown Railway Station. He had 'Yes', he had 'No', and perhaps he had a few rudimentary English phrases, but nothing more.

As he entered the booking hall he extracted from his pocket the piece of paper on which he'd written 'Gaiety Theatre' in his looping German script, and when he reached the grille, which separated ticket buyer from ticket seller, he proffered this paper to the clerk in his railway livery on the other side. The clerk glanced at the paper, issued a single ticket to Westland Row, took the stranger's money and directed him to the 'up' or city platform.

Adolf followed the directions.

A train belonging to the Dublin and South Eastern Railway (DSE) appeared, and he boarded. The carriage was crowded with boisterous people, and there was a strong smell, half saline, half human. His train arrived at Westland Row. Passengers swarmed off, and he followed. He found his way out into Westland Row itself. Like the train, the street was crowded, the atmosphere febrile. As James Joyce wrote:

There is one gay week every year in the Dublin calendar, the last week of August, in which the famous Horse Show draws to the Irish capital a vari-coloured crowd, of many languages […]

> For a few days the tired and cynical city is dressed like a newly-wed bride. Its gloomy streets swarm with feverish life, and an unaccustomed uproar breaks its senile slumber.[1]

He realized that the city was so crammed it might be difficult to find digs later, but there was no time to worry about that now. He *had* to get to the theatre.

He showed his piece of paper to someone. He was directed along Nassau Street, up Grafton Street and down Tangier Lane, a malodorous entry that delivered him right to the stage door of the Gaiety.

He went in, and found the stage door keeper in his little room behind the stage door. Adolf waved his clarinet case or pronounced '*Merry Widow*', and was directed to the green room set aside for the orchestral players. He changed into evening dress.

The audience filed into the auditorium. It was not only a first night, but also the very first night that Dublin would see this risqué confection, and the crowd had high expectations. There was a full house.

Bells sounded backstage and stage managers shouted. 'The performance will begin …'. Adolf took his seat in the orchestra pit. He warmed up his clarinet. His reed had been pared with a razor to the perfect thickness and broken in. He played a few scales. The sound he made was warm and rich. He felt a twinge in his finger.

The house lights dimmed. The auditorium fell quiet. The baton rose in the pit. The conductor surveyed his players' ghostly faces, then moved his head, and the first note sounded. Adolf's first cue arrived and he started to play. Yes, he felt some pain, but he played on. After all, he was a professional.

The interval. The audience rose. Adolf massaged his finger backstage, or perhaps he went to Neary's public house on the other side of Tangier

---

1   Joyce's article (entitled 'La Battaglia fra Bernard Shaw e la Censura' – 'Bernard Shaw's Battle with the Censor') is reprinted in *The Critical Writings of James Joyce*, ed. Ellsworth Mason and Richard Ellman (1959).

Lane. It was traditional for Gaiety musicians to drink during the interval in Neary's, and Adolf did drink, so my guess is that he respected tradition.

The musicians returned to their places in the pit, and the audience to their seats. The lights dimmed, the baton rose again, and *The Merry Widow* resumed. Adolf's finger still hurt, but he played on to the end. The curtain fell.

Though no women were reported to have swooned, and the smelling salts, if ever issued, had turned out not to be needed, the audience, overwhelmed by the sentimental conviction of the story, smitten by Lily Elsie's singing and intoxicated by Lehár's music, applauded heartily. Then the house lights came up and everyone rose from their seats and flowed into the aisles, heading for the exits like a tide going out.

III

Upstairs in the Gaiety, some of the dress circle audience drifted into the dress circle bar for a final nightcap. Here, the barmaid, Margaret Wall, known as Rita, a thin, light, small-breasted woman with a nice face, grey eyes, light-brown hair, pale, clear skin and a wide brow, served them deftly. Her look was a delicate late-Victorian one, and everyone liked her, particularly men. She had a way of making them feel that they should protect her. Her take-home pay was ten bob a week, plus tips.

Back in the orchestra pit, Adolf disassembled, cleaned and put away his clarinet. He tidied away his sheet music. He went back to the green room and changed out of his evening dress and in to his travelling suit. He'd nowhere to sleep, but in Europe it was customary for musicians, if they'd no alternative, to overnight in a theatre box. That was now his plan.

In the dress circle bar, now empty, all customers having left, Rita Wall washed glasses, wiped down surfaces, and positioned tables and chairs. This bar was really a set, and it needed to be dressed for the next performance. That job done, she began to count the evening's takings. It had been a busy night.

The theatre was quiet now. The main lights were off, and the small fire-regulation lights, which had to be on by law whenever everything else was off, were on, and everything touched by their yellow light looked ghostlike.

In the green room Adolf judged it was now safe to make his move. He took his suitcases and padded quietly from backstage to the foyer. Here were the stairs. He began to climb. At the top was the circle. The boxes were off the circle.

He got to the top, stopped, peered ahead, let his eyes adjust, pointed himself towards the boxes and set off again. According to family lore it was the royal box with its abundance of silken cushions that was his intended sleeping spot. To me that sounds like an invention.

In the circle bar, meanwhile, Rita was at the till. The evening's takings had gone down to the manager, and she was checking the next day's float. When she had the money totted up she put it in the till, then locked it.

The bar's doors were open, giving her an unimpeded view of the landing outside. Whether she was actually looking out at the moment Adolf padded past, or whether she noticed movement out of the corner of her eye and was surprised because nobody should have been moving around up there at this time and so looked up, I don't know. But, whatever the case, she hurried after the stranger and stopped him. This was the moment when, according to family mythology, he met his doom and she met hers.

3.

Adolf and Rita's Meeting

I

So what happened? He was a Bohemian who spoke German. She was a Dubliner who spoke English. A nice situation: both spoke the languages of their country's powerful neighbours, some would say oppressors, but not each other's. They couldn't talk to each other. Not a hope. But Rita had the advantage. This was her town, her theatre, not his. She was also twenty-six to his eighteen.

I imagine that a lot of gesticulating and pointing followed. Rita spoke her northside English, Adolf spoke his pitiful pidgin. Rita noticed the cases Adolf carried and pointed to them. They identified him as being of no fixed abode. Adolf grasped her meaning. He pressed his hands together then folded his head onto them, as onto a pillow, the universal symbol of sleep, and then he pointed in the direction of the theatre's boxes. Rita understood. She shook her head, 'No, no.' She was emphatic. He couldn't sleep in a box, she explained – out of the question.

She took his arm, and he let her lead him down the stairs, through the theatre and all the way to the stage door, where the stage door keeper sat in his little office. He was in charge. He would settle this matter.

Rita explained. She'd found the young man beside her in the circle heading for a box. He was going to sleep in it.

'No, no,' said the stage door keeper. No one was allowed to sleep overnight in the theatre. It was against fire regulations.

The next bit of the story was awkward. Adolf was told to go, and Rita was ready to go. Both went out into Tangier Lane. Rita, one imagines, went quickly, she wanted to be off, and Adolf went slowly.

Rita, who had to get home, now strode towards Grafton Street, where the tram stops were. At the top of Tangier Lane she stopped and looked back at the stage door, where Adolf stood pondering. She wondered if he would be able to get a bed. No, she thought, which meant the street for him, and if she hadn't intervened he might be snoozing in a box at that moment, and would that really be so terrible?

She walked back to him. She pressed her hands together and laid her head on them, reprising the universal symbol of sleep. She would take him back with her, she said, to the family home on the northside. Adolf understood her mime, if not her words. He accepted. What else was he to do?

They caught her tram to Nelson's Pillar in the middle of O'Connell Street and then a second to Glasnevin. They got out at her stop. She offered to carry one of his bags, and he gave her the case with his clarinets as it was the lightest. They walked through the gaslit streets to 26 Marguerite Road, home of the Wall family. She opened the door and ushered him forward. He went in. She followed and closed the door behind them.

II

A minute or two later, introductions completed, the parties took the measure of each other.

This was what Adolf saw:

Rita's father was a patriarch with a beard, and looked a bit like the recently dead King, Edward VII. Rita's mother looked old to him, but friendly.

Bridget ('Bee'), Rita's eldest sister, had a wide face, a wide mouth, dark eyes and a swarthy complexion, and didn't look remotely like her. But the other two, Mary Anne and Julia, who were younger than Rita, both dainty, frail and bird-like girls, did. Adolf was told (though he didn't necessarily follow) that Bee was a waitress at the Red Bank Restaurant, where she had good tables, so got good tips, and besides her wage, got eggs and bacon every Saturday to take home, and that Mary Anne and Julia also worked. John Wall insisted. There were no slouchers allowed in his house.

And this was what the Wall family saw:

A youth, eighteen years old. He was five feet ten and a half in his socks. He had an athletic body. His face was a bit bulbous, even pudgy, as Slavic faces often were. His nose was flattened a little and turned down. This was because of an accident when he was younger. He had splendid white teeth, something all of them envied. His skin was sallow. He blushed easily. Already this was obvious, and charming. His hair was very black and brushed back off his forehead. He had black-brown doleful eyes. He had beautiful hands. It was Bee who noticed that.

They also saw a bachelor, but one who was already spoken for. Rita it was who captured him alive in the Gaiety, helpless and unable to speak English, and brought him back to the family home, so that was her claim staked. He was hers. All in all, they concluded, a very innocent nice young man.

Now they'd assessed one another, the evening could begin. The Walls asked their guest where he was from. Adolf wrote 'Moravia' on a corner of the newspaper that Mr Wall had been reading. Since medieval times, Moravia and Bohemia had shared a common history. At home in Markneukirchen everyone would have understood what he meant, but his Irish listeners did not know what or where Moravia was. Adolf

14

tried again. He wrote 'Bohemia' on the newspaper. Old Mr Wall spelt the word out and said, 'Germany?'

'No, no,' Adolf said indignantly, speaking of himself and his people. 'Not Germany, not Germans.'

His English was clearly deficient. The Wall sisters wanted their visitor to talk to them and they wanted to talk to their visitor, and on the spot they decided to teach him to speak English like they did – properly, and with a better class of accent.

So they began. They threw him words and phrases, and he threw them back, mangled and mutilated. At the end of the night he sat at the upright piano in the front parlour and played some popular songs of the day, then the Walls made requests, and he obliged. They only had to hum a refrain or sing a line and he could play it. This was incredible. The Walls were impressed. He was quite a catch, this strange man Rita had brought home on a whim.

The end of the evening came. Mrs Wall made up a bed for Adolf on the horsehair sofa in the front parlour, and offered to wash and starch the dress shirt he would need for the following night's performance. He handed his shirt over and got between the blankets. Creaks and fragments of girlish talk drifted down through the ceiling. The parlour windows had lace curtains, and the light from the gas lamp in the street leaked in palely through the spaces in the stiff material. As he fell asleep, perhaps he began to feel at home. The last thing he noticed was his finger. It throbbed still, but he'd done it. He'd played through.

4.

Rita's Side

Here are the scanty details on the Walls that have come down to me.

Rita's father was John Wall. He was born in County Wicklow in 1850. This made him fifty-nine on the night of Adolf's arrival. He was a bossy, lazy, overweening man who liked nothing better than to set others, such as his daughters, to work.

Rita's mother, Margaret Wall (née Russell), was born in 1851 in County Tipperary.

When and how John and Margaret met is not known to me. Perhaps John's work on the railways brought him to Tipperary? But meet they did, somehow, some way, and they were a natural fit. They both spoke well. They both dressed well. They were both rural, literate and Roman Catholic, though they both tried to look Protestant. They both wanted to live in a rented red-brick house with lace curtains in the windows and a garden at the front, and they both wanted, one day, to have at least one daughter married to a man in the British Army (anything above a sergeant), and oh please God to have one son a lawyer, if they ever had a son that is, (which they didn't). They also shared an idea of themselves as superior to the ordinary Irish person, whom they viewed as only 'good enough to dig holes in the road and to give a cup of tea to in the hand and without a saucer.'[2] The price they paid for this belief in themselves as elevated Hibernians, of course, was that they were terrifically frightened of falling into poverty and ending up in the workhouse. In their eyes there was no fate worse than being forced to join their compatriots at the bottom.

II

John and Margaret married in 1881. He was twenty-one; she was twenty. John was a railway guard employed by the Midland Great Western Railway. He worked at MGWR stations in the country, and at some point he and his wife came to Dublin, where he worked at Broadstone Station, the MGWR terminus. Margaret wanted a son, a not uncommon want. She got pregnant; she gave birth. It was a son, but the baby was stillborn. There was a second pregnancy and a second son, but this too was a stillbirth.

After the two 'lost boys' came four daughters. They were Bridget, born on 14 January 1880, known variously as Bee, Bridie, and Beatrice; then Rita, born on 4 August 1882; then Mary Anne, known as Polly; and finally Julia, who was known as Judy. The younger daughters' birthdates are unknown to me.

Mrs Wall was twenty-nine when she had Bee, and in her late thirties when she had Judy. By Victorian standards she came late to maternity, and carried on having babies to an advanced age. She went on as long as she did because she wanted a son, but after Judy she accepted that she wasn't going to get one, despite her prayers. 'God says No!' she exclaimed when announcing that she would no longer

---

2   All quotes are from my father's 'Autobiog' (as he called them) notes and papers unless otherwise stated. He collated his Autobiog notes and papers at the end of his life.

try for a boy. Hearing this, John Wall immediately vacated the marital bedroom and moved into the box room, and there he slept for the rest of his life.

III

My father's notes on Rita emphasize two qualities. One, she was small and energetic, a dynamo, indefatigable and persistent. Two, her accent was not demotic Dublin but 'better class'. There was Dublin in it, of course, but it was refined, anglicized. The Walls were most emphatically not tenement people; they were red-brick semi people. And this accent-improvement lark was 'a family thing'. All the sisters spoke in the same way. They also shared an extrovert bent and a tendency to show off, which expressed itself in Rita's case as an interest in the theatre and acting.

In 1907 she secured a modelling job at the Irish International Exhibition in Herbert Park, Ballsbridge. It was a World's Fair, intended to improve the trade in Irish goods, and was opened by the Lieutenant of Ireland, Lord Aberdeen, with great pomp, on 4 May 1907. For this job she wore traditional Irish national costume – shawl, three-quarter-length skirt, coloured petticoats and Bo Peep shoes – and had her hair dressed and gathered and held by a band of Irish lace, and a photograph has survived that shows her magnificent hair held in its lace band. There are no details of what exactly she did at the exhibition – perhaps she worked as a greeter and guide, or manned a commercial stand – but her six months at the fair, which was attended by over two million visitors before it closed on 9 November, was *the* great event of Rita's life. Its only rival was a ball in Dublin Castle, the centre of British authority in pre-partition Ireland, which she attended with her sister Bee, and at which she rubbed up against 'the quality', of whom she apparently thought very highly indeed.

The Walls, it seems, were that now most derided of types, the Castle Catholic. The kind of Catholic, that is, who was happy with the status quo, who didn't rock the boat, who went along with British authority and, worse, was willing and indeed happy to support that alien foreign authority because of the material benefits that flowed because of the connection. Fenians, IRB types or anyone who lauded insurrection or talked loudly about Irish freedom made them nervous, and in the family home there was no seditious talk about breaking the union and Ireland becoming an independent nation. If they were anything politically, I'd guess the Walls were pragmatists. Oh yes, in oh so many ways, with their habits of conformity and their readiness to adapt to circumstances for personal advantage, the Walls really were very like the Géblers of Teplice-Šanov.

5.

Courtship

On Wednesday 25 August 1908, Adolf woke for the first time in Glasnevin. Mrs Wall gave him breakfast: stewed tea, dark and brown, and bread, probably smeared with dripping. His shirt was out on the line, she told him, and he thanked her. She then confirmed the arrangements agreed the previous evening.

Because of the Dublin Horse Show, accommodation was either too pricey or not available in Dublin, so for the duration of *The Merry Widow's* run he'd stay at 26 Marguerite Road. He could spend his days practising or resting or doing whatever it was musicians did, and then he could go into town on the tram with Rita in the afternoon and return to Marguerite Road at the end of the evening.

The architect of this plan was Mrs Wall. She had never lost her son-hunger, and now here was an eighteen-year-old flesh-and-blood man-child, and she wanted him in her house. Adolf was happy to accept: the prospect of being kept and pampered, as he knew he would be, delighted him. As much as Mrs Wall needed a son, he needed a mother like her: warm, loving, caring, his own, according to family lore, being a bit of a Tartar.

I have no idea if the complementary needs of Adolf and his future mother-in-law were what kept him in 26 Marguerite Road, but in the absence of romantic love (and there is no mention of love in the notes that have come down to me, or in the notes that my father later made about his life), this was what my father believed had happened. A sonless older woman became obsessed with a young man who was happy to take her attention because his own mother was so cold and hard. Of course there was another explanation that my father didn't consider, for the simple reason that his own childhood was so awful he was incapable of imagining parental altruism: Mrs Wall insisted Adolf stay for Rita's sake. Mrs Wall did it all for her daughter. I suspect that was the truth.

II

On Wednesday evening Adolf played another performance. Every time he pressed his right finger down, it still hurt. It was the same every night for the rest of the run, and in the years that followed when he remembered this period that was what he recalled, though mingled with those memories of pain were memories of his discovery of this new city, which he walked around every day in order to study her joyous, raucous, good-tempered and belligerent inhabitants, her crowded, traffic-clogged streets and her architecture. What particularly caught his eye were the military buildings: there were barracks simply everywhere, and inevitably there were a lot of soldiers marching around or roistering about everywhere, and from what he saw he drew the inevitable conclusion: British military power was quite something.

Sunday 29 August loomed – almost the end of summer. The Wall sisters proposed a jolly to the seaside. Adolf accepted, and what followed, he would later say, sealed his fate.

On Sunday morning, at Westland Row, Adolf and the sisters boarded a southbound DSE train. A whistle blew, and the train juddered out of the glass-covered station and into the light as it followed the rails south. Through the carriage window Adolf saw the backs of inner-city houses (dark, crowded, miserable places), dank yards, lines heavy with sooty washing, then streets with trams and cabs and omnibuses and horses and children, and then, once the train had passed out of the city and into the suburbs, he saw the pewter-coloured sea, boats with funnels, smoke plumes, piled-up clouds and, in the distance, the green, rounded, breast-like Hill of Howth. In Bohemia there were no vistas like this – Bohemia was a landlocked land within a landlocked Empire. The Irish sights made quite an impression.

The party alighted at Killiney Station (Adolf in a suit, smoking a cheroot perhaps, the Wall sisters in their Sunday hats and long Edwardian dresses that gave them the classic hourglass outlines), and set off on their promenade. Whether they crossed the railway line and picked their way over the pebble-strewn strand or went up the Vico Road and then down by the steep cliff path to the small Whiterock beach is not recorded. What is known is what happened next.

At some point during this walk it had occurred to Adolf that he might like to spend his life in Dublin, Ireland. Here were the reasons why:

There was the week he had just had.

There was the journey on the train out to Killiney he had just made. Oh, the vistas.

There was the place in which he now found himself. Oh, the buttery Irish light, the saline smell of the sea, the murmur of the waves as they rolled up and fell back down the pebbly shingle.

There were his feelings for the host family, for Mrs Wall who mothered him as his own mother never had (if true), and for Rita (whatever they might be).

There was his newfound inclination to settle, and his corresponding disinclination to live as a peripatetic jobbing musician endlessly shuttling about Europe and beyond.

There was his sense that the Irish and the Bohemian national characters were similarly melancholic, humorous and irascible. The

Irish were people he could live with, amongst whom he could even feel at home.

And finally, and perhaps most importantly, there was the historical moment. Militarism, and not just of the German variety, was on the rise in Europe. He had no idea, of course, what form that future would take, nor of how terrible it would turn out to be, but he knew that the future might well involve all sorts of unpleasantness, starting with conscription and going on to include fighting, killing, and of course dying.

If things went awry in the manner he feared then Ireland might be exactly the place to be. This was his instinct. But there was a question that had kept nagging at him all week.

'What about the Germans?' he asked in the few words he had at his disposal.

'The Germans?'

'Yes,' he said, 'the Germans.' There was a war coming, he said, as everyone knew, and the Germans were going to rampage around Europe.

Yes, the Wall sisters nodded. They had heard about this too.

So, he said, would they come to Ireland?

Oh no, the Wall sisters replied, the Germans wouldn't come to Ireland. Certainly not.

How, he wanted to know, were they so sure? (Though he couldn't put it into words, he was pretty sure that, like him, they also knew that Germany's armed forces were as impressive as they were terrifying, and as large as they were belligerent).

The Wall sisters twirled their parasols (if they had any) and laughed lightly. They could answer that question easily, they said. The Germans would not come to Ireland for one very simple reason:

THE BRITISH WOULD NOT ALLOW IT.

Adolf had his answer, and his whole life turned. This was the moment that decided his future wife would be Irish, that his future children would be Irish, and that the bulk of the rest his life would be lived out on Irish soil.

6.

Marriage

I

Of the next part of this story there is nothing, either in the Autobiog notes my father made much later, or in the family lore cupboard. Nothing about Adolf's proposal, nothing about Rita's or the Walls' or even the Géblers' family feelings is recorded. Nor is there any suggestion, assuming it was even true, that Rita knew anything about Adolf's feelings for her mother, if indeed he had any. Nor is there anything about his feelings for his future spouse, or hers for him. Indeed, of feelings and affection, of love and romance, there is absolutely nothing, and in that space where an account of those feelings might lie, there are simply these few bald facts.

Adolf finished his Dublin engagement. He was still contracted to the Daly's Theatre production of *The Merry Widow*. He went, to London or Europe or both, fulfilling his contract. He returned to Ireland, possibly in October 1909, and he was certainly in the country on Sunday 22 January 1911, because on that day, starting at 4 o'clock, the Dublin Orchestral Society (conductor Signor Esposito) gave one of their Sunday concerts in the Antient Concert Rooms, and he took the clarinet part in the third item on the bill, Mozart's Symphony in G (which the programme explained had been modified by Mozart for the clarinet, was his most modern work, and was 'characterized by a feeling of sadness and regretfulness'), and the solo part in the fourth item, Henry Lazarus's grand fantasia for clarinet, *Ma Normandie*. He must have then stayed, because he was still in Ireland in the spring when the census was taken.

II

The census styled itself 'A RETURN of the MEMBERS of this FAMILY and their VISITORS, BOARDERS, SERVANTS, &c., who slept or abode in the House on the night of SUNDAY 2 APRIL 1911.' The return for 26 Marguerite Road is a fascinating document, notable as much for its fibs as for its truths.

It is in a single-page landscape format, with several columns for the different particulars. Reading from left to right, the first column on the left is for 'Names and Surnames', the second for 'Relation to head of family'. On the night, there were seven persons in residence: the head of the family, John; his wife, Margaret; their four daughters, Bridget, Margaret, Mary Ann and Julia (as it was an official document, the baptismal rather than the family or pet names were used); and one boarder, Adolf Gébler. Column three, 'Religious Profession', lists all as Roman Catholic, while column four, 'Education', lists all as able to 'Read and Write'.

Columns six and seven, 'Rank, Profession or Occupation' and 'Particulars as to Marriage' contain nothing that is not already known. Column eight, 'Where born', gives Adolf's birthplace as Austria, there not being space to write Austria-Hungary. Column nine, 'Irish Language', is blank – none of them spoke Irish. Column ten asked whether any of the following applied: 'Deaf and Dumb; Dumb only; Blind; Imbecile or Idiot; or Lunatic'. This too was left blank.

Then there remains, unmentioned so far in this account, the column in middle of the census form, column five, which is headed: 'Age (last birthday) and Sex'. The entries don't cavil about gender or the ages

25

of John and Margaret Wall (sixty-one and sixty respectively), but the information given about the daughters is quite a different story.

Bridget (Bee), who was born in 1880, should be listed as thirty-one, but is described as twenty-eight. Margaret (Rita), who should be listed as twenty-nine, is recorded as twenty-six. (Polly's age is given as twenty-four and Judy's as twenty-two, which may or may not have been accurate.) Had the two elder misses Walls forgotten their birthdates, or does the explanation lie with the boarder, who is correctly listed as a youthful twenty-one? By massaging their ages downwards did they hope to make a union seem more appealing? It looks that way.

III

Adolf and Rita were married by Father P. J. McGrath in St Columba's Church, Iona Road, Glasnevin on 23 January 1912. He was twenty-two; she was thirty. The witnesses were Peter Kennedy and Bridget Wall. The new couple started married life in 119 Royse Terrace, Phibsborough Road, which was exactly the sort of rented red-brick home to which Rita had always aspired.

The year 1912 also saw one other marriage, that of Rita's thirty-two-year-old sister Bee to a ship's cook, a man called Daniel (Dan) O'Brien, and two deaths. Adolf's father, aged sixty-four, died in Hagen, Westphalia, though the date, the reason why he died in Germany, what Adolf made of it and whether he attended the funeral are all unknown. Of the other death, that of Rita's mother, though again I don't have the precise date, I'm slightly better informed: while hauling porter bottles home to her husband, Margaret fell and badly gashed her knee. The wound got infected, and she died of septicaemia. Following her funeral, John Wall left Marguerite Road and moved in with his newly married daughter, Rita. I don't know where Polly and Judy went.

Adolf and Rita, besides supporting the dependent they'd just acquired, had rent and their other bills to meet. They took in a lodger by the name of Jack Carney, and his later villainy ensured that his name lived on in the family's annals. Adolf went to work. As he could play just about anything by ear, and was a convivial fellow who felt at home playing in northside front parlours, he hired himself out for house parties. He also started to teach piano, violin and clarinet, and his new wife had a brass plate made and fixed outside 119 that read 'Adolf Gébler Professor of Music'. Although ostensibly commercial, the real purpose of this signage was to represent Adolf as having the same status as doctors and other notables who boasted brass plaques.

IV

By the middle of 1912 Rita was pregnant, and on 26 May 1913 the first child, a girl, Adelaide, known as Ada, was born. When she arrived Ada was red-faced and squished up, but within a year she had turned into an alluring infant with golden hair and lovely even features.

It was now the spring of 1914, and from here on a lot happened. *A lot.*

In April, Rita became pregnant for the second time. In May, one of Ireland's first custom-built cinemas, The Bohemian Theatre, opened. It was on the Phibsborough Road, close to where Rita and Adolf lived. The Bohemian had a small orchestra (piano, strings, woodwind) to provide the music when silent films showed, and Adolf joined as the pianist. The pianist called out the cues, led the other players, and was in effect the conductor, so his appointment was an indicator of his considerable musical competence.

In June, Archduke Franz Ferdinand of Austria, and his wife, Sophie, Duchess of Hohenberg, were assassinated in Sarajevo by a Bosnian Serb. This precipitated a sequence of bellicose ultimatums and actions, on the one hand by Austria-Hungary, and on the other by Serbia, as well as by their respective allies.

From Paris, where he played violin in the opera and practised as a doctor, Charles, his eldest brother, wrote to Adolf in Dublin (a letter my father quotes in his papers, but which I've never seen):

Germany wants some of the great lands of Russia and will go to war with Russia to expand. Young men will die like flies. I will enrol in the French army and fight the occupiers of our 'homeland' Czechland [sic]. *We are Slavs, not Austrians or Germans. One day we will possess our beautiful homeland and put out the Germans who have colonized our soil.*

This was what Charles planned for himself, but for his younger brother, Adolf, Charles envisaged a quite different path. Whatever he did, Charles went on to write, Adolf must not return home, because if he did:

… the people who already have everything will put you in a brave uniform and send you out to be killed gambling on getting even more power and glory and grander uniforms for themselves. It is your duty to escape, [and] *be somewhere else in a foreign country, if you can, when they make their murderous war* […] *They will put you in prison and make you work, but you may keep your life and you must!*

On 28 July 1914, Austria-Hungary declared war on Serbia. Within days, all the great powers in Europe except Italy had mobilized, and the Great War, which pitted the Axis Powers (including Germany and Austria-Hungary) against the Allies (including the United Kingdom, of which Ireland was part), had begun.

V

Sometime soon thereafter, September or at the very latest October 1914, two detectives from Dublin Castle and a single policeman from the Dublin Metropolitan Police walked up to the front door of 119 Royse Terrace, Phibsborough Road. They had come for Adolf, and seeing the brass plaque, they knew they had come to the right address.

One of the three pulled the bell cord or rapped the knocker. I don't know about this next part, but let us say, for the sake of this account, that it was Rita who opened the door.

On her doorstep she saw two men in suits and a constable in uniform while her visitors saw a very small woman with a swollen belly – Rita was now six months pregnant. She was carrying my father and a toddler on her hip, Ada, my aunt.

One of the men asked if they might come in. They were admitted; the door was closed. They had come for Adolf Gébler, one said. Was he at home?

'Yes,' said Rita. Or maybe she said, 'No, but he'll be back.' I don't have that detail, but what I do know is that when they finally got to speak to Adolf they informed him that as the United Kingdom was now at war with Austria-Hungary he was under arrest as an enemy alien and he had to go with them.

This announcement precipitated incomprehension. Adolf couldn't deny it. Yes, he was technically an Austro-Hungarian: that's what his travel papers gave as his nationality, and that's what the census return had said, but in practice he was a Czech nationalist who believed in Czech independence and he despised the Austro-Hungarian Empire and the German Kaiser's expansionist programme. He wasn't an Axis type, for God's sake; that's why he'd come to Ireland and married Irish-but-really-British Rita: it was to escape from precisely that background.

Adolf having made his pitch, Rita made hers. She was British, her toddler was British, the child to whom she would soon give birth would be British, and who was going to feed and support her and her children when Adolf had gone? The police had been arresting German and Austro-Hungarian enemy aliens for weeks and had heard it all before, I imagine, and were bored of having to listen to the same old guff again.

The policeman handcuffed Adolf. They took him to a police station, and from there he was sent on to Templemore in County Tipperary, a

Royal Irish Constabulary (RIC) depot, where he was held with other 'aliens'. This was a temporary recourse whilst a dedicated camp was established.

VI

As the site of their Aliens' Internment Camp on the island of Ireland the authorities had selected Oldcastle in Country Meath, a small town of about 700 people with good rail links north and west of Dublin.[3] Specifically, they used Oldcastle's old Union Workhouse and Fever Hospital. Major Robert Johnston (1872–1950), a winner of a Victoria Cross in the South African wars, was nominated as the camp commandant.

In the autumn of 1914 the hospital had forty-four inmates, so the first step was to relocate these patients to adjoining counties. Facilities were then put in place for the internees, including dormitories where they would sleep, two theatres, some classrooms, tailoring and boot-making workshops, four recreation yards and two playing fields. The place was also fortified by the addition of nine sentry boxes and a barbed wire entanglement around the site that stood at five feet high and fourteen feet wide.

The first batch of prisoners, sixty-eight of them, arrived at Oldcastle Railway Station on Sunday 14 December, and were marched through the town to the camp under the watchful eyes of Oldcastle's bemused inhabitants. They were followed by further batches, and the number of inmates quickly rose to about 600, a level at which it remained for the duration of its existence, amongst them Adolf Gébler, my grandfather. About 500 of the internees were Germans; the remainder were Austro-Hungarians.

---

3   My main source of information on the camp was 'Das Kriegsgefangenenlager/The Prisoner of War Camp Oldcastle, Co. Meath, 1914–1918' by Declan O'Connor, translated by Martin Döll, published in *Die Harfe*, Nr. 130, Spring 2015, pp. 37–41.

The internees came from a mixture of occupations and backgrounds. There were the captains, officers and ordinary seamen from Axis merchant ships who happened to be berthed in Irish harbours when the war started. There were the ten waiters and cooks who had been on the staff of the Shelbourne Hotel. There were several shopkeepers (Adolf subsequently liked to describe them as 'the cream of Dublin's pork butchers'), as well as a good number of musicians, most notably Aloys Fleischmann (1880–1964), who was the organist and choirmaster in Cork's Catholic Cathedral when arrested.

The camp regime involved a lot of hard work, with the inmates either labouring in the camp itself (almost everything the inmates needed was made on the site, from loaves to shoes to shirts, so it took a great deal of effort to keep the place running), or working on nearby farms, where the camp's food was produced. Constructive activity inside the camp was focused on music – hardly surprising given the high number of musicians who were incarcerated there. Remarkably, there were two orchestras (one run by Fleischmann senior) and a choir, as well as several bands to cater to more up-to-date tastes in music. Adolf was certainly in one of the orchestras as well the choir, and he participated in performances given both in the camp and out in Oldcastle itself.

Perhaps the most unusual feature of the regime were the Sunday walks. If 100 prisoners were in agreement they were allowed to march (and that meant march, not walk) to Dromone, about four miles away, where there was a public house at which the internees were permitted to buy a drink. If they were prepared to buy their military escort alcohol, the internees were allowed to stay and buy more than one drink.

The Sunday walks (which, unsurprisingly, proved very popular) provided inmates with some social contact with the world outside. More meaningful contact, though, for instance with their families – and many of the inmates like Adolf had Irish wives and Irish children – was almost impossible, as only one or two fifteen-minute visits per month were permitted. Rita probably never visited Adolf during the years he was in Oldcastle, though she did write to him, occasionally sending food parcels too. Adolf, for his part, took steps to repair the rupture in the only way he knew – though music. He somehow obtained two manuscript composition books, and he filled these with a mixture of popular tunes of the day alongside one or two of his own compositions. His plan, when he was finally released, was to present his daughter and his as yet unborn child with one each, and in his mind these tokens would compensate his children for his absence.

Fleischmann senior, to whom we are indebted for much of what we know about Oldcastle, wrote regularly about the camp in his letters home to his family in Cork. The place as he painted it was not barbaric or systematically brutal (though there were occasional violent incidents) so much as it was stultifying and even suffocating. In a memorable letter to his son, Aloys Fleischmann (junior) (1910–1992), who would go on to become one of Ireland's most important twentieth-century composers as well as the Professor of Music at University College Cork, described Oldcastle as a place of men 'worn down by their fate, robbed of their livelihoods, torn from their families … vegetating like packs of different animals behind barbed wire.' Oldcastle, in other words, was not a place where one flourished, but then that was pretty typical of all penal institutions at the time. Their function was not to encourage development; it was to hold and contain.

When Adolf initially arrived at Oldcastle and discovered it was a hard labour camp with a pretty rigid regime, he was appalled. After all, he had been plucked from a wife, a family, a house and a job. Later, however, he revised his opinion. Yes, Oldcastle was harsh, he would say, but he would also concede that incarceration saved him from far worse horrors.

7.

Birth

Adolf married Rita to escape the Germans, but with the onset of war his motives didn't matter. He was on the Axis side now, no ifs or buts. That is why he was interned, and it made her the wife of one of the hateful Hunnish enemy – an unpopular thing to be, at the beginning of the war at least.

With Adolf gone, Rita now faced the problem of how to survive. She had one child already, and a second was imminent. Her only income was an allowance of 9s. 6d., the weekly payment the War Office made to the wives of interned or enemy aliens. How was she to pay the rent? Step forward Mr Carney, the lodger. He was a charitable soul. He saw her difficulty. He'd help her out. He'd pay it all until she could manage it again. He even undertook to take the rent book down to the rent office each week, pay the monies over and get it stamped. Rita, eight months gone, couldn't ask for a nicer lodger.

Her pangs started in the back bedroom of 119 Royse Terrace, Phibsborough Road, on 31 December, the last day of 1914. Dr Carton, whose name, like Carney's, survives, though in the doctor's case it was remembered for reasons of status rather than infamy, attended her. Approaching midnight, with Dublin's church bells peeling, she delivered her second child, my father. He entered the world right on the line where 1914 sheered into 1915, and as a result there would always be confusion, even in his own mind, as to when exactly he was born. His birth certificate, issued on 25 January 1915, gave his birth date as 31 December 1914, but as time went on he celebrated his birthday on 1 January, even, it seems, in adolescence.

II

About a month or two after the birth, Rita stopped breastfeeding him, and diluted cows' milk was given to him in place of breast milk. His response was alarming. At first, his abdomen swelled up and became rigid. He then went into spasm, his pulse raced, and his breathing became fast and shallow.

Dr Carton was summoned. He thought that the baby should go to hospital and that without medical assistance he might not live, though this advice was not acted on. Meanwhile, news of Dr Carton's dire prognosis spread around Phibsborough, and one of those who heard it was a shawlie, name unknown, an old and wizened woman who smelt of turf smoke and who lived close by in a hovel beside the Tolka that flooded every winter. She enjoyed her reputation as a healer, and was particularly renowned for her knack with sick babies, and she immediately took herself round to Rita's house, where she was admitted to the sick room. Rita and the old woman had never met before, but Rita knew of her and what she supposedly could do.

The sick baby (by this stage, the very sick baby) was given to the visitor. She filled a basin with warm water, immersed the infant and massaged him. She did this for hours until the baby's spasms stopped, his pulse slowed, and then, miracle of miracles, he swallowed a little water. Now that the baby was stable again, the old woman delivered her forecast. 'He can't have cows' milk,' she said, 'he's taken against it for life.' She continued by reassuring the anxious mother that her baby would do all right on goats' milk. On hearing this, Rita remembered the herd that grazed the waste ground behind the terrace where her sister Bee lived. She knew that the goatherd sold the nannies' milk, so there was the supply, almost on her doorstep, and every day thereafter, as she'd been advised, she bought a can's worth (it was cheaper than cows' milk), and fed it to her son in a bottle.

The old woman's prognosis was right: he thrived on goat's milk. Every day he got stronger and better, and his near-death experience became a memory. When he was three months old, Rita felt that he was now strong enough for his first rite of passage, and on 5 March 1915, in St Joseph's Church, Berkeley Road, my father was baptized Ernest Adolph Gébler by Father James Dempsey.

III

His health restored, his initiation into the Church achieved and the afterlife of his soul secured, a new danger appeared in the form of his sister. Inevitably, his arrival displeased her. Why wouldn't it? One day, Rita popped out for a message. She was only gone for a minute or two. When she came back, she found her son in his cot with the pillow from her bed lying over his face. She questioned Ada. 'It was to make him sleep,' the child explained.

These stories about his near-death because of cow's milk and Ada's attempt on his life he would later return to obsessively, because, as he saw it, they spoke the great, terrible truth: right from the start, his was a life lived under the twin shadows of near-fatal lactose intolerance and murderous female malevolence. These were his foundation myths, and they governed everything that followed.

IV

Rita found a girl to mind her children, and went back to her bar job at the Gaiety. She worked matinees and nights. Now that she had a wage on top of her War Office allowance she started to pay rent again. But between her children and her job, Rita was frantic with cares, and so to 'help her', the lodger continued to visit the rent office every week with Rita's rent book and the rent money she gave him to pay in. For weeks, even months, the arrangement rolled on, until one day when he was at the rent office perfidious Mr Carney reported that Mrs Gébler had gone, and asked, since he was living in the house already, if he could take over the tenancy of 119 Royse Terrace.

His weekly visits over many months had given the landlord the impression that he was reliable and virtuous. To make his plea even more persuasive, Carney added that he was now betrothed, but couldn't get married until he had a home, which was why he was asking to have the house transferred into his name.

Although this information seems insufficient to explain what happened next, what happened next did happen – or it is believed to have happened. It is there in the family annals. Rita's name was expunged from the rent book, and Carney's substituted. The lodger was free to marry: all that remained was to take full possession. He returned to 119 and informed Rita that he was now the official tenant and she had to go, taking her children with her of course, and old John Wall too.

That is the story, but it does not seem credible that Carney's stroke could actually work. There are surely parts missing. Why did the landlord believe Mr Carney's canard? Why did he not visit the house and check for himself? And for that matter, why did Rita or John Wall not visit the landlord and tell him that they were still very much in residence? Maybe the dissembling wasn't Carney's. Might Rita have concocted the story about Carney's perfidy so she wouldn't have to explain to Adolf later that she actually just left the house because she didn't like it and wanted a different life? I do not have the answers to these questions. All I know is that in late 1915 or early 1916, Rita, the children and John Wall quit 119 Royse Terrace and moved in with Bee, who since getting married had lived at 43 Botanic Avenue, not far from Marguerite Road.

Number 43 was a red-brick house, two-storey, one in a terrace, and rented of course. Downstairs there was a best room and a back parlour, each about twelve foot square, each with black fire-grates. At the back of the hall, three steps led down to a kitchen, a small, dark room with a wayward range, a grease-encrusted gas stove and a stone sink, as well as an indoor lavatory, which was separate from the kitchen, with a 'flushing system', which made this a superior house. Upstairs there were two good bedrooms, while over the kitchen there was a third bedroom, small, grubby and careworn, and this was the room that Rita rented from Bee. The sisters took turns to use the kitchen, and when Rita was at the Gaiety, Bee minded her children – a responsibility that would later pass to Bee's oldest child, Peggy.

When he was a year or so old, accompanied by Rita, Peggy or Bee, my father began to walk. Or tried to. A vestigial memory of the struggle, an orgy of standing and falling amidst the lawns and paths and flowerbeds of the Botanic Gardens (the beautiful formal gardens near number 43) stayed with him for the rest of his life, and the older he got, the stronger these memories grew.

Recalling Bee, who was so bound up with these memories, at the end of his life my father remembered her as someone round, even squat, heavy, swarthy, generous and unfailingly kind. By the time he wrote these words he was completely out of the habit of praising anyone, and the very fact that he did so suggests to me that Aunt Bee must have been quite exceptional.

V

Ernest was sixteen months old when, at Easter 1916, a number of buildings in Dublin's centre were seized by Irish revolutionaries, and several days of fighting and heavy shelling followed. In later life he was adamant that he did not remember hearing anything, but did remember that food suddenly became scarce and that the adults in 43 Botanic Avenue were appalled at what the rebels were doing to the centre of their city. I suspect that these were not actual memories but rather were what he was told later and then came to believe were things he remembered. As for their veracity, I am sure that they are true. Food supplies were disrupted. More importantly, the Walls were part of the majority whose wishes were not reflected by the Rising, though that event has managed to dominate the narrative ever since. Hunkered down in 43, as fighting continued, I imagine the adults (certainly John Wall and his daughters Rita and Bee) must have raged at what was being done on their behalf, though without their ever having been asked. As they were not believers and had no sympathy with Republicanism, this is not surprising.

8.

Adolf's Homecoming

In April 1918 there was a large anti-conscription rally in the square in the centre of Oldcastle, which was only a few hundred yards from the camp. Several internees got on the roof to watch, and when the speeches ended they were surprised but not displeased when the crowd moved down to the camp's gates and began shouting messages of support to the inmates on the roof. For the authorities, now that Irish popular opinion had swung against the war and in favour of Sinn Féin, the Oldcastle camp suddenly became a focus of anxiety. What if Irish revolutionaries and the internees, who were all suspected (wrongly of course) of harbouring a deep commitment to Irish independence and a longing to help the Irish in their struggle, made common cause? It could be a catastrophe. The only solution was to ship the internees out, and so, the next month, Oldcastle's entire population was sent to Knockaloe Aliens' Camp on the Isle of Man, which had a far stricter regime and a reputation for being harsh.

Eight months later, in November, the Armistice was agreed. Adolf, however, along with all the other internees, was kept in Knockaloe.

There were two reasons. Firstly, the war was not actually over, as what had been concluded was a ceasefire; it wouldn't end until the signing of the Treaty of Versailles on 26 June 1919. Secondly, the government hadn't decided whether these prisoners could stay in the United Kingdom on not.

Adolf had a British wife, and assumed that he could remain in the UK, which was what he wanted. But then on 3 February 1919, according to the Aliens Register for the A Division area kept by the Dublin Metropolitan Police, the Austrian citizen Rita Gébler entered Ireland, though her birthplace, the record indicated, was Dublin. She hadn't entered Ireland, of course, but was living there already. The record just couldn't accommodate that fact. But she was not British, or even Irish, any more. She was Austrian. That was the point.

By this stage it was government policy to deport all aliens back to where they came from, so presumably it was in anticipation of this that Rita changed her nationality. She wouldn't have wanted to be a British national in the new Austrian Republic. Meantime, in Knockaloe, Adolf, who definitely didn't want to go back to his defeated homeland, resisted all attempts to deport him. Eventually, though how he managed this as a foreigner on the losing side is a mystery, he secured leave to remain, and on 5 August 1919 he signed 'An Undertaking of Neutrality', as was required of all aliens:

I,
(name) Adolphe [sic] *Gébler*
(Address) 43 Botanic Avenue, Dublin
(Nationality) Bohemian

Hereby promise and undertake that I will neither directly nor indirectly take any action in any way prejudicial to the safety of the British Empire or to the safety of her Allies during the present war.

Across the top of the form in pencil was written 'Unconditional Release'. Adolf was free to go. He was twenty-nine.

II

There are three versions of Adolf's return to Dublin.

One:

It was evening, late August. On Sir John Rogerson's Quay on the Liffey a crowd was waiting, among them Rita, pale, thin, drawn, and the children. Ada, six, had gold ringlets and dark skin. The other child, Ernest, four years old and obviously the younger brother, had straw-coloured hair and large brown eyes. All the Géblers were in their Sunday best.

From the east, the Isle-of-Man ferry sidled into view and crept up to the quayside. The gangplank was dropped and secured, then down its swaying length flowed the alighting passengers. On the quayside, human churn and hubbub as greeters and arrivals collided.

In the crowd Rita noticed Adolf hauling a battered suitcase, his hair cropped close to his scalp. He'd gone away, she thought, a boyish man, but that had been aged out of him now.

Adolf noticed an emaciated woman looking at him. Who is she, he wondered.

Rita saw this. He doesn't know me, she thought.

Adolf noticed the appalled expression of the woman staring at him. It couldn't be, could it?

'Adolf,' Rita called. Oh yes, it was.

Ada heard the name and jumped into her father's arms. He hugged her, then at some point he stopped and looked at his son, whom he had never seen before, and then at Rita, whom he hadn't seen for nearly five years. He was twenty-nine. She was thirty-seven, but looked much older.

Two:

Rita was on the quayside alone and without the children when Adolf's boat docked. Adolf came down the gangplank, and only when Rita came towards him did he realize that she was his wife.

When they got back to 43 Botanic Avenue, Adolf wanted to see his children: his daughter, Ada, whom he had not seen for nearly five years, and his son, Ernest, whom he had never seen. Rita brought him to the little back bedroom where she and the children slept. When he went in, Ada sprang out of her single bed and into his arms. Adolf hugged and kissed his handsome daughter and murmured, 'Beautiful! Beautiful! How beautiful she is.'

From his cot, my father screamed at the strange man to leave his sister alone and put her down. He didn't.

Three:

No one met Adolf off the boat. He walked alone through Dublin, its centre still wrecked by the fighting that had gone on during the Rising, to 43 Botanic Avenue. Rita opened the front door to him. For a moment he didn't know who she was, and she knew that he didn't know, and she knew why: since he saw her last, in the autumn of 1914, she had grown old and unalluring.

Later, upstairs, Ada jumped into her father's arms and his son told Adolf to put his sister down.

This story of his father's return appears many times in my father's notes on his life in its different versions. Whatever the facts, though, the deep meanings are the same in all the variants. One, Adolf failed to recognize Rita, an annihilating experience after all she had endured. Two, Ada instantly commandeered Adolf while my father, in contrast, failed to secure Adolf's attention at all. This paradigm of Ada folding into Adolf while his son, my father, was ignored, would continue to be the default throughout my father's childhood. Henceforth, Ada was always 'the one' and he was always 'the nothing'.

III

Later on in the evening of Adolf's arrival, or perhaps on a different evening soon after, there was a little party to welcome Adolf home in the good room at the front of number 43. In attendance were Bee and Dan; Judy and her new husband, Frederick Dack (the Irish-born son of English parents, Freddie converted to Catholicism in 1911, emigrated to Winnipeg, Canada shortly thereafter, joined the Canadian Expeditionary Forces in 1914, was posted to France for the duration of the war, and married Judy on 15 July 1919); and Polly and her future husband, Billy Williams, with whom she would later live in England. There was no mention of Old John Wall attending, but I assume that he must have.

During the party Adolf told Bee, 'I am glad to be alive and in the world and to have my children.' He opened his suitcase and pulled out a dozen oranges and sweets and two talismanic treasures: music composition books filled with tunes he'd made up and collected in the camp. The oranges were for the adults, the composition books were for his children, Ada and Ernest. Writing sixty years later, my father said that he still had the composition book made especially for him in the internment camp, but I've never seen it.

9.

A Psychological Audit

I

Rita, before the war, was a well-spoken girl from a superior working-class family whose father was something on the railway and whose people lived in a good rented house. Marriage and motherhood had then coincided with war and catastrophe. She lost Adolf, her house and her place in the world, and ended up squatting at her sister's. Though he could hardly be blamed for his nationality, she held Adolf responsible for the fact that she was left alone to fend for herself and her children, which in turn required her, as she liked to put it now – her tongue, always a formidable instrument, had been sharpened by her wartime misery – to do everything short of walking the streets to keep her children and herself clothed and fed. Oh yes, the Rita Adolf returned to was a careworn, fraught, unhappy woman with an acute sense of grievance, which she vocalized without stinting.

II

For his part, Adolf returned from camp more alien than when he went away. For a start, having spoken only German – and what else would he speak in a camp of German-speakers? – his not very good English had atrophied, which rendered him even less able to defend himself when his wife vocalized her grievances, as she did. He simply didn't have the words from which to build a bulwark to protect himself.

In addition, as an ex-prisoner, he was out of sync with the civilian world. After five years away he had forgotten how to cross the road. He couldn't manage traffic, or money. His table manners had gone to pot. He couldn't eat properly. He didn't know how to relate to women or children. He was out of the habit of everything. That was what incarceration had done. It had institutionalized him, and it had atomized his social skills.

All of this was beyond Rita's ken; she had no notion of what incarceration did. All she saw was her own unhappy story of failure, and all she knew was that she needed care and tenderness. But incarceration was not the humus from which a man who tended to kindness and compassion was bound to spring. On the contrary, incarceration, especially when it violated a man's sense of natural justice as Adolf's had (after all, he hadn't done anything; he was incarcerated simply because of his nationality), could only make a man angry and bitter and selfish and thoughtless, which was precisely how Adolf was when he returned.

Then there was the further complicating factor of how Rita had changed. The lustre she had when he was taken was now gone, and she had become a woman who, if not yet old, was well on her way to that situation. She knew what she had become, and worse, she knew that her husband knew. After all, he'd failed to recognize her, hadn't he? It was terrible, having struggled to keep the family together, as Rita had, and after everything she had been through, to be humiliated in this way.

Well, she would pay him back in turn, she decided. So she did. She paid him back in rage.

III

And then, complicating everything further, were the children. My father heard his mother's bitter words – and there were many of them – and inevitably found himself taking her side. He didn't decide this.

It just happened like that because after their years together that was the only way it could have gone. She was the only parent he had ever known, so he was bound to identify with her. Plus, he had never met his father before. He resented this stranger, and feared that he would come between him and his mother. These circumstances were not conducive to my father and his father bonding. On the contrary, they were inimical to it.

IV

The final party in this maelstrom was Ada. She was older than my father, and her relationship with Adolf was different because she was older. Adolf already knew her vaguely, and she already knew Adolf vaguely. He remembered her from before his arrest, and she remembered him. She was charming. She was loquacious. She loved to draw and to sing, to talk and to dance. She was confident. At every opportunity, now her father was home, she pushed herself onto his lap or got up beside him at the piano. She announced that she wanted to play, and he started to teach her. In return she taught her ex-internee father how to eat with a knife and fork instead of a spoon. She showed him how to cross the road. She explained money to him, the value of the different coins, what they could buy. She tuned into his mangled English. She mastered it. She became his English teacher, correcting his poor grammar, diction and syntax, and his translator, always being on hand to supply him with the words he needed but didn't know, or couldn't remember. She was his assistant, his consort. She smoothed his path, she mediated, she explained him to the world and she explained the world to him.

Rita saw and understood that her husband liked and valued Ada more than he liked and valued her. Ada was an attractive golden-haired angel whereas she was an unlovely drudge. This understanding, the final element in this scenario, caused her to lash her husband mercilessly, which drove him closer to Ada, which reinforced Rita's feelings of rejection and made her move even further away, taking my father with her.

V

This was the family dynamic in the aftermath of the war: it was Rita and my father versus Adolf and Ada. There is another fact, however, that cannot be argued away. Adolf and Rita's problems, despite everything, do not appear to have extended to the bedroom: not long after Adolf got home, his wife fell pregnant once again.

10.

After the War

I

In the autumn of 1919 Adolf and Rita lived in the back bedroom in 43 Botanic Avenue with their two children. Rita worked in the Gaiety, but Adolf could not return to the Bohemian Theatre. The Musicians' Union had boycotted him, probably because he was a foreigner and they wouldn't have him doing work an Irish musician could do. In order to make a living he had to go away. He worked in the west of Ireland, but mostly he went north, to Londonderry and County Down, where he played in cinemas and dance halls.

Sometimes Rita and the children went with him, and Adolf would bring the children to work, which was how Ada, now seven or eight, and my father, now four or five, came to see footage of a volcano erupting. The world was full of fire, Ada whispered to her brother in the darkness. It was under the ground, she said, but one day, just like on the screen, the earth would open and the fire would roar out and that would be the end of the world.

Looking back as an adult, my father connected what he has learnt very early with what he subsequently became in adolescence:

A few years later, when I began to mend my own shoes (boots), I began to realize that it was necessary to always have good soles on boots for the end of the world. The world on fire vision had been forgotten, but the need to be prepared to 'walk' for thousands of miles, as well as live 'in the wild', always remained at [the] back of [my] mind, with a feeling that I would be the last man in the world. There'd be nobody left somehow, but me – with my strong boots.

His other great childhood cultural experience was the Robin Hood story. Someone read it to him – his mother most likely – and he never forgot it.

II

From France came news of Charles: wounded in the trenches he had been hauled to hospital, where it was discovered that he had tuberculosis. His wounds patched up, he was dispatched to a sanatorium, and he wrote from there. Adolf was so moved by this letter that he stowed it in his wallet so he would always have it on him (it remained there for years), and borrowed enough money to travel to France to visit Charles.

When he got there, Adolf and his brother made a plan. When he recovered, Charles would come to Ireland to see his brother, his brother's wife, his brother's children and his brother's new country.

Adolf returned home feeling buoyant. He thought that things were turning and that his luck was picking up. In this, he was deceived. Not long after Adolf got back home to Dublin, Charles died, and the sanatorium dispatched his service box to 43 Botanic Avenue, which he'd given as his home address. When the box arrived it was hoisted onto the table in Auntie Bee's kitchen and the lid opened. Inside were Charles's effects. I imagine these might have included his epaulettes, his gloves, his funny French peaked kepi (if he ever wore one), his tunic buttons, his smoking paraphernalia (if he smoked), his pocket book, his shaving brush, his strop and his cut-throat, though I don't know.

But whatever the things were, Adolf wept at the sight of them, and my father, who was in kitchen, was baffled. How could simple objects do that? He was just a literal-minded seven-year-old who responded primarily to the evidence of his own senses. Thus, one day, around the same time that Charles's service box appeared, he was out in Botanic Avenue when he saw a neighbour making his way uncertainly along the pavement and tapping a white stick as he went.

'Blinded by gas,' he heard someone say, and this he understood, because he was able to see that the veteran's eyes were damaged when he passed.

The next Gébler, a girl, Mary Louise, was born in Londonderry in the summer of 1920. Adolf would always call her Lulu.

11.

Germany

Adolf's mother, now a widow, was in Berlin. She wrote to her son in Ireland. She told him that the Berlin State Opera Orchestra would soon be back up and running, that they needed musicians, and suggested he apply. Her son was responsive to this idea. He wanted to get back into the world of classical music, and why wouldn't he? He had trained for it at the Prague Conservatory, and it was the tradition of both his class and family. The War of Independence was also in full spate in Ireland, with Irish nationalists on one side and the British Army and the Royal Irish Constabulary on the other. It was a nasty war full of tit-for-tat actions. The country's tone was sullen and weary. Now would definitely be a good time to be away.

Adolf applied to the Berlin State Opera Orchestra, and was offered a job playing clarinet. Adolf, thinking that he was going to restart his European musical career, went ahead of his family and stayed with his mother in Berlin.

The family – Rita, along with Ada, my father and the baby, Mary Louise – followed. They had no suitcases; everything was tied up in blankets. They looked like refugees, which in a way they were. The Continental rail system had not recovered from the war, and they spent days waiting for trains and nights sleeping on station platforms. They had no money for 'proper food' as Rita called it as they crawled eastwards. It was a hellish as well as an epic journey.

Eventually they reached not Berlin but Düsseldorf, where they stayed with Adolf's sister, Helen, who was married to Jacob, an interior decorator, and possibly Gretel, Adolf's younger sister. In the streets, though they were disguised in German clothes, they were tormented as Englishers, about whom the Germans, following their defeat and the onerous terms imposed by the Treaty of Versailles, had distinctly negative feelings. Ada and my father were mobbed on their first day at the school where they were sent, and never went back. With no school, no playing in the street and no friends, their time in Germany was a time of piercing loneliness.

II

Helen and Jacob lived near a fish canning factory, and my father, now solitary and tending towards the feral, became adept at stealing freshly pressed boiling cans. As he ran home to Helen and Jacob's he would throw the cans into the air and catch them in order that he wouldn't burn his hands. At some point during this German sojourn, sweets and chocolate, having been rationed, returned to shops. This made a huge impression on him, as did trips to Berlin where Rita and the children visited the opera (alas, there are no details of what they saw), and the family's strange, awkward meetings with Grandmother Maria Géblerova in her Berlin flat. She had no English, and her daughter-in-law and grandchildren no German or Czech. She was seemingly an austere as well as an unfriendly woman.

Rita was hardly better, of course. She complained bitterly to Adolf on these Berlin trips, not only about the brutality of the Germans (which had merit, it was true), but the Germans' strange and alien ways, the tub of sauerkraut under Helen's sink, vinegary and stinky, and Jacob's disgusting habit of emptying the contents of their chamber pots onto the vegetable garden every morning. For all these and other reasons, she said, and even though he had a job, she could not live in Germany. Rita's campaign was as relentless as it was unreasonable, and in the end Adolf had no alternative but to capitulate and return to Ireland.

It was a decision that can't be judged in isolation; it has to be seen within the context of what had happened going back at least a decade. When the Great War started, Rita was the wife of one of the enemy, and her side, as she thought, had persecuted them. When she then came to Germany she found that she and the children were the enemy again, only now, bizarrely, they were associated with her recent persecutors, the victors in the war, and hated by the Germans on that account. Not to have been on any side and yet to have had to endure the level of animosity she endured since 1914 was insupportable. As she saw it, after years of misery, to leave Germany and go back to Ireland and the English language and her people, knowing that this time she would not be vilified, was the only alternative. No other way of living could be tolerated. She was also pregnant, and where that child came into the world was a matter of huge importance to her.

Adolf's feelings about the decision were not so positive. The Berlin State Opera Orchestra represented his best chance, to date, of becoming a serious classical musician, and he was giving that up to return to a country in turmoil and in which he would be a foreigner. On the other hand, on account of his decision, his children, including one as yet unborn, would be back in their language and their culture, and he may have calculated that for them it was worth giving up what he gave up. But of course the problem of not belonging, though it would not be as bad in Ireland as it had been in Germany, would still be there. His children would still have an alien for a father and a funny foreign-sounding surname. They would never completely fit in to the host culture, and for his son, my father, that sense of being at an oblique angle to the Irish norm would always matter.

12.

Back

The family arrived back in Ireland some time in the summer of 1922, and just in time for Rita to give birth, most probably at 43 Botanic Avenue, to the fourth Gébler child, my father's sister, Olive. Owing to the Civil War then raging between the forces of the Irish Free State, who supported the Anglo–Irish Treaty under which the state known as the Free State was established, and the Republican opposition, for whom the treaty represented a betrayal of the Irish Republic because the new entity did not include the six Ulster counties that had become Northern Ireland, the western wing of the Four Courts had been destroyed in an explosion, and with it the Irish Public Records Office, so my aunt's birth could not be registered, and indeed would not be registered until the summer of 1947 when she needed a birth certificate to get married.

II

It was still the summer of Olive's birth. It was a temperate day, mild, sunny, with a breeze. A neighbour boy came into the back garden of

43 Botanic Avenue where my father was playing, and he had with him a 'sail boat'. It was only a small object, five or six inches long, with two triangular sails and a pencil-thin mast. The visitor explained to my father, now an eight-year-old, that this was not a boat but a yacht. The boy was very particular on this point, and once he was sure that my father had grasped the word he offered to show him the not-a-boat-but-a-yacht in action.

The zinc bath in which the children were bathed every Friday night in the kitchen was kept in the garden. It was located and filled from the garden tap. Once it was full, the visitor knelt on one side of the metal oval rim and my father on the other. The surface of the water was smooth and still and clear; through the water the zinc bottom showed as a dull gunmetal grey, and there was a smell of carbolic soap too, which the zinc had absorbed over years of use and now gave back.

The visitor set his yacht down carefully on the water. Being weighted (it had a keel of course, but my father had no idea about that), it sunk low, while the ripples produced by the launch moved outwards and died away. There was a small pause, a moment of grace, the vessel poised, the water level like a mirror, two pairs of eyes staring, and then a miracle as the small sails attached to the pencil mast billowed slightly and the yacht started to move of its own volition across the water towards him. It was thrilling and lovely, and he had to have one of these miracles for himself immediately. Unfortunately, the visitor wouldn't part with his. No, that was never going to happen. That left only one alternative. He was good with his hands. In the back bedroom, using matchboxes, thread bobbins, bits of orange box and pieces of domestic detritus that he'd scavenged, he had made a townscape of cramped little terraces and streets clogged with carts and drays, omnibuses and trams. If he could do that he could manage a boat. He would do it himself.

The visitor gone, he found a piece of wood, all rough and knobbly, not smooth or lacquered, and about twice as long as the visitor's yacht. He hacked away at it, and something like a hull emerged, with pointed prow and rounded stern. The shape of sorts having been made, he faced a new problem. The sails. Where would he find them? And the mast. And what of the hole in the middle into which the mast must fit? How was he to make that? There was only one man he could approach, though he was known to dislike young children, his grandfather. He approached the patriarch with his poorly whittled hull, and despite his reputation, Old John Wall gave advice in his gruff voice, sourced sailcloth and a mast, and helped to fit the mast and rig the sails. Job done, they went together out of 43 Botanic Avenue by the little gate at the rear, across the waste ground and down to a little pool at the side of the brackish Tolka.

The river chortled as it ran, but in the pool the waters were stiller, safer. He knelt, set his yacht on the brown surface and let go. He had not forgotten the moment of grace at the bath tub, the miracle as the small sails billowed slightly and the yacht started to move of its own volition; this was not only what he now expected but what he was absolutely convinced would now happen. But instead, not enjoying the benefits of a keel, a concept neither he nor his grandfather understood, with the first puff of wind his vessel rolled sideways and the sails went splat onto the water. He tried and retried to sail his yacht, but every time the wind blew it went over. It was only during the occasional moments when the wind held back that it floated unsteadily, sitting far too high out of the water, but these moments were few, and were never long enough to give him pleasure.

He carried his yacht home. He was bitter, he was disappointed, but the next day, thinking that the fault must have been in the hull he had carved, he found another piece of wood and started whittling again. Later, he would identify his obsession with seas and seafaring as beginning at this moment. Although there may be some truth in that, I think it would be more accurate to see his yacht-making as part of his lifelong obsession with things, which, unlike people such as his mother (who had just betrayed him by having yet another baby), were utterly reliable and consistent. A mechanical object could go wrong, but you were able to control it and fix it. And despite going wrong, it would always be more reliable than humans. In an uncertain world, here was something to hold on to.

III

As 1922 shaded in 1923, life became very difficult. The Musicians' Union boycott was still in place, which meant that Adolf could not work officially (assuming he could even find any work), whilst the Civil War made it difficult for him to make even an informal living in Dublin as a musician, playing at parties, teaching privately and so on. As a result of these problems, Adolf and Rita decided to leave Dublin and go to Wexford. It would be safer in the country, and Adolf would teach country people, who were desperate for music, obviously, because they were far from civilization, and in return the country folk would pay him with sacks of potatoes. That was the plan – and to make it more likely that they would thrive they would not take John Wall with them. He would stay with Bee, and at some point thereafter, though I have not been able to find the date or any other details, he died.

13.

May Geraghty

I

Sea View Cottage, in the south-east corner of the island of Ireland, with views over Rosslare Bay. This was where it started, the slow seeping into his understanding of the troubling ways of the adult world.

A Sunday morning. Late-ish. He was seven years old. Adolf and Mammy still in bed. He thought, I hope Dada is not doing that thing to Mammy, on top of her....

He entered the bedroom. It was as he feared.

'Go away,' said Adolf, 'we don't want tea.'

Scorched by his father's anger, he withdrew.

And then, which he bracketed with the bedroom and his parents in bed, there were the bloodied cloths steeped in water in the bucket behind the kitchen door that appeared once a month, hung about for three or four days, then vanished and were forgotten until they appeared again a month later. He knew the bucket was connected to what went on in the bedroom, only he did not know exactly how. Not yet.

II

Adolf was contracted to teach piano to May Geraghty, the daughter of the strong farmer whose place lay not far from Sea View Cottage. In return for teaching May, Farmer Geraghty agreed to supply Adolf with sacks of spuds, which Adolf transported home slung over the crossbar of his old policeman's bicycle.

One day Adolf brought his son to Geraghty's, and my father met the pupil. She was a pale-faced girl with freckles and straw-coloured hair, blue eyes, and a red tongue that she often stuck out and wagged at other children, dogs, cows, and even her own father behind his back. She was eleven or twelve years old, a head taller than him and starting to have bosoms. They became pals, and he started hanging around Geraghty's with his new friend whenever he could. May taught him to sing 'Going the Road to Sweet Athy', and he taught her bits of Gilbert and Sullivan he had learnt from Adolf. They went bathing in the little river or on the great strand, and they hung around the farmyard. The cows doing their dung were a source of endless interest. May attempted to teach him to milk. He wasn't very good at milking, unlike May, who could milk like a man, he noticed.

III

He was over at Geraghty's but alone when he spotted an egg under a hedge, brown and smooth and enticing. He touched it. It was warm. He made a decision. He wouldn't find May. Instead, he'd claim this treasure and spirit it home. He took the egg, bolted back and presented his booty to his mother.

'That belongs to somebody,' she said. 'Did anyone see you take it?'

'No.' This was true.

That night in bed he worried about the egg. Had he done wrong? Was he in trouble? The next time he saw May he confessed.

'I took your egg,' he said, and then he explained how he had found it, fallen for it, stolen it.

May told him not to worry as everybody had a few hens who laid out in the summer. Finders, keepers – that was the rule, she said. He wasn't convinced.

A couple of days later when he was up on the hill above Geraghty's he saw her coming out of the farmyard, and he ran down, ducking and hiding behind hedges in order that when he got to the bottom he would be able to emerge and meet her accidentally.

He duly appeared like magic before her, and she was surprised, not having seen him coming.

'Put your hands out,' she said, 'I've something for you.' He did as he was told. She took two eggs from her apron pocket and laid them onto his palms, saying she had got them from a hen who was nesting out. So it really was all right to take eggs if they were lying around, it seemed. Then she asked him to keep a watch out for foxes and to tell her if he saw one. The hens who laid out were at risk, she said.

Another day. He fell in the farmyard and split the skin of his knee. Lovely May stroked his leg to take the scalding pain away, wiped his moist eyes and kissed his cheek. Then she gently washed his bleeding wound at the drinking trough in the yard, tied her handkerchief over the wound with her yellow hair ribbons and walked him back to Sea View Cottage, holding his hand the whole way.

That evening, though, his mother only gave him cursory attention. Grumbling that she was rearing her family 'in a cow shed', she just tied bits of torn cotton around his knee. Later that night, when the candle was blown out and his head had snuggled into the pillow, he remembered everything about his saviour and started a 'made-up story' in which he saved May's life. He would go on telling himself made-up stories that fulfilled his deepest wishes for the rest of his life.

IV

The Geraghtys' farmhouse, a Saturday night. My father was in the kitchen with May. She had half a glass of beer, and now and again she let him take a sip, saying 'Just a sip, mind.' Adolf was in the parlour pounding the piano so hard he could be heard in the kitchen. He played a succession of two-steps, quicksteps and foxtrots, while revellers flew about in the kitchen and May took my father out into the middle of the floor and swirled him about too.

Later, Adolf entered the kitchen with his fiddle and together with a tin whistle and an accordion player he breezed through a succession of Irish jigs and reels. He could play the traditional material as well as his usual popular and classical repertoire, and it was that facility to do both that earned him the moniker by which he was addressed not only that evening but all the time now – 'Adolf the Music Master'.

V

It was Sunday, late August, and it was dry.

Adolf, Rita and the children (Louise and Olive in a pram perhaps) were walking along the track to Geraghty's. Adolf had his bicycle. His spuds were due; he was going to collect them and wheel them back.

Along the route they came to a gateway. The whole family stopped to look into the field beyond. A few days earlier the grass had been cut and left to dry, and today, using a Model T like a tractor, Geraghty was raking the grass into seams that ran across the field.

Adolf had seen cars, but it was in this moment, seeing what a car could do in a field in place of a horse, that he realized the beautiful utility of the motor car. It was truly a magical machine, and it could do magical things.

Geraghty stopped and got out. Adolf spoke to him, the words tumbling out. He couldn't be doing with the bicycle any more, he said, and he must, he absolutely must, have a car. How could he get one?

Easy, Geraghty answered. He had another Model T in a shed back at the farm, which he would be happy to sell to Adolf, and oh no, it wouldn't be sore on Adolf's pocket.

And what about driving itself? Adolf asked.

Nothing to it, said Geraghty. Would Adolf like a go?

What, right now?

Yes, said Geraghty.

Of course he would, said Adolf.

Adolf got into the driving seat. Geraghty showed him the controls. There were three pedals. The left one was for both forward speeds. Press it right down and one was in low gear and went slowly. Allow the pedal to rise fully up and one was in high gear and one went fast. Hold the pedal at halfway and the car was in neutral. The middle pedal was for reverse. To switch from forward to reverse the driver just took his foot off the forward pedal and depressed the reverse one. The right pedal was the brake. There was also a lever on the road side of the driver's seat. This had to be fully forward for high gear, otherwise the left pedal would only rise to neutral. Throttle on the steering wheel. All clear?

Oh yes, said Adolf. He shoved the lever forward, released the left pedal and veered off. As he careered around the field Rita and the children raced after him screaming, Stop! Stop!

Later, Adolf and Geraghty went back to the farm to view the car that was for sale. It was one of the early basic models, the kind popularly known as flivvers. It had a standard chassis, a banquette seat under the hood for four passengers, and a pan at the back for luggage. It was missing one of its artillery wheels, the kind with wooden spokes, but Geraghty's price was good – five pounds, payable in instalments – and Adolf didn't think the missing wheel would be a problem. He knew where to source one.

Adolf got a second-hand wheel and two side screens to enclose the cab. He brought everything to the farm and Geraghty did the fitting. They were very simple, these flivvers, and so easy to work with.

The work done, the crank was turned. The engine started. Adolf climbed into the driving seat. He drove away. He made a lot of noise as he went, and did not seem to be in complete control, but he got home without incident.

He parked outside Sea View Cottage and went in. He found Rita in the kitchen in a fury. The cottage was a pigsty, she said, yet his lordship, Adolf the Music Master, could afford to buy a motor car! This was followed by more of the same. Adolf said nothing. He couldn't, because what she said was true, all true.

14.

The Misses Ashley-Ryder

I

The world was full of secrets. How were people made? Where did they come from? And what exactly were the feelings that men and women had for each other, and then, arising from such feelings presumably, what was the secret thing they did with each other? These things fitted together, only my father didn't know how exactly. And then there was his father's elusiveness. Adolf was always vanishing in the flivver, only to return hours later, often somehow mysteriously altered. It wasn't to Geraghty's he went. It was somewhere else. But where? How could he find out?

The flivver had a tray at the back for luggage. If he stretched himself out on the pan just before Adolf made one of his unexplained journeys, his father would drive away not knowing he was there, and take him to wherever it was he went, and then he would know.

II

It was the day when he knew Adolf always went off in the flivver. A bit before the time Adolf normally left, my father stretched out on the pan at the back. When Adolf came out of Sea View Cottage with his clarinet cases, he did not see his son lying there.

Adolf stowed the cases and cranked the Model T. The engine caught. Adolf climbed into the front seat. The flivver sank slightly rightwards with his weight, then rose. Under the hood a slight kerfuffle as the lever went forward and the left pedal came up, and then the car trundled off. On the pan my father, lying stretched like a corpse as the Model T drove on, stared up at the blue and white sky and the different kinds of cloud streaming overhead.

The car slowed; he felt this. Then he was aware that Adolf was steering through a gateway. Once inside the gate he knew where they were. It was not that far from Sea View Cottage, a long walk really, and he had been here once before on a visit with Adolf. He knew there was a gravel drive with trees on either side, and at the top there was a big grey house, three storeys high, and steps leading up to a wide front door that had a knocker and a fanlight overhead. Inside the house there lived a nice woman called Cynthia Ashley-Ryder, and she was a Protestant – somehow he had picked that up. Cynthia had an elder sister called Gwen, but everyone called her Blossom. She was not like a grown-up at all, but a child in a grown-up's body.

The flivver stopped. There was a faint smell of oil and metal and steam. Adolf got out, retrieved his instruments, crunched over the gravel, climbed the steps and pulled the bell rope. Very far away, deep in the house, my father heard the bell's answering tinkle, and then, a bit later, he heard the door opening and Cynthia's voice, warm, friendly, hopeful and feminine. Adolf remarked that he hoped that he wasn't late for the clarinet lesson, and Cynthia said no, he wasn't, followed by something about Blossom. Her sister, Cynthia said, was curious about Adolf. She was curious about the lesson. Last time Blossom sat in, and this time she would want to sit in again. Blossom was a child who, once she got a notion in to her head, could not be deflected. However, Cynthia had a plan. They would use a different room from the one they used last time, a room in a distant and obscure part of the house, and she hoped that Blossom would not find them there. This would allow them to have their time together without her interfering, hopefully....

Adolf went inside and the door closed. My father slipped off the pan and flitted round to the enormous glasshouse, which he remembered from that initial visit and wanted to explore.

He opened the glasshouse door and stepped forward. Moist, warm air folded around him. He closed the door behind him. The light was green. There was a taste of chalk. He began to walk. Brick shelves on either side lined with pots filled with moist, dark earth, and out of the earth all manner of things were growing. He was both overwhelmed and moved by his sense of life burgeoning inside this cobwebbed glass cavern.

He knew that the clarinet lesson was of fixed duration, so he had to return to the flivver and stretch out on the pan before the lesson finished. He had no watch, however, and was unable to judge the time. Inevitably, he miscalculated.

He was slinking across the gravel when the front door opened, and out onto the steps came Adolf, Cynthia and Blossom (Adolf and Cynthia's efforts to evade Blossom having failed), and his father saw him. At first Adolf was disgruntled and shouted his displeasure. So he'd got there on the pan; did he now propose to get back by the same method?! Did he not know how dangerous it was?! What if some idiot had hit the flivver from behind on the way there or hit them on their return? What if he were thrown out onto the road?

Adolf then stopped abruptly and turned to Cynthia. He had had an idea, he said. Next time he would bring the boy. What did she think about that?

Cynthia turned to Blossom. What if Adolf's little boy came to play with her next time Cynthia had her lesson? Would that be a nice idea?

Blossom clapped her hands. She was delighted. The plan was sealed.

And so Adolf started taking my father to the Ashley-Ryders', and while he and Cynthia had their lesson, and what my father called in his notes their 'loving time', he and the child-woman, Blossom, played together. Their play was baby play mostly, with Blossom the mammy and he the baby. The Ashley-Ryders' house had a huge bathroom, and now Blossom had a baby she yearned to wash her baby in the bath, but my father wouldn't have that, obviously, as that would have involved undressing.

III

Although Adolf drove there, the Ashley-Ryders' house wasn't far from Sea View Cottage – at least, not going as the crow flew, across the fields. My father now started walking over on his own to visit. Blossom was still agitating to bathe her baby, and one day he was struck by inspiration: he slipped on his bathing trunks and then he went over, and Blossom had her dearest wish granted. She washed her baby in the white-enamelled cast-iron bath.

IV

He was with his father driving up or down the Ashley-Ryders' drive when they passed a paddock inside which a stallion, having scrambled up onto the back of a mare, was grinding his belly against her behind. He was shocked first by the violence and then by the realization that this belonged with the Sunday mornings when Adolf and Rita were in bed and Adolf didn't want him in the room. It seemed it was a universal, this getting-on-top-of-the-lady thing.

The world was slowly yielding up its secrets, and there would be more to follow, he was sure of it. With this came another feeling, not necessarily at this moment but not long after, and this was the certainty – as comforting as it was essential – that one day he would escape his family and get out into the world, and that out there he would not just be free but he would be a somebody.

15.

An Incident

I

Night. A country road. Adolf driving, my father beside him. All was calm, all was quiet. The engine puttered, and the world that slipped past and under them was all black bar a little splinter of road top and hedgerow lit by the flivver's acetylene headlamps.

Suddenly, a man ran out into the middle of the road. He wore a hat and a coat. In one hand he carried a sack, and in the other he held something. The man made a downward motion with this hand that held this something, the universal sign for Stop. Adolf braked. The man darted to the driver's side. The 'something' was a black snub-barrelled revolver.

'Republican Army,' said the man quietly. He then explained that he was an Irregular. This made him an enemy of the Free State. He waved his sack – dynamite and ammunition for his comrades. Unfortunately there were checkpoints to pass before he could make delivery. Until now he hadn't known how he'd do this, but lo, here was salvation – Adolf the Music Master. He travelled around Wexford's roads willy-nilly, teaching

67

these ones, playing with those ones. The Free State soldiers knew and liked him. Well, here was Adolf's chance to aid Ireland. He could take the man and his sack through. It would be a peach. The Irregular waved his revolver again.

Adolf turned to his son. He told him to get out and walk slowly back up the road they had just driven down. Eventually he would reach Sea View Cottage. He was to go inside.

'Say nothing to anyone,' said Adolf.

'Not a word,' said the Irregular, who had crossed from the driver to the passenger side while Adolf had been talking. 'Understand?'

He nodded. He understood all right. He got out and stood at the side and watched as the Irregular backed into the seat, swung his legs around and lifted the sack onto his lap.

Adolf engaged the car in gear and began to creep up the road. Though his son could not know this, the explosives had made Adolf nervous. He feared they were unstable and liable to explode if subject to jerky movement. That was why he drove so slowly, so carefully.

II

My father did not want to walk home in the dark. Seeing the car crawl off, he realized that he could avoid this.

He strode forward. The flivver was easy to catch up with. The next part would be easy too: there was no rear-view mirror (when Adolf wanted to see behind him, he literally stuck his head out and looked back), and the back window in the hood was just a pane of yellow celluloid, small and high up, so there was little chance he would be spotted in that way either.

He grabbed the edge of the hood and stepped carefully up onto the pan. Job done. The flivver moved on, and he rode, staring ahead. At first there was darkness everywhere other than where the light from the lamps fell, but then, in the distance, far away down the road, he saw kerosene lamps, their yellow and orange flames trembling. It was the first checkpoint. Adolf slowed as he approached, and my father crouched and balled himself very small and pushed himself against the back of the hood. The flivver was just moving. He heard voices, Adolf's and the Free State soldier's. Then the flivver sped up slightly, and as it passed the soldier didn't notice him crouched on the pan, but after they passed my father saw the soldier's outline as he stared away up the road into the darkness, his rifle hung on a strap over his shoulder, the lamps standing on the road, and a wooden contraption with a sign on it. Then, as the flivver moved forward, the soldier and the lamps shrunk and finally vanished, and it was all darkness again. He stood and rode until they came to the next checkpoint, where he hid himself again. The flivver passed through the second and third checkpoints without incident.

Later it was another country road, an especially lonely one. Adolf stopped. Bent low, Ernest could not see but he heard the Irregular slip out, say something and walk off. He lifted his head to look over the top of the hood. The Irregular was walking off, the darkness folding around him, then he was gone. Ernest was safe. He jumped down, darted along the driver's side of the flivver and presented himself to his father – ta-da!

Adolf blanched.

'Why did I send you home?' asked Adolf. He lit a cigarette. His father now answered his own question. Because he wasn't thinking. If he'd been thinking he'd have known his son couldn't be trusted to do what he'd been asked. Oh yes, he should have kept his son close.

A pause. The engine trembled. The acetylene lamps hissed. Adolf tapped the seat next him, his usual place. Ernest went around and got in.

16.

Miscellaneous

I

He was at school. The teacher was a nun. She had a leather strap hanging from her girdle. He had done something. A bad thing. 'Put both your hands out,' she said. He had to. He knew that. So he did. She whammed his palms a couple times. It hurt. Terrifically. His eyes watered. He thought he wanted to pee. He went back to his desk, sat, and put his stinging hands between his thighs. And then he made a decision. He wasn't going to bother with school any more. It wasn't worth it. And so he didn't.

Thereafter, when he went he didn't bother listening but sat dreaming or staring out of the window. He took nothing in, and was certainly unable to answer the nun's questions. Before long he became known as one of the slow ones, one of the no-hopers who were allowed to sit quietly and not much bothered by the nun as long as they didn't bother her in turn by being noisy or disruptive.

Of course word from the school found its way back to Sea View Cottage. In the school's estimation he was probably not very bright.

The judgement went uncontested by Adolf and Rita. Adolf was too busy with his own concerns to be bothered to do anything about it, while Rita, given her default deference to anyone in authority, just assumed that if the teachers said this then it must be right. After all, the school surely wouldn't have said what they said if it wasn't right, would they? No, it was the truth and she accepted it.

What was not considered by Adolf and Rita was of course that school was not just about academic learning; school was also where a child was socialized. By not participating, not only was Ernest not learning about matters academic; he wasn't learning about how to get along with people either. But his parents didn't worry about that. They just assumed that, being not much interested in learning, it followed that he was not much interested in people (though he had a few pals, like May), and that was that. He was just a solitary creature who was largely content with his own company.

II

First thing each morning in the school holidays, he got up and ran outside, and under great rolling cloudy skies he chased through the fields, the bog lanes, along the cliffs, the beaches, past rock pools, past the sea. When it came to getting out and running free he was like an alcoholic with his first drink. He had do it. He had to get outside, partly to escape Sea View Cottage and his parents' sniping and Ada bossing him, and partly because of the elation and sense of anticipation that flooded him when he got outside. This was the feeling that something would happen – he didn't know what exactly, but he knew it would. The day would unfold and offer gifts, either personal or occult. He might meet a pal, or he might find a magic object. He already had a talisman that he kept in his pocket at all times, a brass cross (which wasn't a true cross because a small portion of the end of each arm was bent up at a slight angle), which made him generally lucky, he believed, but what he really wanted was something that would grant his wishes when he rubbed it, and one day he was certain he would find it.

III

There was a cabin near Sea View Cottage where an old woman lived. She was 'dangerous mad'. Those were the words used to describe her: dangerous mad. He was warned to avoid her.

He had a friend, Tom Cummins, a couple of years older, about ten years old, who lived in another cottage nearby. Tom's father worked for the council on the roads. Together with Tom he gathered sticks from a wood, made these into bundles, and carried them to the old woman's door. Knock, knock, knock. The door opened. The woman's face showed in the space between door and lintel. She was grubby. She reeked of turf.

They had sticks, the boys explained. Would she have them? She would of course, she said. She took the sticks, went off, returned, and pressed a clutch of small tarts into their hands. As she did she whispered, 'Keep away from people, they're no good.'

The boys carried the tarts back to the wood, found a spot, sat down and set about eating. The pastry was very hard; a combination of spit and dextrous gnawing was required to get through the crusty edge. The filling when they reached it though, and which they'd assumed was jam, turned out to be treacle, strong and bitter but strangely delicious. He and Tom were delighted by their first experience of enterprise, and thereafter they returned to the old woman's cottage often, sold her many bundles of sticks, and received many cakes in return. He never told his parents though.

IV

He was ready for music lessons. Ada was by now playing little tunes and 'owning' the piano, so Adolf said, 'We do not want two piano players – Ernie will play the fiddle.'

He was given an old fiddle. He didn't like the thing, or the sound it made. He got as far as 'Red Saffron' in the music book, with Ada accompanying him on the piano, then he gave up. He didn't want to practice. He still longed to be on the piano stool though, and he never stopped believing that his place up there had been usurped.

V

A gang of children milled about in the road near Sea View Cottage. One of the children, a girl, had a go-cart made of pram wheels and rough bits of scavenged timber. Her brother, Neddy, with a bucket on his lap for the blackberries that would be picked shortly, was strapped into the go-cart. Neddy was about his age, seven or eight. There was something wrong with his legs, and a blanket covered them.

Neddy made one of his typical spittle-choked sounds. His sister unhooked the old billycan dangling from the back of the go-cart and wheeled her brother through a field gate, and then behind the hedge so the other children couldn't see. After a minute or two, brother and sister returned. He knew that if he were to sniff the billycan it would smell of pee. That's how Neddy did his number ones. He peed in the billycan, and then his sister emptied it. Everyone knew this.

The children trekked to a nearby hill where the hedgerows were famed for their heavy, succulent fruit, and picking commenced. Neddy's sister parked her brother in a little sand quarry at the side. 'Don't rock!' she said. Neddy nodded as if he understood. He would go on nodding until she returned. Neddy was known for this too.

Neddy's sister went off. My father, in the meantime, doubled back to investigate a bird's nest he'd noticed earlier. The nest was empty. He retraced his steps. He could see children straggling up the hill ahead of him. Some had started little fruit piles on the road. Somebody, the sister probably, would get the bucket later from Neddy and gather the berries up.

As he passed the quarry entrance, he glanced in. The go-cart was on its side, and Neddy, who was strapped in, was on the ground on his side.

He tiptoed over the sandy, pebble-strewn quarry floor. He feared that he would find Neddy with frothy spit billowing from his mouth, or worse, dead, whatever dead looked like.

When he got to him, he saw that Neddy was lying quite still, his eyes closed under his fringe of black hair. The blanket had fallen away, and he saw the cotton shorts Neddy wore and his spaghetti legs.

Neddy opened an eye and looked up. He had a lopsided face, one eye too low, but because of the way his cheek was pressed into the quarry floor his face appeared straightened. It occurred to my father that Neddy hadn't shouted or screamed, and he realized that Neddy had been waiting for help.

He pushed the go-cart upright, and Neddy along with it. He spread the blanket over Neddy's legs. What did he do now? Leave? Stay? As he wondered he felt his hand being taken. He looked down. Neddy, with both his hands, had grasped his.

My father began to cry involuntarily, the tears hot and salty. Was this on account of his realization that life was cruel and unfair? It really didn't seem just that Neddy, having toppled, should have to wait, his face in the dirt, for someone to come and set him back upright. Or perhaps what provoked his tears was the realization that Neddy's family cared about Neddy much more than his own seemed to care about him. The tears may not have been for the other: they may well have been for himself.

VI

He came home to Sea View Cottage from the lanes with a sock missing and his shirt muddy, which provoked a tirade from Rita about thoughtless children who lost their socks and muddied their shirts, just pleased themselves and did what they wanted. Rather like his father, as it happened. Another time he returned with a sack of spuds he had 'found' in a field, and she shouted, 'So this is what's become of you! You've become a tinker!'

When his father came home he heard from his mother another kind of tirade. These concerned a husband who pleased himself buying motor cars and what have you, while his wife had to live in what was called a cottage but was actually a cabin with a leaking roof.

Rita was changing. She was ageing. Her hairline was receding. This left her forehead higher and squarer. Her eyes were becoming more mournful, her lips thinner, her mouth more curved down at the corners, her face narrower and showing pallor, her body smaller. She was shrinking with misery, and might one day become nothing. And yet, her son noticed, despite the rows and the raging, sometimes his mother and father touched one another's shoulders, or held hands, or glanced at one another with softened expressions, and then on 31 July 1923 the fifth Gébler child came, a girl, Iris, who would later be known as Irene.

17.

Tramore One

I

Around the time of Irene's birth, a letter arrived from Adolf's younger brother, Hermann. He was looking for opportunities. Adolf wrote back that Ireland was the future due to a marvellous combination: the inexhaustible appetite of the Irish for moving pictures, and the shortage of good musicians able to provide silent films with the music needed to come alive when projected. Adolf added that he was planning a move to Waterford or nearby, where the prospects for a musician willing to accompany films were mighty. If Hermann wished, Adolf concluded, he could come to Ireland, live with him and Rita, and make himself a lot of money.

In the high summer of 1923, shortly after the birth of Irene, the family left Wexford and moved to Tramore, a resort town outside Waterford. They rented a house opposite the graveyard on Church Road. 'Church Villa' was a draughty, shabby, two-storey house – it had been built with certain genteel pretensions around 1850 – with a mouldering conservatory running across the back in which nothing was growing. At the side was a carriage house, inside which sat a 1900 Wolseley motor car, complete even to its brass standby oil lamps, all dusty and cobweb-covered. When it was raining my father and his siblings sometimes played in it. In the roof space of the carriage house, reached by a steep set of rickety stairs, there was an attic with a fire grate where servant boys would once have boarded, and here he and his sisters liked to ape adults, swanning about and smoking cigarettes made of brown paper.

II

As in Glasnevin, as in Rosslare, Adolf was soon accepted by his neighbours as 'one of ourselves' because of his willingness to play on any old piano anywhere such popular tunes of day as 'Ma! (He's Making Eyes at Me)' and 'Horsey! Keep Your Tail Up!'

As it was the holiday season there was an open-air cinema on Tramore beach, and Adolf played piano for the films. He wore a straw boater and a blazer for the shows, which added to the occasion. My father, eight years old, took the hat around to the audience in their deckchairs and collected their money.

III

Sometime in September the open-air cinema folded, and Adolf found work as musical director of the orchestra of Broad Street Theatre (later the Savoy Cinema).

It was a Saturday. Adolf had to play the children's show, which was probably in the morning, and for this it was just him, the other musicians only coming on in the afternoon. He went in, bringing his two elder children with him. According to his terms and conditions, they came in for free as long as they didn't sit in the auditorium and take seats from paying members of the public – they had to sit beside him below the screen, hidden from view by dusty green baize curtains hung from brass poles.

The cinema was filling up. The shouts of the swelling child audience were incredible. From his chair beside Ada he watched his father. Adolf had a newspaper on the music holder on the piano, lit by a special light. He read, sometimes running his finger across the columns of news print, and at the same time he smoked a Jamaican cigar – the smoke was blue, its smell strong and bitter.

The auditorium's gas lights faded. The fire curtains covering the screen glided away. The audience's volume rose then fell. Adolf's hands moved on the keyboard and stirring chords flooded out. The projector whirred and a white beam of light appeared in the darkness, and hundreds of millions of motes danced inside the seam as the film's opening frames, shimmering and jerky, appeared on the screen.

Adolf's upturned face was lit by the gauzy light from the screen. The end of his cigar glowed. His music sounded out, rich and thrilling. He looked back at the newspaper and read on while continuing to play, and then he lifted his eyes back to the screen again, and this was how he did it when at work in the cinema. He read and played, played and read….

My father and Ada got off their seats. If they watched the films from here it would give them a crick in the neck because they were so close to the screen. They slipped through the curtains and went into the auditorium, located two empty seats near the front, and sat. This was a far superior spot from which to watch, and if the usherette came they could easily vanish back behind the curtain like fish startled by a shadow.

The first subtitle showed, and the entire auditorium of children, including Ada beside him, chorused the words together. And having started, they did not stop. Every subtitle was shouted out, and so, as he sat there, he, an illiterate, began to understand that the sounds he was hearing and the shapes he was seeing were connected, and that was how, not instantly but after many matinees, he learnt to read. And once that happened he became frantic for books, newspapers, stories, anything with writing, while simultaneously he took up the pencil and began to form his own letters, and from there he progressed to writing words, sentences and paragraphs. School must have played a role, though there's no mention of one in the account he prepared later. As he has it, the cinema was where he got his education. It should be added, of course, that what he achieved was well below what he should have been able to achieve, given his age. Had Rita and Adolf been more attentive it might have been different. He might have got an education and fulfilled his potential. But harassed and burdened as they were with their own cares, they preferred to let their son follow his own wayward course, for which he would never forgive them.

IV

Alongside his work at the Savoy Cinema, Adolf continued to teach, and with his better pupils he formed an octet. One of the ensemble's members was Hannah, who played the violin. She was a very good musician – so good that Adolf thought she should go professional. She had a warm intelligence, as opposed to Rita's, which was a bitter intelligence. Hannah was in her thirties, unmarried.

Hanna's surname was Winton, and hers was a minor 'ascendancy' family. The Winton house stood in neat parkland. Hanna lived here with her sisters and brothers and parents. The octet rehearsed there, and my father went along with Adolf. While the musicians played he roamed about, and as at the Ashley-Ryder house there was a greenhouse (all big houses had one in those days, it seemed to him), and he was at liberty to eat what he wanted. He gorged on apples and black grapes, though he took care to keep his fruit eating hidden from his elder sister and his mother. The only rule was that if he found the greenhouse door open he was to leave it open, and if it was closed he was to leave it closed.

Rita was unimpressed by Adolf's music making. She had stock phrases that she muttered whenever he was about and could hear. These included, 'My husband, he's everywhere except at home,' and 'It's well for some, but I can't amuse myself going to rich people's houses to play music. No money comes from that.' Rita never went to the Wintons' house, but when the octet gave public performances playing well-known pieces by Schubert, Schumann and Brahms, she did attend.

V

Hermann, having left his wife, Irma, behind in Frankfurt, arrived in Ireland on 17 October 1923. He lodged in Church Villa, where he agreed to contribute towards his keep, and secured work as the musical director of the Coliseum Cinema. As autumn slid into winter, the house was difficult to heat. The fires and the range seemed to eat coal, and the scuttles were no sooner filled than they were empty. It was incredible how quickly the fires gobbled the coal up.

Then my father and his sharp-eyed elder sister Ada saw Hermann spiriting coal upstairs. The next time Hermann was out, Rita searched his room. The bottom drawer of his wardrobe was filled with coal. It transpired that he had been taking their coal upstairs and then returning it to the household as his contribution!

VI

He was in the Savoy. This was not a children's show so it must have been evening. The film was running, the accompanying music was sounding. A pair of women's bare breasts appeared on the screen. They hung there, white and round and extraordinary, and from the reactions around him in the auditorium he sensed again what he had already begun to intuit: the body's private parts had a colossal power in the complex lives of men and women and their relationships to one another.

VII

It was a fine day. He and Adolf went off in the flivver. He fell asleep in the front seat. When he woke, the flivver was parked on a country road. He saw country gates and a country bridge. He heard footsteps and voices, Adolf's and Hannah's.

'Hannah,' he heard Adolf saying, 'I have children. What can I do? You know I can't …'.

He cautiously half-lifted an eyelid and there they were, Adolf and Hannah. His father wore a suit. Hannah wore a cloche hat and pearls. They were holding hands. Their faces looked the same, he thought. Like brother and sister, he thought. There was a comfort. Siblings didn't have loving times like grown-ups, did they?

VIII

One of their neighbours in Church Road gave him a she-pup. She was small and brown-eyed, and her soft, furry stomach was lined with tiny nipples. He brought the she-pup home to Church Villa. 'Take her away,' Adolf said. 'Take her to the sea and drown her.'

He went to Tramore Strand. There was a statue on the beach commemorating an army transport that sunk out at sea with great loss of life. As so many soldiers and sailors had drowned here, he thought, this was just the place to drown the she-pup.

He took off his shoes and socks, waded out a bit and threw the she-pup in. He expected the pup to sink, but she didn't. She held her head up and frantically struggled to a seaweed-covered rock, and then scrambled up onto it somehow.

Since she had refused to drown he had no alternative. He lifted her off the rock, carried her back to Church Villa and brought her inside, hidden up his jersey. In the kitchen he met Adolf.

'You can take the pup out from under your jersey,' said his father.

There was nothing he could do. He brought her out. His emotions were churning. First there had been excitement and joy when the neighbour gave him the pup. Then there had been the desolation when he was told to drown her. Then had come the elation that followed the she-pup's refusal to drown, which surely cancelled Adolf's order. And now, after all he had been through, he was back where he had begun, about to be told yet again that the pup couldn't stay and that he was to get rid of her. He could fight and struggle against his fate but he could not escape it. He was always found out, wasn't he, or so it seemed to him now.

18.

Tramore Two

The second summer in Tramore. The day was bright; the sun was high and warm. Adolf packed the flivver with kids, my father included. Adolf checked he had the bag of oranges and apples for later. He had. Adolf turned the crank. The engine fired. Adolf jumped in. Adolf drove off. He was taking the children to the beach. Not the one at Tramore; another one, with interesting rock pools full of marine treasures, fish of all kinds, creatures in shells, trembling shrimps, and most prized of all, bony crabs with spindly legs and pale pink shells.

The road to the sea turned and twisted and went up and down. The flivver slowed down whenever it climbed and sped up whenever it went down. This motion went on till the final brow was crested and, glory of glories, there was the sea stretched out ahead, green and flat, smooth and glass-like, and above it the sky, blue and lovely, with great clouds lying on the distant horizon, flat on the bottom and fluffy on top.

Adolf slowed, changed into low gear and nosed the flivver onto the track that went down to the beach. It had been made so that seaweed could be carted up, and it was so steep the kelp gatherers never filled their carts more than a quarter full: that was the maximum that horses could haul. The track clung to a cliff face, and on its left side there was a sturdy parapet wall with occasional gaps.

The car moved forward and down. So precipitous was the track that the flivver's front was instantly noticeably lower than the rear. My father's stomach felt light and fluttery. He heard the little stones, lifted by the slow turn of the flivver's wheels, striking the car's underbelly. It sounded, he thought, like a fistful of pebbles hurled at glass. The tyres also made a unique noise as they turned, a funny, hollow booming. Occasionally he heard the special sound made not by wheels turning but when the tyre itself was somehow hit by a stone.

Then came a cough and a wrench. It was not external; it was inside the flivver, in the undercarriage below the floor pan. The frequency of the little stones striking the undercarriage sped up. The sound made by the tyres moved from a growl to a rumble, and the rumble swamped the tyres' airy interior noise. There was a sense of motion, of growing speed, and then, a hurtling forward movement. There was a smell too. It was a scorched smell, acrid and bitter, oily and rubbery, and with the smell there was smoke rising from below, nasty, thin, insinuating smoke with a taste like fish bones when they were burnt. It was the brakes. They were on fire.

'Hold on!' Adolf shouted. He steered left and got the flivver's left side into contact with the parapet wall, and as the flivver's body and the stone now ground against one another, a terrifying noise was made. There was a gap coming, and Adolf steered out to avoid the gap, then brought the flivver back and ground its left side against the wall again until it finally came to a lurching shuddering halt. There was a moment of quiet. Adolf did not move, but remained holding the wheel tightly, staring forward. Next thing there were squeals and grunts and gasps from the children crowded beside Adolf. A little girl started to cry and said that she wanted to go home.

Adolf stepped out of the car. He was shaking so much it looked like he might topple over, but he reached forward and put his hand on the flivver's bonnet, and he stayed, leaning like that, for ages. Then he straightened up and started to circle the flivver. He was obviously going to inspect the damage. My father scooted out and joined him at the front, where he saw that the left front wheel was completely ground away, and all that remained was the stub of the axle. He also saw that the left front mudguard was gone, and the left side of the car was mangled. The little girl was still crying. Adolf called out. There was no need to cry. They had survived. They had lived. They were safe.

In the post-mortem that followed, Adolf speculated on the cause of the catastrophe. On an incline, by keeping the car in gear, engine compression acted as an additional retardant to the small two-brake drums on the Model T Ford's back wheels (it had none on the front). But if the driveshaft broke, and Adolf thought that was what had happened, the engine compression effect was lost, and on the steep downhill track the two rear brakes weren't strong enough to bring the car to a stop.

Adolf later returned with a party of adults to try rescue the car. His companions were amazed that the car hadn't gone over the edge. The car itself was a write-off; it was not even worth towing away. Anything useful was cannibalized, and the remains were heaved over the wall and onto the beach below. The track was now clear for the carts of seaweed to make their slow, weary way to the top.

II

To replace the Model T, Hermann and Adolf bought a little two-seater Perry motorcar, and then fell out over the repayments. There was a row in the kitchen, and then the brothers retreated to separate corners and wept bitter tears. Adolf fulminated in English. 'I should have remembered,' he said, 'Hermann was so mean with money. First stealing the coal and now crying about five pounds!'

III

Fourteen months after the birth of Irene, on 25 September 1924, a sixth Gébler child, Adrian, was born. Quite why the unhappy couple Adolf and Rita had as many children as they had is a puzzle. Though Rita was a practising Catholic, if not an especially pious or devout one, Adolf was an implacable opponent of nefarious dogma, so it seems unlikely that Church teaching had anything to do with this high birth rate – not if he had anything to do with it at any rate. I doubt that it was ignorance either – both knew what needed to be done to avoid conception. Perhaps the explanation was that Rita used intimacy to secure and smoothe her unfaithful, truculent husband, and the children were simply the product of that strategy. Or perhaps it was that Adolf, who drank and had an overweening and even bullying temperament, simply insisted on sex and Rita had to comply. Or perhaps Rita and Adolf's was a marriage that thrived on conflict. First they rowed and then, in the privacy of the marital bed, they reconciled and were happy until the next argument. Their marriage would certainly not be unusual in alternating grinding conflict with momentary erotic amity.

19.

England

Rita's sister Judy, and her husband, Freddie Dack, now lived in Walsall, close to Wolverhampton, and her other sister, Polly, and her husband, Billy Williams, also lived somewhere in the English midlands. Because of these connections, Adolf sought work in the region and was eventually engaged as the pianist at the Scala Cinema, Wolverhampton, commencing on Thursday 24 September 1925 at a salary of £5. 10s. 0d. per week.

The position was probationary, but he passed, and moved to a sister venue, the Agricultural Hall Cinema, a theatre in the Snow Hill area of the city with over a thousand seats and an organ for accompaniment.

Rita and the children left Tramore and Hermann and joined Adolf in England[4]. For my father, the move was a miserable experience. In Ireland, thanks to a regime of benign neglect at home, he had largely escaped the

---

4   Hermann remained behind working at the Coliseum Cinema, and later became a teach-
    er in Waterford city and a viola player with the Cork Symphony Orchestra, which was
    founded by the son of Adolf's fellow internee – oh, what a small world was Ireland – Aloys
    Fleischmann.

rigours of school discipline and structure, but in the English midlands he couldn't. At the school to which he was sent he was assessed, judged to be well below where he ought to be given his age and, though he was nine, going on for ten years of age, he was put in a class of five-, six- and seven-year-olds. And if this weren't bad enough, he also had the wrong clothes – Irish ones, whatever they were, and not English ones. He was thus, when he started, the new 'ill-dressed' big boy in the baby class, for which he was harried mercilessly by boys his age, and the bullying, once it had started, just ran on, though the reasons for its starting were long forgotten. In Ireland he hadn't been much involved with school, and on that account hadn't connected with his peers. Now in England there was an opportunity to rectify that deficiency, only this didn't happen. His outlier status made him a focus of obloquy, with the result that rather than being socialized, which would have brought him closer to people, he was ostracized and vilified, which pushed him further away.

Later, his persecution at school fused with memories of Ada at home denigrating him as an ignorant and stupid dumb-cluck to form one of his key ideas. His siblings were largely cherished at home and as a consequence they all flourished at school. He, on the other hand, was singled out as the family's fool (Ada being the chief persecutor), and the result, inevitably, was all that followed. He would never forget this.

II

I don't know where the Géblers lived when they first arrived in Wolverhampton, but it wasn't long before they secured a council house on the Low Hill estate. After Sea View Cottage and Church Villa, this was a minor miracle. However, this good fortune wouldn't and couldn't help the marriage, and it was in this, the first good house they'd ever had, that Rita's 'guerrilla war' against Adolf now began in earnest – or perhaps it had always been like this but only now was my father noticing these things. Rita's principal weapon was her tongue, and her principal charge was that Adolf was selfish, feckless and profligate, and as a result his family had to go without. Her favourite technique was to denounce Adolf to the children as if he were absent when actually he was present. Two lines have come down to me:

'Oh, your father can afford his glass of beer in the pub after closing while his poor children have holes in their shoes and wear cast-off clothing.'

'Oh, your father does what he likes, but we make do with nothing.'

Adolf's English was no match for hers, especially when she was aroused by her own invective. His response in these situations, therefore, was often to remain silent and to act as if he didn't care to reply because what he was hearing was not worthy of a response. This was a mistake, for Rita was able to argue that his silence confirmed the justice of her case.

Adolf's other strategy to protect himself from Rita was to inure himself with drink, and when Adolf was drunk, as often he was, he did not keep quiet. Rows erupted, plates and cups were thrown, furniture was overturned, and sometimes blows and kicks were traded.

Yet despite this terrible marital life, intimacy was not totally extinguished. Not long after the move to Wolverhampton my father was in his parents' bedroom. He was rummaging about as children will, and at the back of the top shelf of the wardrobe he found a round box that he guessed might be for face powder or some sort of cosmetic, but when he opened the box he found it contained a little rubber thing with a rim, which rose to a point in the middle. It was like a coolie hat, and though he had no word for it, and though he did not know what it did exactly, he knew it was something to do with that thing that Mammy and Daddy did when they had their bedroom door closed.

III

The early Wolverhampton years were the time when Adolf was at his most prosperous.

Film music was mostly live and mostly improvised. The musician looked at the screen and, as the film rolled, the musician played. Timing was vital. Sometimes the music had to anticipate the visuals, other times not. Tact was also important: the music couldn't be crass, couldn't underline. It had to aid but never force. And it was an all-or-nothing business, this accompanying malarkey. When the music worked, the ability of the moving pictures to enchant and to mesmerize was enhanced, but when the music failed, the images lost this capacity and an audience's pleasure was diminished, even ruined. Improvisation demanded inventiveness, along with skill, fluency and technique, and not all musicians had these virtues.

Adolf knew the problems from the inside (he had been an accompanist since before the Great War), and he knew that the obvious solution (and he was not alone in thinking this) was the bespoke score. With this material on their music stands, accompanists would never fumble as they struggled to watch and improvise. All they would have to do was watch out for the cues, sight-read and play. To make such scores required composition and orchestration skills, which of course he had, and so, inevitably, on behalf of his employer, Associated Provincial Picture Houses, or APPH, who in turn were owned by the conglomerate Provincial Cinematograph Theatres Limited, along with his usual playing duties, he began viewing forthcoming films and creating scores with separate parts for the different instrumentalists. As well as using these himself, he was also able to sell them to other cinemas when they showed the same film.

Unfortunately, there were so many films it was impossible for a single musician to generate bespoke scores for every single one. But Adolf had an ingenious solution to this problem. All the material he wrote was returned to him after the film for which it had been written had finished its run, and was then broken up and organized, with the help of Ada and my father, into a library wherein everything was catalogued by theme – 'Storm', 'Chase', 'Araby', et cetera. This material was then rented out to accompanists who would use it as a guide from which to improvise. He also recycled this generic material into the new bespoke scores that he wrote. Oh yes, this was a model where not a note went to waste. It worked brilliantly, the money started flowing in, and the family left Low Hill and moved to a better area, the Old Fallings Road, Bushbury, where Adolf bought a new jerry-built detached house, constructed to sell rather than to last, on the never-never.

He named the new home Villa Bohème, a nod both to his homeland and Puccini's opera *La Bohème*, which he loved more than any other piece of music.

Now there was cash at last, Adolf bought a maroon Singer saloon motor car, a small, sleek, lovely thing, and a wind-up gramophone with a big trumpet, and lots of heavy shellac 78s, mostly Jazz, mostly American artists, and on Sunday nights in Villa Bohème, my father, Ada and their friends had little foxtrot parties. Fats Waller, with his exciting stride piano style, was their favourite. In his notes, my father wrote rhapsodically, which was not his characteristic register, about these times:

> *The Twenties*
> *To be ten and eleven and twelve years old in the twenties … you fell in love with those girls in the Shantung* [soft, undressed Chinese silk] *square dresses to the knee, artificial silk stockings* [viscose rayon], *garters, low-heeled strapped shoes, shortcut straight hair with two points caressing the rouged cheeks, who, at the drop of a steel needle on to a His Master's Voice 78 ('Wind it up!') danced the exhilarating Charleston … To turn over from childhood to adolescence in the twenties meant to be marked for life.*

IV

The garden of Villa Bohème was filled with rubbish left by the builder, and my father cleared this away and established a garden. He was good with his hands. He had always made toys, and since he found a cobbler's last (a tool for the manufacture and repair of shoes) in a rubbish dump he had always fixed his boots. He had a knack for understanding how things worked, particularly complicated mechanical and electrical things, and as he grew older his competence grew. Among other things, he now made himself, from scavenged components, a crystal radio set that he listened to at night when he was in bed. From all around the world strange music and new voices flooded out of the earpiece and into his head.

20.

Apprenticeship

I

The story of the cinema was one of continuous technological and aesthetic improvement, and as everyone knew in the late twenties, synchronized sound would be next.

Currently, shots of characters speaking were followed by inter-titles with what they had just said written out for the audience to read. All other sounds (waves on a beaches, horses galloping, et cetera) were suggested by music. In pursuit of verisimilitude, some films came with a soundtrack pre-recorded on gramophone records, which would be played through speakers to the audience in the auditorium as the film was showing. It was a crude system, and couldn't work for dialogue because there was no system for synchronizing image and gramophone record: there was no way with this system of making the audience *believe* they were hearing exactly what they were seeing.

However, as Adolf knew, as everyone knew, what was coming was a system that would allow a picture and a pre-recorded soundtrack that came with it to run in tandem simultaneously. This system would offer audiences not only images with matching sounds, but pictures of characters talking that synchronized exactly with what they were heard saying. Once that happened the talkies would have arrived and film really could be said to replicate life.

For musicians, who had provided most of the sound world of the cinema up to then, the talkies would be a catastrophe. However, for those with the right technical expertise, it would be a wonderful opportunity. Silent films were massive, but the talkies would be even bigger.

At least, so Adolf thought. And so, with one eye on this future ('A projectionist will always have a job,' he liked to say), and the other on his son, whom he believed was good for nothing except superior manual labour ('He can do anything with those hands of his, but don't ask him to think'), he wangled my father the position of apprentice operator, as the trainee projectionist was called, at the Agricultural Hall Cinema. As Adolf had done so much business with APPH, they presumably took his son partly as a favour to Adolf, though they might also have found my father's mechanical aptitude persuasive.

II

Although legally he was not meant to start work till he turned fourteen, which as he had it was on 1 January 1929, he actually started at the Agricultural Hall Cinema some time in the summer or autumn of 1928, when he was thirteen.

His working day started at ten. His first job was to cart the rubbish from the previous day down to the basement and heave it all into the furnace. Then, in the projection booth, or operating box, he spent an hour or so cleaning out and oiling the projection machines.

From twelve to two, in cotton gloves, he was at the rewinding table. His job, in order to reduce the number of irksome reel changes, which interrupted the flow of the screenings, was to make up the big split spools for the shows by joining shorter lengths together. In order to get material into the right order he had to put what would be projected last onto the spool first, and what would be projected first, last. Besides sequencing, he also had to ensure that the material was emulsion-down as he wound it on (if it was emulsion-up, then the geometry was reversed and all movements were in the other direction from the way they had been shot), and that any nicks or tears in the film were identified and repaired, otherwise there was a danger that the film would snag and then snap during projection. And if all that weren't enough, the nitrate film was unstable and liable to combust if handled carelessly, so he had to be extremely gentle with it.

He had to have the reels checked and ready in time for the first matinee. At about 1.30 p.m. people started to drift into the auditorium. So they would not have to sit in silence there were gramophone records provided, and his job was to play these over the public address system until the time came for the projectionist to dim the lights and flick the projector on, which started the screening (as the trainee he was never allowed to perform these tasks).

Thereafter, he would be in the carbon-arc-fume-filled operating box, where, amidst the ceaseless clatter of the projector, he spent his time rewinding end-out reels that had just been projected so they were front-out again and could be projected at the next show. His working day lasted until 10 p.m. (as the apprentice operator he got away an hour before the adults, who finished at 11) and he worked six days a week. His salary was fifteen shillings a week, and for every day without a film breaking or a mechanical breakdown he got a bonus, paid every six months.

III

In February 1929, APPH was brought by Gaumont British Theatres, a company with a progressive outlook and a modernizing agenda. At the Agricultural Hall Cinema they were still playing records with pre-recorded soundtracks, but the talkies were coming to town, and soon, now that Gaumont were in charge. The first talkie in Wolverhampton, following the installation of a sound system, was *The Singing Fool*. It opened at the

Agricultural Hall Cinema on 12 August 1929, and because of record audiences, management retained the film for a second week.

Adolf's life as an accompanist was over. His sheet music business folded. On top of that, he couldn't get teaching work as all over Britain thousands of musicians recently made redundant by the talkies were offering lessons for next to nothing. Having no income, he was unable to make the repayments on Villa Bohème, and the house was repossessed.

He had to do something, and for want of anything else he took the lease on a grocer's back in Low Hill, where the family had started when they arrived in Wolverhampton. It was a terrible time to go into retail: the Great Depression had started, the economy was shrinking and unemployment was rising. His customers were poor and had no money, and he had no alternative but to offer credit. He hobbled along until his debts become insupportable, at which point, inevitably in this story of financial calamity and social decline, he was declared bankrupt.

Adolf could go no lower. Now the only way was up, and what would allow him and his family to escape poverty and catastrophe was an offer from a most unexpected source.

21.

The Letter

I

Ireland, known as the Free State, was now a nation, more or less, and like all proper nations, she had a state broadcaster, 2RN[5]. The state broadcaster, like all proper state broadcasters, had an orchestra and, according to family tradition, sometime in 1931 or 1932, someone from the orchestra wrote Adolf a letter.

2RN's ambition, the letter began, was to create a world-class national orchestra, and in order to achieve this ambition they were looking for top instrumentalists who had a superb technique, a beautiful tone and a wide experience of the classical repertoire.

Someone at 2RN, the letter continued, had remembered Adolf (presumably this would be the pre-Great War Adolf, the Adolf who lived in Glasnevin, who at innumerable parties banged out on the pianos in the front parlours of red-brick houses the popular material of the time – Gilbert

---

5   This was the original name for Radio Éireann, from the call sign, which was allocated, at that time, from London. Hence, Cork was '2CK' and London '2LO'. Dublin couldn't get '2DN' as this has already been allocated (to Durban), and had to settle for '2RN'. That this phonetically recalls 'to Éireann' is entirely coincidental.

& Sullivan, Irish standards, Moore's Irish melodies and so on – and who had a rented house with a brass plaque outside that said 'Professor of Music'), and this was the reason for writing to him. The orchestra's management believed that he was exactly the sort of musician they were looking for.

The letter went on to inquire if he would care to return to Ireland, join 2RN's orchestra and play a leading role in the establishment of what would become one of the world's great orchestras, yours sincerely, blah blah….

II

Adolf was excited, and so was Rita, who was homesick and longed to go back to Dublin. But what about their oldest son, my father, then fifteen or sixteen years old? He was not yet a fully fledged projectionist, but he would be one day, and once he was he would always find work and earn a decent wage. The cinema was booming, and projectionists were always in demand. It was inconceivable that he should abort his apprenticeship, but equally it was inconceivable that Adolf should spurn 2RN. There was only one solution to this problem.

The family would return to Dublin, where Adolf would restart his career as a classical musician, while my father would stay and live with his aunt, Judy Dack, and her husband, Freddie, and their only child, Walter (then eleven years old). The Dacks managed a pub, the Rose & Crown, for a local brewery, lived above the bar and had room for a lodger. The only problem was location.

The Rose & Crown was in Pleck, Pleck was in Walsall, and Walsall was six miles from Wolverhampton. My father would be hard pressed to afford the fares and to pay Judy for his keep on fifteen bob a week. Step forward Billy Williams, husband of Rita's younger sister, Polly. She and Billy were also living in the midlands, and Billy owned a Douglas motorcycle that he either never used or no longer used. My father, Billy said, was welcome to it, and hey presto, that was the transport problem sorted.

My father went to the Williams' home to collect the Douglas. Billy Williams showed him how to start it and where the brake and the throttle were, and gave him some rudimentary advice about cornering.

The Géblers, 1908.

John Wall (Rita's father) standing next to Judy. To the bottom left of the picture is Polly, and to the bottom right is Bee. (The couple with the baby are a German couple.)

Ernest has written 'Adolphe's brother Herman (*sic*) and Erma (*sic*). They were married but he left her when he came to Ireland. A (*sic*) UNPLEASANT MAN.'

A photograph of Ernest Gébler, seventeen-year-old apprentice cinema operator, 1931. The photograph is of his shadow and was taken with a home-made pinhole camera.

119 Phibsborough Road, the house where Adolf and Rita began married life and where Ernest was born, pictured in 1914 or 1915.

Marianna Gébler (née Blaschitz), 1922.

Adolf on a bicycle on O'Connell Street with a child (probably Adrian) in 1931 or 1932.

Ernest in 1936, aged twenty-one.

Rita, Ada and Ernest, c. 1918.

Rita Gébler (née Wall) dressed for the Irish International Exhibition, Herbert Park, Ballsbridge, 1907.

Bunny Jones, Rudolf Jones's wife, Ballybrew 1940s.

Ernest, 1933.

Ernest and Ada, 1916.

Maria and Wilhelm, 1881.

conditional Release

G.O. 5612 & 5614.

RELEASE FORM No. 1.

Undertaking of Neutrality.

I, ...*Adolphe Gebler*.......................... (name)

(Address)....*43 Botanic Avenue Dublin*....

(Nationality)...............*Bohemian*..........................

hereby promise and undertake that I will neither directly nor

indirectly take any action in any way prejudicial to the safety of

the British Empire or to the safety of her Allies during the present

war.

................*Adolphe Gebler*.........(Signature).

....Aliens' Camp,

Isle of Man.

Date..

C. & F.—1,000/1/18.

[stamp: KNOCKALOE ALIENS' CAMP 5 AUG 1918 ISLE-OF-MAN]

Adolf's 'Undertaking of Neutrality', stamped Knockaloe Aliens' Camp,
Isle of Man, 5 August 1918.

Adolf seated on the running board of the Model T. Standing are Constance Wynford and Miss
Kenny, the 'Classical Music Trio'.
Taken in Waterford, 1922.

Ernest and Ray Scutt (seated) in the Agricultural Hall Cinema during
its demolition, 1931.

Adolf (the third man from the left, seated, wearing a bow tie) with the
Oldcastle Camp Orchestra. This was taken after four years of internment (1917-1918).

Adolf conducting Oldcastle Aliens' Camp Orchestra.

Rita, 1930s.

He then set off, never having driven a motorcycle in his life. The journey, he later wrote, was a 'paralyzing experience', but he made it back to Low Hill where the family, who had not yet left, were living.

III

I have never seen the fabled letter from 2RN that summoned Adolf back; I have only heard of it by repute. However, in the light of Adolf's mediocre career as an orchestral player in Dublin, I do not believe that such a letter with such a message ('Dear Genius, come and play for us') ever existed.

What I think arrived from Ireland was an invitation to tender ('2RN needs instrumentalists, and if you are available perhaps you might let our bookings secretary have your contact details, including a telephone number …').

Something like this arriving at the moment it did would have seemed like a Godsend: Wolverhampton had ended badly, and Rita wanted to go home. If the family returned it would make Rita happy, and Adolf would be able to slough off the taint of failure and bankruptcy. In Dublin, after all, he still had contacts.

Then, in addition, there was the relationship between Adolf and his eldest son. It may have seemed felicitous to Adolf at this point to put distance between himself and my father. Now of course there was no actual position guaranteed in Dublin. I suspect, however, that Adolf persuaded himself, which was not hard, that he had a very good chance of securing a position. After all, was he not exactly the sort of player the 2RN orchestra were supposedly in need of? And this sense of certainty, I think, then metamorphosed into the fantasy that he had been offered a position, which had the great virtue of not only flattering Adolf, but making his actions necessary and impersonal. He had to go back to Dublin, taking the family, because he had a position he would have been insane to decline, and he had to leave my father behind to finish his apprenticeship, because it would have been insane to abandon that at this moment.

This fiction, assiduously cultivated, eventually became gospel in the family. Even my father believed it.

22.

The Early Thirties

I

Adolf, Rita, Ada, Olive, Louise, Irene and Adrian returned to Dublin and rented a house in Drumcondra. The garden was full of snails. Their neighbours were unfriendly and disapproved of them because they were not properly Irish. And of course the Géblers didn't help themselves either. When he was sober, Adolf was perpetually dour and scornful, and when he was drunk (which he was regularly), he was sarcastic and awkward. Rita was bitter and argumentative, though never belligerent, and the children, with their flat English midlands accents, were simply too noisy and too rumbustious for their peaceable Hibernian neighbours.

II

Back at the Agricultural Hall Cinema, my father's main friend was the second operator, Ray Scutt, who had been the apprentice prior to him. Ray was known as 'Smelly Ray', and to while away the time while he was machine minding he read cheap paperback thrillers and romances.

One summer afternoon, when it was particularly hot in the operating box, my father noticed one of Ray's books that the second operator, having read, had abandoned, as was his habit. My father picked the book up and began reading bits of it. He had told himself stories in childhood and given himself much pleasure in the process, and he now discovered that the reverse of that transaction, the importation of narrative into the psyche, was just as efficacious. Before long he was fascinated, and in that mildly entranced state the grind of machine minding was forgotten.

Thereafter he started reading Ray's abandoned books systematically, and in this way he began to slow process of turning himself into a writer.

III

On 19 September 1931 Gaumont closed the Agricultural Hall Cinema. My father helped to decommission the plant and strip out the fittings that could be sold. The Agricultural Hall was then demolished and work commenced on building a new cinema on the site. During this period my father stayed in Wolverhampton. Perhaps he went to another Gaumont cinema. The new and magnificent Gaumont Palace Cinema opened on the Agricultural Hall Cinema site on 5 September 1932, and my father returned there and resumed his apprenticeship.

IV

Following his return to Dublin, Adolf had played with the 2RN orchestra from time to time. In the language of the day he was a temporary augmentee clarinettist, brought into the woodwind section on an as-and-when basis to support the permanent players, Frederick Ashton, M. Egan and J. O'Rourke (who were all Free State Army members, as were most of the 2RN orchestra).

After some months of this ad hoc involvement, and judging that he had proved himself to the orchestra, Adolf applied for a permanent position. He was ideally suited. At that time the orchestra wanted to recruit high-class players who were not in the army or from a military background, and Adolf was certainly musical enough, and he was a civilian. Unfortunately, he was also argumentative, disdainful, difficult and caustic, and in addition he was a indefatigable drinker, and it was for all these reasons, I imagine, that the interview panel decided not to recommend him for a post.

His failure to secure a permanent position was not the end of Adolf's involvement with the orchestra, and he continued to play with them when he was requested to. This must have grated with him, but he had no choice. He needed the money. Of course he could not support the family on a temporary's salary, so he found other work: as a bandmaster at the Irish Transport and General Workers' Union, rehearsing, conducting and developing the union's brass and reed band; composing incidental music for Dublin theatre productions; and teaching privately. It was not much of a living, but it was something.

V

Back in Wolverhampton, my father was becoming interested in girls. Every day now, at work, when he played records over the PA system before the first matinee, he foxtrotted and waltzed in the operating box, holding imaginary partners in arms. In anticipation of the staff dance, he bought a suit, a dark one, but when the night came he spent the evening on the edge of the dance floor, not having the neck to ask any girl or woman to dance on account of not being sure, even after all his practice, that he could carry off the actual dancing bit. It was a lonely, bitter night.

On Sundays he used his Douglas to go with the nineteen-year-old Ray Scutt to Rhyl, the resort on the north coast of Wales. He and Ray went to click with girls, but never managed that feat, always returning to Pleck on Sunday evenings disappointed.

At this time he never read anything but a newspaper, or the cheap paperbacks Ray read at work and then abandoned. He had no interests and he did nothing but work and sleep and go on fruitless expeditions to meet girls. Fundamentally, he was lonely, gut-achingly lonely. He still had his crystal radio, the one he had in Villa Bohème, and because he hoped to hear his father playing (a point of connection, an antidote of some sort to his loneliness), he started to listen to 2RN regularly, and in that way he began to hear Irish songs and Irish airs that he had not heard for years.

Since early childhood he had heard many kinds of music, everything from Beethoven to popular dance songs ('Tea for Two', 'Ma, He's Making Eyes at Me'), but this Irish material affected his psyche more deeply than anything he had ever heard before. This was partly because of its own virtues, its ancient melodies and stirring lyrics about hurt and loss, and partly because of the memories it provoked – his childhood, flying around the Geraghtys' kitchen with lovely May, Adolf sawing away at his violin.

He then heard that the family had fled Drumcondra, apparently forced out by their neighbours who objected to their noisy, bohemian ways, and had taken shelter at Auntie Bee's. He remembered 43 Botanic Avenue, and that point of connection coming on top of the loneliness, which had been made all the more acute by what he had remembered when he listened to the crystal radio, made him decide that he must somehow return to them.

23.

My Father's Scheme

I

He consulted 'The Major', as the Gaumont Palace Cinema's manager was known. He told The Major that he wanted to go home. The Major pointed out that the apprenticeship was given as a favour to Adolf, and that he was expected to finish it. If he just upped and went to Dublin, there was every chance that he would be returned by his father at the request of management. There was only one way to ensure that did not happen: he must be sacked. And to be sacked he would have to do something wrong. The Major suggested that he left the switches in the operating box in the wrong position when he knocked off in the evening.

So he did.

He received a warning.

He left them off a second time.

He received his second warning. One more mistake and he was out.

He left them off a third time. He was told that he could work to the end of the week, and then he was to go. He was out.

All the staff knew that he had done what he had done deliberately. Whatever else he was, he was not slipshod. It was a ploy. He wanted to be released so he could go home to his family in Dublin, his funny German father, his thin, worn-out mother and their brood of kids. Everyone in the Gaumont Palace Cinema understood this, and on the last Saturday The Major organized a whip-round. The staff stumped up £3. 15*s*. 0*d*.

He took the money, expressed gratitude, shook everyone's hand and roared off on his Douglas in the direction of Walsall to spend his penultimate night in the Rose & Crown.

On Monday morning he left the midlands (to which he never returned) heading west, for Wales, specifically Holyhead on the island of Anglesey, the point of ingress for Irish travellers entering England and egress for Irish travellers returning to Ireland, from time immemorial.

Whether he had communicated with his parents I don't know, but somehow I suspect that, given how he'd got himself sacked, he had not. He was going to surprise them.

II

Somewhere in Wales, a mountain road, steep and winding.

The Douglas crawled upwards. A sense of height. Tiny fields on either side. Sunlight, and then – and this was literally like stepping out of one room and into another – he found himself in cloud, a world of wet vapour so dense and enveloping he could see only a few feet ahead.

The mountain's top. He knew he had reached it because instead of the front being above the back, the motorcycle was level. He went forward for a while, and then the front dropped and the back was higher and he knew he had started the descent on the mountain's other side. He went slowly, carefully, and then, reversing the experience of his ascent, the cloud stopped and he was back in the sun, and he sped up.

Later. He was wet from the cloud and he wanted to dry off. He parked up and went into a field and lay down. A party of Welsh children passed, saw him lying on the grass and laughed. He was tired, and the Welsh air after that of the English midlands was soporific. He fell asleep....

Farther on. The drive-chain broke. He dismounted and began to push the heavy motorbike.

The first garage he came to did not stock chain links like his. He pushed on.

The second garage said they could order the links he needed from their supplier, but it would be a day or two before they would arrive. He was impatient. He wanted to be on his way, so he put clay links on instead. They were not the right size, but they were good enough. They got him to within two or three miles of Holyhead before they broke. He dismounted and walked on, pushing the bike along the road and through Holyhead's outskirts – a place of low cottages, alternating with the odd pub or commercial premises. It was dark now. He did not know the actual time, but he knew it was late because there were no people around in Holyhead's streets.

He abandoned the motorcycle outside a police station and walked on, following signs for the harbour. He arrived at the quayside just in time to see the Dublin boat, lights strung along her sides, steam and smoke gushing from her funnels, pulling away, the stretch of water between her stern and the quay's edge churned white by her propellers. He spent the night on the quayside, walking about, trying to keep warm, staring into the dark, from which the next vessel would appear.

Very early the next morning, the miracle happened. The next boat loomed up. It was not the one from the night before. It was a different one, old and dishevelled, the cattle boat.

The ship tied up, then gangplanks were dropped, and down these, slipping, sliding, bellowing, flooded hundreds of shit-smeared cattle who were then penned on the quayside to await onward transport to abattoirs. He purchased a single ticket. It cost him ten shillings. He boarded. The boat smelt meaty and cloacal and primeval.

A few hours later, the boat docked at North Wall. He disembarked. He had not been in Dublin since he was a boy, and he did not know the way to Glasnevin. He asked someone and they told him.

He set off. He walked along the north bank of the Liffey. He passed the Custom House, amazed by its glory, and went up O'Connell Street. The empty city at this early hour was eerily sad, eerily beautiful. Neither his mother nor father had ever spoken of Dublin as the overwhelming, exhilarating city he was traversing now. He couldn't understand why.

He arrived at Auntie Bee's front door. He knocked. How the family received him and what was said about his aborted apprenticeship is not recorded.

What is not in doubt is that he was allowed to stay.

24.

A Rocky Start

I

My father wanted work. He needed cash. He wanted to impress, and perhaps to contribute to Auntie Bee's housekeeping costs. He started looking and he found work as a projectionist at the Capitol Cinema in Prince's Street, just off O'Connell Street. Unfortunately, the projectionist he replaced was in dispute with the management and had been laid off or dismissed. Perhaps he did not know this when he took the job, or perhaps he did know but did not realize that there would be consequences. But there were, and Adolf had to go to his friend Frank Robbins, Irish Citizen Army stalwart who fought in the Easter Rising, 1916, and now a functionary in the Cinema and Theatre branch of Irish Transport and General Workers' Union. His son was totally ignorant, Adolf explained, and he knew nothing about union cards or trade union membership or working-class solidarity or anything like that, and that was why he mistakenly took the job at the Capitol cinema, and he was very sorry.

The apology was accepted, and an understanding was reached. My father's transgression would be written off as an act of youthful folly, and once the furore died down a union card would be forthcoming.

Adolf returned to his errant son and broke the good news. He had to lie low and wait till his misdemeanour was forgotten. Once enough time passed he would get his union ticket.

II

He had never had any truck with religion, but passing the time tramping about the city's streets – to get his bearings he walked obsessively backwards and forwards between the slum tenements (the buildings once obviously lovely) and the drowsy, prosperous suburbs – my father saw that the people of Dublin very much did. From this observation there arose the idea that he should embrace their religious practice because this would bring him closer to the place and her people. It would cement something. It would make him a citizen.

This idea having taken root in his mind, he entered a church. He talked to the priest. Confession and First Holy Communion followed. When he left the church he felt as if he were on air. He had subsumed himself into Dublin. He was ecstatic, euphoric.

An afternoon, a day or two later. He was in another, different church. There were tinker children there. They were barefoot. They were dirty. Their clothes were ragged. As he observed them, it hit him. They believed they would be rewarded later for the faith they professed now. Despite his recent induction into the Church, however, it suddenly seemed to him that, given what Catholicism offered, which was probably not true, or was indeed actually untrue, what was actually happening was a scam designed to dupe and then control the gullible like these children. The rewards promised in the future would of course never be honoured. This insight destroyed his religious infatuation in an instant, but his feelings for the city survived.

25.

Books

In the toilet of 43 Botanic Avenue, a book with a string threaded through the tunnel between the spine and the shelf back (the part that would show when a book was on a shelf) hung from a nail. The back cover was gone, as were about half of the pages. They had been used as toilet paper, with users tearing from the back inwards.

He looked to see what the book was called. According to the front board cover, which was black and red and gilt, it was called *Bleak House*, and the author was Charles Dickens. He did not recognize the title and the author, but he did recognize the book's provenance. It was from Woolworth's, and was one in a series of cheap imprints of the classics. It retailed for 6*d*.

He leafed through the prelims. The paper was soft, yellow, cheap, coarse and porous. He reached the first page of text, and started to read. The quality of the print was poor, smudgy, but the words were wonderful.

Until this moment all he had read in the fiction line had been Ray Scutt's discarded paperback thrillers and romances, books that were popular, efficient and banal. The first page of *Bleak House*, on the other hand, with its account of soot-benighted London in mourning for the sun, was dense, rich and intoxicating.

He undid the string around the nail and left with the half-book. Its theft was noticed immediately. Auntie Bee questioned him. He had been in the water closet. Did he know where it had gone? He looked blank. No, he said, he did not. But of course he did. The half-book was hidden under his coat.

He slipped out of 43 and went down to the River Tolka, to the place where he had tried to sail his home-made yacht as a child. He had privacy here. He read more, and over the next day or two he read on to the place where the pages stopped, somewhere in the middle. It was a shame not to have the rest, but enough had been read, and it had happened. He had always known what a 'story' was – after all, he has been telling himself stories in bed at night since childhood – but now he knew something that he had not known before: there was such a thing as 'a quality story', a story built out of words that were carefully chosen and artfully deployed, and as a result of the care with which it was made was not only effective, like a popular novel, but lovely, even beautiful, thrilling, stirring, moving. His half-experience of *Bleak House* was the beginning of his life as a writer, the moment in which his future was determined. Later in life (much later) it struck him: *Bleak House* had the effect it had, vaulting him into literature, because there was nothing between it and everything else that he had read before. His emptiness and his ignorance gave *Bleak House* a power it would not otherwise have had. Deficiencies did sometimes have their uses.

II

Back in 43 Botanic Avenue, on a little shelf in the front sitting room, he discovered more books. He gobbled them up. The author was someone called Zane Grey, and all his novels presented an idealized version of the American frontier during the nineteenth century. One of them was Grey's bestseller, *Riders of the Purple Sage*. These 'cowboys', as he learned to call them, made an impression. Grey was an adroit storyteller, and his narratives were full of colour and incident. But they were at the same end of the spectrum as Ray Scutt's discarded paperbacks. They were efficient, but they were coarse. *Riders of the Purple Sage* was not *Bleak House*, and Zane Grey was not Charles Dickens.

He had started to discriminate. He was becoming a critic, and a self-conscious one. He dimly perceived, hitherto unrealized and unacknowledged, that he had no education. He did not understand that world. He knew that Adolf did, and he realized that he must make more of an effort to learn from his old man, despite their difficulties, but in the meantime he would make a start himself. He had to repair his deficiencies.

Lad, he said to himself, you'd better start your education.

But where? he asked.

The library, he answered himself.

The closest library was the Capel Street Library in the north inner city, and shortly after he had realized what he had to do, he walked down to pay his first visit.

The library (established at the end of the nineteenth century by Dublin Corporation as part of its drive to provide education to the city's proletariat) was located in the bottom of a classic red-brick Dublin Georgian town house with sash windows and a glass fanlight above its handsome door. It was the kind of dwelling Sean O'Casey's characters inhabited in his plays, the kind sometimes referred to as tenements, and indeed the library's upper storeys were tenanted.

He went in. The library's interior smelt of gum and ink and wet tweed, which was really the smell of dog pee and turf dust.

He sat down and read the newspapers (*The Irish Times* and *The Times* from London) and then, having made the necessary arrangements at the desk, he went to pick a book from the shelves to take home. He had already decided against *Bleak House* because of a feeling that some spell would be broken if he read the second half. Furthermore, as long as it was unread, then he could pretend to himself that anything and everything he read was part of his search for the second half of Dickens's great novel. To deny himself would lure him to read on.

He borrowed a sociology book, and so it started, the process of educating himself, and the practice of reading, which was to continue for the rest of his life, on and off. This visit to the Capel Street Library was the first of hundreds.

26.

Developments

He was still walking frantically. One day he was at the top end of O'Connell Street when he noticed a dray (the flat kind with four wheels used by coalmen) near the Parnell Monument, and he saw there was a small man standing on the dray who was addressing the crowd gathered around him and coughing when he was not talking into a handkerchief.

Curious to hear what the man was saying, he joined the back of the crowd. The man, though he would only discover this later, was Peadar O'Donnell.

An Irish Republican, a veteran of the War of Independence and the Civil War, O'Donnell was one of the anti-Treaty Irregulars who occupied the Four Courts in 1922 and who miraculously escaped at the end of the siege. He was later interned by the Free State, and later still he was a hunger-striker who used starvation to attack the Free State for locking him up and keeping him in the conditions in which they kept him. In other words, Peadar O'Donnell's was an Irish revolutionary's life that spanned the gamut. And, unusually among Irish Republicans, he was also a man of the Left. This was evident in what he was now saying, and my father found himself not only interested in but in agreement with what he now heard.

II

He returned to listen to Peadar O'Donnell a second and then a third time. When the third meeting broke up he was approached by Bernard (Barney) McGinn (who would later have a play, *Remembered Forever*, produced at the Abbey). Barney wondered if he was interested in the mix of Irish Republicanism and socialism he had just heard O'Donnell promulgate.

In his flat English midlands accent, which greatly intrigued Barney, he said yes, he was intrigued, and he was invited by Barney back to Mallin Hall (named after James Connolly's second-in-command, Michael Mallin) to meet like-minded people. This was his introduction to Dublin's socialist and Republican circles.

III

The Géblers were allocated a corporation house. They left Botanic Avenue and moved into 2 Offaly Road, Cabra.

One day, alone in their new house, my father searched the wardrobe in his parents' room (he was an incorrigible snooper) and there, behind Adolf's old folded shirts, he found his mother's Dutch cap (old, no longer used, the rubber slightly perished), Marie Stopes's pioneering work on human intimacy and contraception, *Married Love*, and an anthology of Lenin's writing in paper covers. The last was his father's, he believed, though how Adolf came by it he had no idea. Over the following days, whenever he got the chance, he took the Lenin out and read it, always taking care to put it back exactly as he had found it. He was impressed by the dead Bolshevik's incendiary ideas and unwavering certainty. Lenin knew what was wrong and he knew how to fix it too.

27.

Into the World

In 1934, Hilton Edwards and Micheál Mac Liammóir, proprietors of the Dublin Gate Theatre, which was in the Rotunda at the top of O'Connell Street, commissioned Adolf to write incidental music for their forthcoming production of Shakespeare's *Julius Caesar*.

One October afternoon, not long before the opening night (which was 22 October), Adolf, who had to deliver the violin part, suggested to his son that he might like to come down with him to the theatre and see a rehearsal. My father agreed, and from Cabra they walked in, Adolf carrying the score in his briefcase.

When they entered it, the Gate's auditorium was dark, and smelt vaguely of perfume and make-up and the dust of the bucket seats. The stage on the other hand was bright, lit by the merciless working stage lights, and in the middle of the stage stood two men: they were in costume, speaking lines. Adolf explained to his son that these two were the only begetters of the Gate: the tall, angular one, who was playing Julius Caesar, was called Hilton Edwards; the sinister, saturnine one, who was playing Mark Anthony, was Micheál Mac Liammóir.

My father, who did not know who they were or why they were important, was much more interested in the young actor much closer to him in age who was sitting to the side of the stage reading a book, and who was seemingly disconnected from what was happening, although clearly, because he was in costume, he had something to do with the play.

After a few minutes this actor snapped his book shut, jumped up, stepped forward onto the stage and started to speak Shakespeare's words: his diction was smooth and perfect, his presence hypnotic, and his manner overpowering. He was stylish, self-possessed, persuasive, and it was obvious that should the circumstances demand it, he could be brutal. The man was James Mason and he was playing Brutus, and as he listened and watched, my father thought that here was exactly the sort of man that he would like to be one day.

Later, there was a rehearsal break. Adolf, Edwards and Mac Liammóir discussed their musical business. He stood on the edge of their circle while they did. This done, Adolf introduced his son. He explained that his lad was a skilful carpenter, could make literally anything with the capable hands that the gods had gifted him, and was brilliant with machinery of any kind. In response, Hilton, who knew exactly what Adolf was angling for, asked if my father might like to come and help out backstage. There would be a small emolument to make it worth his while, he added, and if he got a job, the theatre work could be fitted in around it. My father accepted.

II

His union card came through, and then through his friend Freddie Smith, whose sister was an usherette in the Camden Cinema in Camden Street, he gathered that there was a projectionist's job going there. He applied and got the job.

The Camden was not a purpose-built cinema but a nineteenth-century building converted in 1912. It had an unusual layout:

> Patrons accessed the auditorium via a tunnel-passageway under the screen and, on entering the hall they were immediately struck by the light from the projector.[6]

Famously, patrons avoided being dazzled by moving backwards up the aisle, which allowed them to search for a seat while simultaneously keeping an eye on the film playing on screen. The cheap seats at the front of the auditorium were wooden, those at the back upholstered. Heating was provided by a solid-fuel stove at the rear. When it rained, the stallholders of Camden Street would take refuge in the cinema and drape their shawls over the stove to dry them. The cinema was 'generally considered to be flea-ridden' and he always referred to the cinema as 'the fleapit'[7]. But work was work, and he counted himself lucky to have got it given the miserable state of the Irish and the world economy. The manager was a Mr Geraghty (no relation of May), a 'small, fat, very country-voiced bit of a fuss-pot.'

III

His elder sister Ada, the sibling of whom he was most in awe (Irene, the youngest, was his favourite though), was also enjoying good fortune. Firstly, she was in work. Like her mother before her, Ada was in the theatre on the hospitality side, working in the coffee bar at the Abbey Theatre. And secondly, she had met someone. His name was

---

6 Keenan, J., *Dublin Cinemas: A Pictorial Selection* (Picture House Publications, 2005), p. 34. *Dublin Cinemas* contains a wealth of information about the Camden Cinema, and I have relied upon it heavily.
7 *Ibid.*, p. 34.

Joe Armstrong. He was born in 1906 in Little Mary Street in Dublin's inner city. His family were poor, but indefatigable in the pursuit of education. With the help of his mother, Joe got to and through teacher training college. When he met Ada he had recently graduated and was working as a schoolteacher. The job came with a salary and a pension, albeit both small. For Ada, Joe represented a way to leave the life she had endured, which was rackety, insecure and impecunious, and switch to the sort of life she yearned for, which was secure, comfortable and bourgeois.

28.

Home

I

Like his daughter, and notwithstanding his left-leaning politics, Adolf also yearned for a better, more bourgeois life – or one that looked like it was any rate. He was now making money (he was both composing and working as bandmaster at the IT&GWU), and he took a very long lease on a modest terraced house, 3 Cabra Grove, just a few streets away from the corporation house in Offaly Grove. The whole family (Adolf, Rita, Ada, Ernest, Louise, Olive, Irene and Adrian) moved into the new house.

Unlike most of Dublin's terraced streets, Cabra Grove had houses on only one side of the road, so rather than facing other dwellings, the properties looked out onto a bit of grass. Cabra Grove was also a cul-de-sac, and so there was no through traffic.

The acquisition of 3 Cabra Grove therefore represented social advance: this was a superior house in a superior terrace (built speculatively) in a superior location. For the family, however, given the dysfunction of Adolf and Rita, this may not have mattered much.

Relations were bad, each had a negative picture of the other, and neither was backward when it came to expressing their opinions. Rita felt that her life was impoverished and impossible and that her husband was to blame. Adolf felt that his life had been an artistic and financial failure and that Rita was to blame. Rita held Adolf responsible for failing to provide for her and his six children. Adolf held Rita responsible for hobbling him with her impossible demands, which stopped him thriving and flourishing musically and aesthetically. Rita identified Adolf's drinking as the real reason for his failure to thrive as a musician, which in turn was the reason the family were often so poor. Adolf defended his drinking as both the only pleasure available in a life of unvarying marital misery and failure, and the consequence of her endless criticism: she drove him to it, literally.

Now in middle age, and with their arguments well worked out, Adolf and Rita were perpetually fractious with one another. Rita carped and complained, sniped and denigrated when in his company, while he, in reply, blustered and bullied, boiled and fulminated. It was awful, ugly, exhausting and draining, but there it was, in plain view, every day, every night: she undermined, she scoured; he lashed, he threatened; and it never stopped, this ceaseless warfare between the two parties, for animosity now formed the bedrock of their relationship.

Because of the unrelieved friction, Adolf decided to construct a couple of rooms for himself in the attic of 3 Cabra Grove. Ostensibly these were to be places where he could practise and compose, but once they were done they became a lair to which he could withdraw to drink alone, and thereafter this was very often what happened. This marked a new low point in the marriage.

II

Most evenings, now my father had started at the Camden Cinema, he did not return till late, and as he turned into Cabra Grove and dismounted, he invariably saw, standing at the far end of the cul-de-sac

118

in the dark, Ada and Joe. It was she who insisted on this as their place of courtship, and Ada being the dominant one in the relationship, Joe had little choice but to comply.

One reason for this self-imposed exile from the house was Ada's anxiety about class difference. Joe was working class whereas her family were higher up the class scale. If they acted in a way that was superior, Joe would feel uncomfortable, and she wished to spare him that.

But much more important and much bigger than this was her parents' dynamic and the way they got on (or, more accurately, did not get on), and Ada did not want Joe to encounter this. She did not want to bring him into a house where he would either find her parents quarrelling, or, which could be even worse, her mother alone in the kitchen, bitter and mournful, and her father alone in his attic eyrie, maudlin and gloomy with drink. She wanted to keep him ignorant of the stock from which she sprung in case it put him off, and that was why she insisted that they did their courting outside at the end of Cabra Grove.

III

At some point, the furtive evenings in the dark lost their allure, and Ada and Joe took the plunge. They went to Bray, a seaside resort town outside Dublin, where no one knew them, and they rented a bungalow, where they lived in sin together while Joe continued to teach in Dublin, his private life unknown to his clerical superiors. Given the time and the state of Ireland then, this was a considerable act of defiance.

29.

Unhappiness

I

In early childhood my father had suffered from giant hives, hay fever, red eye and abrasions, and other wounds were often very slow to heal. At eight years of age all these problems vanished and his health was good until, aged fifteen and coinciding with his family's departure for Dublin while he stayed on in Wolverhampton to continue his apprenticeship, he developed atopic dermatosis, bony plates or scales in the skin on his ankles, and the hay fever also returned. This episode of ill health lasted a year or eighteen months, then the problems cleared and he had excellent health again until, not long after he'd returned to Dublin, he contracted amoebic dysentery, which precipitated colitis, inflammation of the colon, and he began to experience bloating, abdominal soreness and the violent rejection of certain foods, along with problems with the skin on his hands, elbows and knees, which kept drying, reddening, splitting and weeping. These symptoms would appear, annihilate him (though he would keep working – that never stopped, he had to work, he had to make money), then vanish.

He sought help, haunting several Dublin hospital outpatient departments. The medics patiently examined his sore skin and swollen belly. In the case of the former, eczema was suspected, but what was going on in his guts they were unable to determine. As to why these scourges afflicted him, the medics could not say.

He had some answers of his own, of course.

It was something he ate. That was possible. After all, he was intolerant of milk.

It was his job. It was monotonous and exhausting. It was killing him.

It was the war at home. His parents' rows stunned everyone in the household into misery.

It was thwarted ambition. His ambition was to become a writer, but that was stupid. He could never escape the force field of his personal circumstances – family, job, ignorance, class, and his domicile, Ireland.

It was deliberate self-sabotage. His symptoms were his body's attempt to dissuade him from trying to make a life in literature because that could only lead to failure.

All these explanations were credible, but which was the right one? He did not know. All he could do was struggle on.

II

In the operating box in the Camden Cinema, for as long as the film was projecting, and unless the film snapped or ignited or there was some other disaster, the time was his own. He could do what he wanted, and what he wanted was to improve himself, and so that was what he tried to do.

He read books, the ones he felt he ought to read, Malory's *Mort D'Arthur* and Shakespeare's *Sonnets* for example. He taught himself shorthand so he could squeeze even more words out in the intervals between the spool changes, and he started to write, stories mostly, his plan being to sell these to magazines or newspapers and make money. His first stories were not very good. Also, they were written by hand in capital letters. He offered one or two to putative editors in this form, and they told him to bring them back once he had them properly presented. Submissions, he was led to understand (and he was ashamed he did not already understand this), had to be typed, and for them to be typed meant that he had to have a typewriter.

He combed Dublin for a machine and, in a shop in a side street near Trinity's front gates, he found an Oliver out of a solicitor's office that was perhaps thirty years old. It had a platen nearly a yard long, was particularly suited to copying using carbon paper by a process known as manifolding, and was on sale for £4. Where was he to get a fortune like that? But then, incredibly, Rita, who to her knowledge had no known relatives left alive who had as much as a halfpenny to their name, was willed £60 by a distant relative. Suddenly, miraculously flush, she bought him the machine.

Now he had a typewriter he could write, and he started a novel about a couple trying to forge a life in a Dublin tenement that would eventually become *He Had My Heart Scalded*. Initially, he couldn't afford a ribbon so he pounded out his copy using the carbon and backing sheet system with the carbon acting as the ribbon. Later he acquired a ribbon, but it was dried out and he had to ink it himself before it would work. It was fortunate he was so technical.

III

Diary note, thirties vintage, undated:

Working in the operating booth or the operating box every day – is it a better or worse way of paying rent than living in the artistic garret on handouts and other people? Anyhow, where would I find a patron? – Even if possible?

The whirling machine and now and then raising your eyes from the book or the scrubbed page and seeing at the end of the beam below the old scratched images of Fred Astaire and Ginger Rogers in 'Top Hat' dancing away …

Elegantly tip-tapping to popular music with good melodies is preferable to solitude. It gives routine to the day. Here I am not alone but not intruded upon.

Fair cinema goddess of this place, view my supplicant attitude with grace and grant unto me …

IV

Later still, with money he had saved, he bought a much better typewriter than the Oliver, a proper writer's typewriter, a Remington. He had no study, so he put a table on the landing under the little window over the front door of 3 Cabra Grove, and when he was not in the Camden Cinema, this was where he sat and typed his copy up.

It was mid summer, 1938. He was typing, tap, tap, tap. Adolf, drunk, angry, belligerent, enraged, came up the stairs and along the landing behind and then reached out and took hold of the Remington. Adolf explained that a family could only accommodate one artist, and he was that artist, so the typewriter had to go. His plan was to fire it out the little window and, with luck, into the road. His son resisted, and Adolf did not succeed.

V

My father left 3 Cabra Grove and moved into a room in a cottage in Castleknock near the River Liffey that was owned by a family called Hoey.

He was no longer a satellite caught by Adolf's gravitational pull. He was free to be his own artist. *He Had My Heart Scalded* was finished. He

123

submitted it to Jonathan Cape. They returned the manuscript. In their covering letter they explained: 'Obscenity and blasphemy must be written after the commercial fashion to be commercial.'[8] He submitted the book to Heinemann, who said no, followed by other English publishers, who said the same.

After the slew of rejections, he put the novel away. Henceforth he focused on four things: his projectionist's job, turning himself into a writer of journalism and short stories that the local Irish press would favour, working backstage at the Gate Theatre and helping out at the New Theatre Group (founded 1938), an offshoot of the Left Book Club, which offered audiences workers' theatre with an anti-fascist orientation.

8   Taken from a letter by Ernest Gébler to the socialist Thomas O'Brien, who was then fighing in Spain, dated 23 September 1938. It is quoted in Klaus, H. Gustav (ed.), *Strong Words, Brave Deeds: The Poetry, Life and Times of Thomas O'Brien, Volunteer in the Spanish Civil War* (O'Brien Press, 1994), p. 182.

30.

The Emergency

I

September, 1939. The Second World War, or 'The Emergency' as it was known in the Free State, had arrived. He still had his ailments, but he was determined that these would not prevent him from participating. He believed in the fight against Fascism, and the need to defeat the warmonger Hitler, and he was on the point of crossing to Britain to enlist (he wanted to be an RAF engine fitter, and he knew such a role would suit him; he was good with machinery) when he realized the awful truth: the RAF's disgusting food would make him so ill he would never get through basic training.

That decided him. He could not go. It was unfortunate, but the body was the body, and if it was not up to the task then that was that. It was a decision that did not trouble him very much. Perhaps, at an unconscious level, he believed he was doing nothing more than emulating his father: after all, seeing out the war in neutral Ireland had been Adolf's practice last time around, so why should he not do the same? Was that so terrible?

II

Spring 1940. In the hospital in Bray, Ada gave birth to a boy, John Armstrong. She and Joe, the child's father, were not married. According to the norms of the day, Ada and Joe were degenerates and their infant was in peril. So policemen came. And a priest. To the hospital. To Ada's bed. Where she lay with her newborn baby. The visitors explained the purpose of their visit: they wanted to take the child away. They wanted to take him out of the clutches of the sinful parents who had had the temerity to bring him into the world without marrying one another and who would obviously not give him a proper Catholic upbringing; they wanted to give him to those who would provide a proper upbringing and thereby save his soul.

The forces of authority tried every variety of cajoling. First they seduced, they flattered. They spoke of the joys of a life free of sin. Then they talked of what they could do for the infant. They promised the world. They promised heaven. They promised God. Ada refused to accept their blandishments: she would not relinquish the baby. They switched tack. They insinuated and threatened the worst. They elaborated on the pains and agonies of sinfulness, not to mention what could be done to make life in this world unpleasant. But Ada was made of the right stuff. She did not waver. Not for a second. She refused and refused and refused, until in the end, worn out, knowing they could get no further, perhaps feeling ashamed, the representatives of State and Church retreated, leaving the mother with her baby.

III

Mary Watson was the child of Irish parents who had been in service in the south of England when she was a child. The family returned to Ireland when she was a young woman, and she met my father. He was on the lookout for a girlfriend, and she seemed like a good candidate. Like him, she was not fully Irish. She was an outlier. Also, he hoped that because she had been brought up outside Ireland she would not resist intimacy with the same indefatigable zeal with which girls who had been reared in Ireland did.

He and Mary began to socialize, and my father quickly learned that his assumptions were wrong: Mary proved elusive physically. She was also parsimonious about her personal details. She would not tell him where she lived, for instance, and in order that he would not be able to discover where she lived she would not let him walk her home.

One night he was with Mary in the pub. She went to the Ladies. He noticed that she had left her handbag behind rather than taking it with her. He did not agonize about what he did next. As he saw it, he had no alternative. Those who withheld had only themselves to blame if others unmasked what they kept hidden. If you kept secrets you should expect to have them exposed.

He opened her handbag. He looked in. He saw an envelope. Eureka! He pulled it out and read the address and discovered that Mary Watson lived in a corporation house on a housing estate. He would never have guessed. Her superior voice had tricked him and made him think her social status was much higher than it actually was. Not that his discovery of the truth changed his amorous feelings. Not a bit. He was smitten.

He slipped the envelope back. Mary returned, and they went on talking. She never knew what he'd done, and he never let on what he knew. He continued to court her. At some point he proposed marriage – perhaps he'd decided that was the only way he'd ever get her into bed – but she declined.

She didn't say why, but he suspected that it was his choice of profession. She declined him because she simply did not believe he would ever make a living as a writer. As he had three-quarters expected it, he wasn't troubled by her refusal. They remained friendly, and at Christmas 1937 she gave him as a present *The Universal Dictionary of the English Language*. This was not only the first proper dictionary he had ever owned, but also one of the earliest affirmations that he'd ever had that literature might be his future. For a poor girl from a corporation estate with her own private doubts, this was a generous as well as an expensive gesture.

IV

My father left Castleknock, went back to Cabra Grove for a while, then lodged at 225 Phibsborough Road with the sisters (Mona and Lucy) of his socialist friend and Spanish Civil War veteran Tom O'Brien, and finally took a room in a house in Ashtown. It was the back room on the top storey and stretched the width of the house. It had a fire, in front of which, turf blazing away in the hearth, he entertained Mary Watson. The other top room, the front one, was occupied by a small, active, bright-eyed woman somewhere in her seventies, and her bedridden husband. This couple barely impinged. They had no radio and they spoke in whispers, and his only contact was when he met the woman on the stairs, or when, once or twice, she knocked and asked if he had six pennies for a sixpence. She needed the change for her gas meter.

One morning, when he woke, he heard the woman crying, and then he heard her tapping on his door. He pulled his trousers on and stuck his feet into his shoes. He rushed to his door and opened it. There was no one there. She was gone.

He looked across the landing. His neighbour's door was open. She was back in her room, he realized. He crossed the landing and called 'Hello' through the open doorway. Then he stepped into the room and saw a double brass bed with an old man lying in it and the old woman nearby, weeping.

The old woman began to talk. She was only away for a few minutes when she went to the shops, but she should never have gone because now look what had happened. At least, she thought it had. She wasn't sure. Could he check her husband, and if he was as she feared he was, would my father please do the thing with the eyes?

He thought that if the old man really was dead then it should be a doctor who did this next part. He also knew that the poor could not afford doctors, and that was why she had come to him.

He had no experience in this area. He was not even sure where to look for a pulse. He opened the man's heavy nightshirt and put an ear to his white, bony breast. It felt cold and inert and dry and lifeless against his cheek. He held his breath. He listened. He heard nothing. This might mean the man's heart had stopped beating. But equally it could be the case that his heart was beating but he could not hear it.

He straightened up, still unsure. This was when he noticed that the man's eyelids were not moving. He had his answer now.

He nodded to the woman to confirm, yes, it was as she suspected. She let out a wail, threw her apron over her head, and speaking through the material told him that he must absolutely do the thing with her husband's eyes because that was what she could not do, and he had to do it with pennies, of which she had none.

He ran back to his own room. His loose change was on the mantelpiece. He had no pennies, but he had some ha'pennies, and he thought they would do. Failing that, he had some silver that he could use.

He took all the money and retraced his steps. The old new widow was still by the bed, sobbing under her apron. He approached. It was one thing to have put his ear to the man's chest earlier, but this was different. He felt queasy. He used the edge of a ha'penny to coax the first eyelid down, and then capped the socket with the coin. With another ha'penny he attempted the trick on the other side, but this eyelid refused to close down completely. A narrow slit remained, through which a sliver of dead eye showed. He started to sweat. He dropped the second coin into place.

It was only later that he realized what the point of the coins was: they were to cover the eyes, which saved one having to close them.

V

The switches were off in the operating box. The auditorium was dark. The stove at the back was damped down. The takings were locked away. It was the end of another day in the Camden Cinema.

He wheeled his bicycle out the front entrance, pulled the grille across and chained it. The premises were secured for the night.

He mounted and wearily navigated his way through the little lanes until he reached Patrick Street, which would take him to the Liffey. There was a yeasty smell from the Guinness brewery down on the river. The chain clanged inside the guard as it turned. The road was quiet. There was little traffic, and only occasional pedestrians. Ornate cast-iron street lamps stood at regular intervals along the edge of the pavement. The light from the lamps was pale and wavering, and it fell in the shape of a bell, illuminating principally the post itself and the paving stones around the base. In between the cowls of light thrown down by the street lamps, the darkness was heavy and thick.

Closer to the river there was a slight decline. The going was easier. Nicholas Street was so silent he heard the smooth soft sighing of the tyres. There really was no one stirring. The Christ Church Cathedral loomed up on his right ahead of him. Suddenly, a notion. Why not? There was no one to see.

He stopped, dismounted and walked with his bicycle to a black back wall of Christchurch, somewhere on Winetavern Street. He pushed the kickstand down and left the bicycle. He took the piece of chalk out of his pocket that he had used earlier to mark which cans had their contents spooled the right way and which had not, and he turned to the wall and he wrote 'HELP' in block capitals. Then he remounted and started the long haul home, Richmond Bridge, Dorset Street, Cabra Road, Navan Road, Ashtown….

The following night, cheered by the special message he alone understood on the Winetavern Street wall, he wrote 'HELP' on another wall, and the next night he did it somewhere else. He continued in this way, writing 'HELP' in different spots until he had his whole route marked with his unique chalk signs. Now his long, bleak, night-rides home had purpose and continuity and familiarity. His chalk marks made him feel at home and, rather like a monarch, he waved to this 'HELP' or that 'HELP' as he progressed homewards.

Then, one night, there, shockingly, under the first 'HELP' he had made on the old black Winetavern Street wall, also in chalk, was a message: 'MEET YOU UNDER BUTT BRIDGE TONIGHT AT 11.30.' He stopped. Had someone been following him and watching what he did at night? He looked behind him, up Nicholas Street. Nothing. No one. He reread the message. Could he tell anything from the script? Did he recognize the writing? No, he did not.

He pedalled off. What was he going to do? He came to the bottom of Winetavern Hill. There ahead of him was the bridge. Did he cross the Liffey and go straight home, or did he … yes, he did.

He turned right and cycled along the quays all the way to Butt Bridge at the bottom of Tara Street. He stopped, got off the saddle, lifted his bicycle onto the pavement and tried to see under the bridge, but from where he was that was impossible.

He noticed, however, some steps at the side of the bridge. He left his bicycle propped on its kickstand and went carefully down the steps, which were stone and slime-covered, all the way to the bottom. At the water's edge he smelt the strong Liffey smell of rot and mud and ooze and brine and human waste. His heart raced. He was ready to run. He looked under the bridge. All he could see, and he could not see much as there was no light down there, was the Liffey's surface, dark and black. He realized that there was only one way to get under Butt Bridge, and it was in a boat.

He went back up the steps feeling vaguely relieved. He got on his bicycle and rode away. He crossed the river and began to pedal homewards through the north inner city, and as his route was different to the usual one he did not have the consolation of his chalk marks on the long haul to Ashtown.

VI

St Stephen's Green, early afternoon. The sun was shining and all the trees were in leaf and he stared at the patterns of light and shade that lay across the path as he walked along. He heard his name, called out in an accent that was slightly arch and rich. He knew that voice, looked up, and saw, as he expected, the possessor of that voice, Micheál Mac Liammóir, walking towards him. And then he saw … well, it was hard to be sure at a distance, but once the actor got up to him he saw that he was not mistaken. The actor was in full stage make-up. The effect in the open air and away from the Gate's normalizing lights was unnerving, even sinister.

They talked, and as they talked a boy passed, and as he passed he muttered to Micheál Mac Liammóir, 'Eh, mister, is it right you're a sixty-sixer?'

He knew what this meant. So did the actor. Sixty-six was slang for anal sex, so a sixty-sixer was a man who indulged with other men: in the vocabulary of the period, a queer. My father understood, furthermore, that what had inspired this was the make-up. The actor's proclivities might have been well known, but it was his appearance that had instigated the nasty sniping. He also saw that Micheál Mac Liammóir was shaken and appalled by what had happened. He had not expected it, and it had caught him off-guard.

So what to do? He could make his excuses and walk on, or he could help. He plumped for the latter. He indicated a nearby fountain. Micheál could wash his face there. He led the actor over. He waited while the actor washed the sticky make-up away – a long and tedious process. Finally, the job was done: Micheál Mac Liammóir lifted his clean, shining face, dripping and pale, into the sunlight. He was *so* grateful, *so* thankful. Oh, what would what he have done without my father, he said, and he would not forget his kindness, oh no, never, never.

VII

In 1941, Ernest Blythe, sometime Ulster Presbyterian, sometime Republican, sometime supporter and enthusiast for Hilton Edwards and Micheál Mac Liammóir's Irish-language theatre in Galway, and sometime Minister of Finance in W. T. Cosgrave's (and Ireland's) first government (famously, Blythe balanced the Free State's books by, among other measures, reducing the already miserly old-age pension by a shilling), was appointed managing director of the Abbey, Ireland's national theatre.

Mac Liammóir (who had not forgotten my father's helpfulness in St Stephen's Green) and Edwards decided that their young stagehand, who wanted to write, and the Abbey's new director, who needed plays, would both benefit from a meeting, so they set one up.

My father went along. Blythe spoke at length about the dramas of the Irish Revival; he described them as plays with hens under the table, and said that while those plays were fine and dandy in their day, time had moved on, tastes had evolved, and now something else, something a bit different, needed to be on the Abbey's stage. What Blythe probably had in mind were plays that made money, but my father thought he meant plays with a modern European and particularly a Russian/Chekhovian bent, and so he proposed a play about lies, the illusion of freedom they offer, and what they actually deliver, which is the end of free will. *She Sits Smiling* (as the play he was talking about came to be called) is set in a Dublin boarding house owned by Mrs Quirke, a widow with grown-up children. Her eldest, Peter, a fantasist, pretends to one of the lady boarders that he's a murderer when really he's only a thief, and when the boarder threatens to report him to the police his mother reveals to Peter the great lie about his dead father that she has had custody of over the years while she has sat smiling in her guest house. Because of the nature of what his mother has disclosed, Peter is left with no alternative but to propose marriage. The ploy works, the boarder accepts, and at the play's end we know the marriage will be a disaster, as do the parties, but we also know it will go ahead.

A commission for *She Sits Smiling* was issued, though there was no contract, no advance and no guarantee of production.

31.

A Friendship

I

Mid war. He boarded a cream-and-white Dublin bus for Bray. His plan was to visit Ada, who had just had her second child, Ann (b. 1942).

The bus was slow, the journey long, and he got talking to another passenger, Rudolf Jones.

Rudy, as he was known to his friends, was born in 1917. He was a bit younger than my father, though in career terms he was more advanced. Rudy was a published writer of thrillers. In 1936, under the name John Ross, he had published his first, *The Moccasin Men*, in Britain. He had gone on to produce eight more, and then the war came, at which point his thriller life stopped because paper was rationed. But no matter. Rudy was now a journalist on *The Irish Times*, where he wrote newspaper copy instead of thrillers, and for this he was paid enough to support an enviable life. He was married, he had children, and he lived with his family and his younger orphaned brother in a Dublin mews house behind Fitzwilliam Place. He also rented Ballybrew, a stonecutter's cottage in the hills above Bray.

My father was intrigued and excited. Rudy was exactly the sort of person he wanted to be, and as a projectionist living in a rented room with a gas ring, it was inspiring to see the life Rudy supported with words. But it was not just his success to which my father responded: he also recognized that Rudy was like himself, an outlier, a Bohemian, and someone who was untethered in conventional Irish terms, being neither Catholic nor Republican. If Rudy succeeded with those disadvantages, then so could he.

Rudy also realized that he had bumped up against a like-thinking person and, such persons being thin on the ground, he knew that one needed to cleave to them. He invited my father to visit the cottage.

II

My father borrowed an old bicycle from Joe Armstrong. He cycled up to Johnny Fox's pub, and turned left onto Military Road, known popularly as the Devil's Elbow on account of its kinks and corkscrews. He followed the road down to the Glencullen Bridge, crossed the Cookstown River and started up the road on the far side. The going was steep, but he hadn't gone far before he saw Ballybrew on his left. He only saw the roof because the cottage was well below the road. He went through a gate. In front he saw tiny, bumpy fields that fell precipitously to the river. He turned back on himself to face the road, and there it was: a tiny, stone-built cottage – Ballybrew. He leant his bicycle against the wall and removed his clips.

Inside the cottage he found Rudy, Rudy's wife, Margaret, known as Bunny, their four children, Rudy's much younger brother, Jack, and Jimmy O'Grady, the landlord, sometime stonecutter and aspiring poet. The cottage comprised two bedrooms, a tiny lobby where Jimmy O'Grady slept, and a living-room-cum-kitchen with a fire. Ballybrew was chaotic and crowded, and the children made an awful racket, but the visit was a success. The Joneses liked him, and he liked them.

Over the next four or five years he visited Ballybrew regularly and frequently, often staying over when he had no work at the cinema. Rudy and Bunny also gave great parties at Ballybrew with excellent gossip, plenty of drink, and music. My father attended and enjoyed these. The Joneses' set were artistic, rackety, convivial, enlightened, liberal and unconventional. The company of such people was enlightening, even liberating, plus it was a relief to mix with people whose opinions and

135

mores were precisely the ones he was groping towards himself. Socially, for the first time ever, he felt comfortable and that he belonged.

III

When the relationship began, my father thought Rudy would help him – and he did. He dispensed advice, talked books, made introductions, gave counsel. But then, as time passed, and my father and the Joneses became more enmeshed and more intimate, the master–apprentice relationship metamorphosed in to something different.

As he discovered, the Joneses' marriage was unusual, at least to him. Rudy had relationships outside his marriage, and, my father suspected, Bunny had relationships with Rudy's friends to pay her husband back.

Rudy was often away, and when he was, Bunny was unhappy. In my father Rudy saw a way to solve the problem of Bunny's unhappiness. He encouraged my father to drop by the mews as often as he wanted to cheer Bunny up, and he invited him to stay at the cottage when he was away to keep Bunny company. My father obliged. Initially he thought he was just being a good friend, but then he came to believe that Rudy hoped he might become Bunny's lover, or at least Rudy would not have demurred if such a development had occurred – nor, he came to believe, would Bunny.

Initially he kept his distance. He was inhibited by old-fashioned, courtly notions of respect and propriety. It just would have been wrong to go with Bunny, wife of his friend, married woman and all that, no matter what signals he was receiving. So although they were often alone in the cottage at night when Rudy couldn't get back due to his pursuit of assignments for the paper, he kept his relationship with the belle of Ballybrew, as he called her, idealized, fond and non-sexual.

But this situation did not last. At some point they became intimate, though there is nothing in the papers to indicate under what circumstances or for how long. There is only a simple acknowledgement written much later in November 1963: yes, he and Bunny were lovers, but there was no love.

32.

Sally Travers

At the Gate Theatre, my father graduated from scene-builder and set-painter to stage manager, specializing in sound. His job, during performances, was to provide effects and noises-off, and to cue up pieces of recorded music.

In 1945 the Gate company mounted Thornton Wilder's expressionistic play *The Skin of Our Teeth*, and during every performance he was under the stage producing the many effects the play required. His raised profile in the Gate brought him into contact with the actress Noelle Middleton. A Gate fixture, she was from Sligo, and ten or eleven years younger than him. She had a lovely old-fashioned face, was very pretty, a little gauche, and a bit stand-offish and proper, but in an encouraging rather than discouraging way. He was still seeing Mary Watson, but he liked Noelle Middleton better, and before he knew it his liking turned into something deeper. He classified his feelings as love (he wanted to believe it was love), but he was also a realist. He wanted a relationship that involved sex. Of course he did. And then, when he thought about that, he realized he was going to get no further with Noelle Middleton than he had got with Mary Watson.

II

His attention was then caught by another woman, and this other woman was in no way backward when she caught his attention.

Sally Travers, a Polynesian girl with a lovely temperament and a delightfully straightforward manner, was the daughter of Micheál Mac Liammóir's sister, Christine, and the celebrated English stained-glass maker and restorer, Martin Travers. Her mother had died in 1934, and four years later, when she became independent, she had come to Ireland to begin her theatrical apprenticeship under her uncle. At the Gate, over the following years, she did everything – she acted, danced, sung, built sets, made props and costumes, and helped out backstage. When she and my father started to knock around she was about twenty-four or twenty-five (five years younger than my father), and having been about seven years at the Gate, she was an established member of the company.

His new status as Sally's possible boyfriend gained him entry into the social world of Hilton Edwards and Micheál Mac Liammóir's, because when Sally attended social gatherings in their house in Harcourt Terrace she automatically brought him along too. At one of these he spotted Micheál Mac Liammóir's two-volume Odyssey Press edition of Joyce's *Ulysses* on the actor's shelves, and let their owner know that he coveted them. Micheál Mac Liammóir, never one to pass up an occasion for a grand gesture, took the volumes down (they were small, neat books bound in green covers) and gave them to their admirer.

But the gift was not innocently given. The next time they met, Micheál Mac Liammóir took him aside. 'Sally's very, very fond of you,' the actor said. 'You will never hurt her, Ernie, will you?'

My father said nothing, just shook his head. He had no intention of hurting her. He also liked Micheál the man as opposed to Mac Liammóir the actor, and he wanted Micheál to believe that his feelings for his niece were genuine.

III

He finished his play, *She Sits Smiling*. He sent it to the Abbey. It was neither dismissed nor taken up. All he got was a vague indication of interest.

What he needed was a commission for another play. One day, backstage at the Gate, he overheard Micheál Mac Liammóir lamenting that 'there was no play about the Mayor of Galway, James Lynch Fitzstephens' who hanged his own son, Walter, for killing a Spanish visitor from the balcony of his mansion in 1493.[9]

'Well, who better to write that play than you, Mr Mac Liammóir,' my father said.

'No,' said Micheál Mac Liammóir. It would take too long to research, and besides, he liked to lie back and write things out of his head rather than retelling stories that already existed. 'Why don't you do it?' he suggested, and then he could play the James Lynch Fitzstephens part.

My father agreed. He knuckled down. A few months later he had a finished play, *The Spaniard in Galway*.

He showed it to Hilton, who liked it, and committed himself to a date for production. He also commissioned Adolf to write incidental music. But a month or two before the production date Hilton told my father that Micheál was being difficult about the play, and he had better hear what Micheál had to say, and that when he went to talk to Micheál to hear what he had to say he was to tread softly as Micheál was depressed because of being overweight, on a diet, off the drink and suffering from 'romantic troubles'.

My father went to the actor's home. The actor received him lying on a daybed with his outdoor make-up on, and his first words were not, as usual, 'Dear boy', but 'It's such an unsympathetic part!'

The Spaniard in Galway, he realized, was not going on.

---

9 For a fuller account of this, see Ernest Gébler's letter titled 'A Great Story' published in *The Irish Times* on 5 December 1983.

33.

Publication

The war was over, and publishing was resuming in Britain. One day he saw an advert in the *New Statesman*: 'Established publisher invites unpublished manuscripts of novels of style and substance,' or words to that effect. The publisher was Sampson Low, Marston & Company, and they could be reached at an address near Fleet Street, London.

He sent his unpublished first novel. About six weeks later a letter came back. The letter's author had read his novel, *He Had My Heart Scalded*, liked it very much, admired particularly its refreshing simplicity and lyrical style, and wanted to publish it.

Sampson Low, the letter concluded, wished to start a distinguished fiction list with mainly new authors, and they wanted him to be one of the authors on that list.

The letter was signed: Dorothea Benson.

First, elation. Rent and outgoings consumed the wages he got from the Camden Street Cinema and the token he got from the Gate. He didn't save: he couldn't. But perhaps, he imagined, Sampson Low might give him enough to enable him to leave work and write full-time. What a boon that would be.

Then the doubts rushed in. Perhaps there was a catch. Perhaps he would have to pay the publishers to publish it rather than the other way around.

After several days of procrastination he replied to Dorothea Benson. Was there a catch? She wrote back. There was no catch – this was a proper offer.

What she didn't tell him yet, but which he would find out in time, was this:

The first reader at Sampson Low had rejected the novel, affixed a pro-forma rejection slip and put it on the rejects table to await postage back to Ireland. Fortuitously, before the typescript disappeared to the post room, Dorothea Benson picked it up for some reason (clairvoyance? instinct? the title?) when she happened to be passing the table, read it, liked it and decided to override the reader's decision and to publish it.

II

Now he had a publication offer, he knew that the next thing to do was write a second novel, a follow up to this first (and most likely uncommercial) debut novel.

Rudy gave him counsel, his advice being in two parts:

One, he should write something for the US. Americans bought more books than anyone else, and on top of sales there was Hollywood: if a book were made into a movie the author made even more money.

Two, US citizens were self-obsessed narcissists, and what they wanted to read about more than anything else was themselves and their story. As an example of a recent popular novel that had tapped into the American appetite for all things American, he cited *Gone With The Wind*.

So, Rudy continued, what the astute author did was to bring points one and two together and write something specifically hagiographic about America's past. As the subject that would do the job brilliantly he suggested a novel about the non-conformists of mostly English descent who, in the early seventeenth century, crossed the Atlantic aboard the *Mayflower* and established a settlement at Plymouth, Massachusetts, and were, because of what they had done, subsequently revered by WASP types as the founding fathers and mothers of the United States of America. There, said Rudy, was a story for American narcissists and therefore a guaranteed bestseller in America.

My father didn't care for what he heard (why write about America for Americans?), yet, ever the pragmatist, he decided he had better look into it. So one wet Dublin day, wearing his old black overcoat with the green mouldy shoulders, he took himself down to the Royal Dublin Society library in Ballsbridge and went to the stacks where the histories of European seventeenth-century exploration were shelved.

He had no plan. He just went along the shelves, taking down whatever book caught his attention and looking at it. Then, when he lost interest, he put it back and moved on.

As he browsed he knocked a book off a shelf. It landed at his feet. It looked old. He put aside what he was reading and picked it up. The title and author were on the spine in warm gilt lettering: *The Story of The Pilgrim Fathers as told by themselves, their friends and their enemies* by E. Arber.

He opened the book and found himself at the start of a contemporary document that Arber had included, which was titled '*REASONS AND CONSIDERATIONS TOUCHING THE LAWFULNESS OF REMOVING OUT OF ENGLAND INTO THE PARTS OF AMERICA.*' It was written by Robert Cushman, London agent of the colony at Plymouth, Massachusetts from 1617 to his death in 1625, and a key figure in the early colonization of America (hence he and his kin were commemorated with a huge granite column on Burial Hill in Plymouth, Massachusetts).

Cushman's text was directed at would-be but hesitating New World colonists, and argued that the occupation of territory already occupied by Native Americans was Bible sanctioned. Many of his readers probably agreed. If the Bible said it was all right to settle lands already occupied, then it must be all right. But then Chushman yoked to the religious sanction an economic argument that the poor, and it was the poor to whom he was appealing principally, would find particularly persuasive.

In the Old World, said Cushman, 'The rent-taker lives on sweet morsels; but the rent-payer eats a dry crust often with watery eyes.'[10] Readers would have recognized the truth of that: in the Old World wealth was unequally divided: worse still, which Cushman emphasized, personal virtue was no defence against catastrophe: 'Even the most wise, sober and discreet men go often to the wall.'[11]

However, and this was the kernel of Cushman's argument, the poor rent-payer who suffered hardship and want through no fault of his own and who shifted from Old to New World, would exchange poverty for plenty.

It was this part of Cushman's polemic that got my father's attention: hadn't he always been a rent-payer and never a rent-taker, exactly the same as the would-be pilgrims Cushman addressed? In other words, he and these pilgrims who had lived 300 years earlier were similar.

After this realization he had his moment of prescience. He might tell the story of the journey of the colonists to America on the *Mayflower*, and this would hopefully be of interest to Americans, but his focus would not be on the colonists as America's founders but on their poverty, which was what obliged them to undertake the perilous journey they undertook. At least, so he thought. All that remained was to make sure he was right. He would borrow the book and read it.

He did, and what he found out was that he was right.

---

10 Arber, E. (ed.), *The Story of The Pilgrim Fathers, 1606–1623 A.D.: as told by themselves, their friends and their enemies* (Houghton, Mifflin & Co., 1897), pp. 504–505.
11 *Ibid.*, p. 503.

III

This kind of story, 'the book you need will always find you by falling at your feet', is a story often told by writers, and my father certainly told the story throughout his life whenever he got the chance.

Interestingly, however, in his accounts he always omitted to mention that the idea of writing about the *Mayflower*'s voyage was Rudy's idea in the first place, and that without Rudy's prompt he would not have been anywhere near the shelf with the Arber sitting and waiting for him in the first place. No doubt he told himself that leaving Rudy out made the story seem more uncanny, more occult, which was true. But leaving Rudy out also meant he never had to acknowledge that the idea for the book was actually his friend's.

34.

London

My father resigned from the Camden Cinema, immersed himself in *Mayflower* material and churned out stories and articles for Irish newspapers. A first copy of *He Had My Heart Scalded* made its way to him, somehow, in Dublin. He took it round to 3 Cabra Grove, and with great ceremony put it into Adolf's hands – a novel, filled with his words, and with his name on the front. Adolf didn't say much, or perhaps he didn't say anything, but his expression spoke. He was surprised at what his son had done, that he had pulled it off.

Some weeks later, when he was back at the house, Rita told him that despite her bad eyes she had read his book. She didn't say if she liked it, though she did say 'I don't know how you got to know people like that!' meaning his characters, who were mostly poor people from Dublin. He was grimly delighted by her observation. The mother figure in the novel was modelled on her, though transposed to a different milieu, yet his mother had failed to recognize herself on the page. It was amazing what writers could get away with.

He Had My Heart Scalded was published on 20 September 1946. The print run was 5,000. It was reviewed positively on the BBC and by English critics ('A first novel and an uncommonly good one. The social background is painted in with realism so fierce and with understanding so deep as to make the book notable,' said Howard Spring in the *Daily Telegraph*), but was less well received in Ireland.

As he had it, the main naysayer in Ireland was Christine, wife of Edward Pakenham, Sixth Earl of Longford, a writer and, together with her husband, a major shareholder in The Dublin Gate Theatre Company.

> *Christine Longford smuggled a copy of* 'Scalded' *in and reviewed it with loathing in a Dublin literary magazine – not that one should suppose her cushioned life on rents* [on properties] *that extended from Stephen's Green to Monkstown had anything to do with that. Dark Days.*

What particularly stung was this damaging assertion: 'The author knows little about Irish life, or Dublin slum life.' He quoted this line for the rest of his life, though of course this may have been what he chose to imagine she had said rather than what she actually said. A copy of the review would resolve the matter, but I've never been able to locate it.

The novel – and he always blamed Christine Longford for this, believing it was only because of her review that it came to the attention of the authorities in the first place – was then:

> *Banned in Ireland* [...] *not for sex –* [it contained] *little or nothing of that – but for its descriptions of life in a typical festering Dublin slum house, an obscenity in itself* [...] *along with fifteen other books including* The Age Of Reason *by Jean Paul Sartre and* Come into My Parlour *by Dennis Wheatley.*

In Britain, however, where it wasn't banned, the book sold 4,566 copies, and eventually it would earn him £226. 5*s*. 11*d*.

Meanwhile, he had been reading his Arber and some other books about English non-conformists that he had managed to obtain in Dublin, but he knew that in order to write the book he wanted to write he needed to research the subject in depth, and there was only one place he could do that: the library of the British Museum. He estimated that the research and writing might take two or three years, and the work obviously would have to be done on the other side of the Irish Sea.

He said to Mary Watson (a little half-heartedly as she had declined his offer of marriage) that he was going over to London, and that if she came too they could live together and see how they got on. They had never had sex (condoms being unobtainable), but she knew that if she went with him they would. That was the deal, but she didn't want to run the risk of getting pregnant and all that that entailed, so she declined. My father dropped her after that, and cheered himself up by thinking what a dull, boring woman she was – no sense of adventure, no spunk.

Coincidentally, Sally Travers was also thinking of relocating. She said to him, 'I'm going back to London, just to see. Why don't we go at the same time?' They were not exactly lovers and had not slept together (fear of pregnancy again), but he knew that she had had relations with ('knocked around with' in the language of the day) one or two other men while at the Gate, and he knew that if he agreed to go with her they would become lovers. That was the deal. And he accepted.

II

Before he could go, however, he needed travel documents. The Irish passport office issued him with a passport on 16 January 1947. The given name he was now using, different from his baptismal one, was Adolphus Ernest Gébler. His visa to enter England was issued by the United Kingdom Permit Office, Dublin, on 30 January 1947, and on 17 February 1947 he arrived at Holyhead, where his passport was stamped. He travelled on to London.

The first problem was where to live. Sally had an elderly godmother, a Miss Parker, who owned a big stucco house, 2 Palace Gardens Terrace, in Notting Hill Gate. Together, they visited her. Miss Parker, assuming they were an item (which if they weren't yet, they soon would be), offered to rent them a basement room with a double bed (and threw in the use of her kitchen). They moved in and started their life together.

III

Spring, 1947. London was frozen. Snow lay thick on the streets. He learnt how to jump the turnstiles in tube stations, which allowed him to travel on the London underground without the expense of a ticket. He found a guarantor and obtained a card for the British Museum Reading Room, which in addition to access to the reading room allowed him the use of a desk and the right to request books from the stacks. He knew that Marx had spent many years in the very same seat writing *Das Capital*; he searched out this sacred spot, and over the years that followed he would often break from his own work in order to contemplate the place where Marx laboured.

He started. He read widely – documentary materials from the period of course, but also the competition, those books about his subject already published, 'the ignorant romancing of the Hemans and the Longfellows' as well as the histories produced by a 'long line of religious axe grinders and puritan historians,' such as The Revd George B Cheever (1807–1890), pastor of the Church of the Puritans, Union Square, New York, and a notable Christian abolitionist, whose book *The Pilgrim Fathers, or The Journal of the Pilgrims at Plymouth, New England, in 1620*, though it enjoyed classic status, 'made me want to run as far away from the *Mayflower* as I could get!'[12] The upshot of his encounters with the opposition was incredulity: why, he wondered, had no American writer,

---

12 These comments come from the account of how he came to write *The Plymouth Adventure* that appears on the back dust jacket of the hardback Doubleday edition (1950).

drawing on materials in one of the great east coast libraries, never thought to write a true documentary historical novel about the *Mayflower* as he was doing? He knew now that he really was on to something.

His novel earnings were insufficient to support a life of research: he had to earn money. He wrote short stories in what he called 'a ready style' with titles like 'Wicked Irishman', 'A Little White Devil', 'You'll Die Howling', and 'Enter Prosper Dominick'. These stories were exactly as their titles suggest – popular, contrived, sensational, and he sold them at a rate of a couple a month to publications like *Lilliput*, a popular English magazine that always included a couple of black-and-white female nudes in each issue, as well as to those Irish newspapers with whose editors he was still in contact.

And of course, when all else failed, he had the financial safety net that Sally provided. She was acting, dancing, designing: she made money. She supported him, and did so despite the fact that the relationship didn't really work – not on her side at any rate. One day he found her crying in their basement room, and when he asked her what the matter was, she said she was crying because he didn't love her, and she could not understand why.

The problem started with physical attraction. Sally, in his mind, was a bit 'ugly', though he conceded that it was a nice ugliness. In his opinion she had the soul of a very feminine girl and the body of a male athlete, whereas what he wanted was someone the other way round, someone with the body of a very feminine girl and the mind of a male athlete. Nothing was said, but she knew that she was not his type. And to make matters worse, he was very much her type.

So there was a mismatch between them. This wasn't simply about looks; it was worse. He didn't see her as a lover: he saw her as a sister, and so when they made love it felt like incest to him, though he conceded that this was the old Puritan ingrowing toenail at work – seeing her in terms of sisterliness was a ploy by his unconscious to inhibit intimacy, to stop him letting go.

But on another level, difficulties notwithstanding, the relationship worked, though the effort to make it work was mostly Sally's – she loved him more. They did things together, they shopped, they walked in London's lovely parks, Hyde Park, Kew Gardens and Primrose Hill, and they listened to records, both liking folksy, countercultural stuff and jazz. They were both captivated, for instance, by 'Fine Brown Frame' sung by Nellie Lutcher (1948), which they first heard in Sally's recently deceased father's house.

From my father's point of view, the best part of The Sally Years was the hours he passed in the cellar room, then later in 51 Colet Gardens (one of a row of eight late-Victorian artists' studios built of red brick and terracotta, with decorative wrought iron and leaded light windows where he and Sally moved in 1948 or 1949), tapping out his *Mayflower* novel on his typewriter, Debussy's *La Mer* playing over and over on the HMV wind-up gramophone. He used this piece to flood his psyche with the 'atmosphere' of the sea in order that he could then write the sea. To guarantee the music was as rich as it could be he made a point of using only white bamboo fibre needles and changing them after every play. To get the sound that inspired the word required him to focus on the technical.

Sometime during this period he found a second-hand ledger in a junk shop. It had been partially used for bookkeeping, but was mostly empty, and thereafter he occasionally used it as a journal ('Must not every serious writer keep a journal?' he wrote at the front). He also used the ledger to list the music he listened to. In addition to Debussy, Hindemith, Bach and Vivaldi were favourites. Much of what I know about this time in his life comes from this source.[13]

---

13 The ledger was removed from my father's house in Dublin sometime in the 1990s by Stan Gébler-Davies, son of my father's sister, Olive. In 1997 the ledger was given back to me along with several letters by Stan's daughter, Clancy, for which I am extremely grateful.

35.

Family

Marianna, sometimes Marianne, whose actual forename was Maria and whose surname was Blaschitz, and who was about to become the second Mrs Adolf Gébler, is about to enter the story, and so, before we meet her, here is her history in her own words, her gloriously mangled syntax preserved:

Mother is maid in scullery in shop keeper's house and the son of her employer give her baby. Mother is dismissed when the baby shows. I am that baby. I am born December 3rd, 1905, in Pellau, Austria. Life is hard. I have time in orphanage. Time with mother too. Then the First World War, then the peace, terrible in Austria, bad money, no jobs, then the Germans come in, then the next war happens and by 1945 I have had enough. I must leave Austria. In 1946 or 47, through employment agency in Austria, I find family in Dublin called Maguire who wants German speaking woman as 'maid of all work' and to look after two children and 'help them learn German'. I have good Austrian references: I get job: I comes Dublin to home of Mab and Leo Maguire. Nice people. Leo is singer on Irish radio. He know Adolf. I meet Adolf in the Maguires house. The rest like they like to say in Ireland is history....

That meeting in the Maguires' was sometime in the late forties, and at that meeting Marianna told Adolf that she was a socialist in Austria and that she was persecuted by the Nazis. Adolf, who believed her of course, being both lonely and left-leaning, was much affected by the account she provided of her sufferings.

Just as important as what was said was the medium in which it was said. The two foreigners spoke in German, and for Adolf, who had been swimming in English for decades, to speak in his mother tongue again (though a Czech nationalist), which had encoded within it the cultural humus from which he had sprung, was a joy. Adolf's subsequent relationship with Marianna owed as much to the reconnection to German high culture through the agency of language that it afforded him as it did to sexual attraction and loneliness.

II

When half his *Mayflower* novel was written, my father decided to go with Sally to Ireland for a holiday. This was in late August or early September 1948.

In Dublin they didn't go to stay with Adolf and Rita at the crucible of misery that was 3 Cabra Grove, but went instead to his elder sister Ada's house.

They expected to sleep together on the sitting room floor, but, perversely, Ada wouldn't allow it. Alongside this capricious and illogical imposition of propriety, his sister was unfriendly, curmudgeonly and critical (behaviours, of course, at which he also excelled), and he came to the following conclusions:

Her life had been a long sequence of let-downs. She was unhappy. She was unfulfilled. His life, on the other hand (living in London, writing a book, writing for newspapers and magazines like *Lilliput*), he imagined she thought was the life she should be living. And compounding the problem of envy was her sense that the natural order had been violated. In the family, her position was always higher and his lower (he being totally uneducated in her view, and rather stupid), but now the polarity was reversed and it hurt, it stung – or so he thought, or wanted to believe, and that was why she acted as she did.

III

He brought what he'd written of his *Mayflower* book and gave it to Rudy, his only mentor, to read. They discussed it on the steps of the Mansion House in Dublin.

'It'll have to be rewritten,' said Rudy, who was not impressed. 'It drags. We'll have to do a job on it. Get some action into it – fights, more sea.'

He was disturbed, shaken and angered by Rudy's verdict. He decided that not only would they not do a job on it together (indeed, Rudy would never ever again be shown material he had written and invited to offer an opinion), but he would not change course. As he was going, so he would continue. He would finish his book exactly as he had planned to finish it.

36.

His Inner Life

I

My father returned to London, but found it hard to write. The inertia and paralysis he felt reminded him of 'standing before an onrushing train and being powerless to move.' But he made himself go on, and somehow ground out the words.

II

Written in his ledger:

12 January 1949
When I was about fourteen I used to sole my own boots with very thick leather and stud them with nails. This was a bolster against insecurity. It was inconceivable that the world should always continue to run on smoothly. Earthquakes, catastrophes, might come at any moment; or, simply, I might have to leave home. So, without reasoning it out consciously, I was ever prepared to set forth, walk

hundreds of miles without getting my feet wet, dry shod in the cold wet desert that would replace civilization. Desert islands, Swiss Family Robinson, were all my hopes; the only way I could prepare was to keep the soles of my boots thick and very strong. Nails for my spirit's insecurity.

III

23 January 1949:

A LETTER NEVER POSTED

My Dear Mother and Father,

Indeed I am aware our relations have been always more than a little strained. But the true causes of this state of affairs I am afraid you have both very conveniently forgotten. You are two people who stupidly and wholly selfishly indulged your positive dislike, if not hatred, of each other from first to last, never, to my knowledge, having once curbed your indulgence in this passion when it might have saved this particular one of your children a day's heartache. Aldous Huxley (a very good writer you will undoubtedly never have heard of) once remarked that practically everyone's childhood is neurotically disastrous if not in one way then [in] another. But there are degrees, my God, there are degrees. However, your fear and resentment towards 'intellectual people' has not allowed you to learn the meaning of such words as 'neurosis', despite Mr Joad[14] in the 'Sunday Despatch', so it is hardly much use my trying to explain myself that way.

Let me merely say then that a child, from the age of five to twenty, cannot be an almost daily observer of the kind of despicable

---

14 C. E. M. Joad (1891–1953), an English philosopher and broadcaster famous for his appearances on *The Brains Trust*, a BBC Radio wartime discussion programme.

and grossly stupid screaming and delph-smashing that he witnessed in our home and [then] *in* [later] *life regard his parents with indulgent and unjaundiced eyes, because he cannot escape without some degree or other of maiming of the soul …*

Your Son

37.

She Sits Smiling

I

The Abbey still had his play, *She Sits Smiling*. In the early spring of 1949 the Abbey posted the manuscript along with a printed rejection slip to his London address. He immediately sent it off to the BBC, and on 9 March he got a contract back from the BBC: they were going to broadcast *She Sits Smiling* on the radio. On the very next day, 10 March, he finally got a title for his *Mayflower* book: in his ledger he wrote, 'I think it should be called *The Dream of Poor Men, A chronicle novel of the voyage of the Mayflower.*' He later explained that the dream was 'The dream of poor men to be rich in distant and fabulous lands.'

II

On 18 May 1949, *She Sits Smiling* was broadcast on the Home Service. A few days later, he received a letter from Ada. 'You've been lucky,' she wrote. 'Your play will have been heard by millions. You must have made money.' She went on to explain that she wanted some of the money she was certain he had made.

His first reaction to the letter was to remember the things Ada had done that he had resented. He recalled, for instance, that she had never expressed interest in *He Had My Heart Scalded* or in the *Mayflower* book:

> It was as if such things didn't exist. Her nasty personality 'welcomed' you, offered a cup of tea, but never mentioned those lynchpins of my life.

She must have judged his novels to be unimportant, he decided, and so she felt free not to notice them: a play on the BBC, on the other hand, was prestigious, and that was why she was able to acknowledge it and ask for the money she thought it had earned for him. It irked him, of course, that she should draw this distinction, as he believed that everything he wrote had the same value.

He also decided that the demand for money was a safe way of expressing the jealousy she must feel: he, the stupid younger brother, was now suddenly a success, whereas she, the clever elder sister, was not. To obtain money would restore the previous order and ameliorate her resentment. Not that he was going to give in to her demands. Of course not. He declined to send her the money she asked for, and in response she informed the BBC by letter that her brother, the author of *She Sits Smiling*, was an IRA sympathizer and a card-carrying communist.

> Was she mad? No, not mad – coarse minded, grabbing, jealous and bound [by] a nice malignant streak. She, after all, had bought a typewriter and expected to also become a writer, though she never let me know that.

38.

Success

July, 1949. My father finished *The Dream of Poor Men*, as his *Mayflower* book was currently titled. A copy went to his agent to hawk around the publishers in New York, and on 15 July he personally gave a carbon copy of the text to David O. Selznick's London agent, Jenia Reissar. In his journal (the one in the ledger) he wrote, 'They might use the research in it as basis for a film and [hire] me along with it to write the treatment.'

London was hot. 'The sun has been beating down on London every day for perhaps two months now. Escape, escape.' On 27 July he went to Ireland for a holiday. He explored the east coast and Waterford, from which the family were driven by poverty a quarter of a century earlier. By 26 August he was back in 51 Colet Gardens, where he and Sally lived.

In October, Lee Barker at Doubleday made an offer on the novel (and paid an advance when it was accepted), after which the Literary Guild, a book club, gave notice that the book would be their book of the month in May 1950. But the path to publication wasn't entirely smooth: Doubleday didn't like the title *The Dream of Poor Men* because,

as he wrote in his ledger, 'it is too difficult to remember as a title …
and it sounds like a proletarian novel. Dear oh dear,' and they insisted
on a new title: *The Plymouth Adventure*. Doubleday also required him
to excise 'most of the references to the first settlers' lowly origin.' He
obliged, but bridled:

> *It's all so false, the letters I have to write – it feels as if I was
> pandering* [...] *making friends with some individual for ulterior
> motives and in whom I have not the slightest interest.*

II

As well as believing that his dealings with the American publishers were
somehow false and shoddy, he was also troubled by his sense that his
own feelings were wrong:

> *The thing was done for money and has already exceeded* [my]
> *wildest hopes – the Literary Guild alone guarantees a minimum
> distribution of something near a million copies and payment to me
> of something around eight thousand pounds. Fantastic. Why feel
> so forsaken?*
>
> *The end of years of struggle to achieve a certain effect leaves one,
> as it were, in a vacuum? Or is it that the success of achievement is
> never, in the experiencing, as profound as expected. I walk through
> the park and tell myself, convince myself that the thing is done –
> there is money (1,500 dollars advance) in the bank to prove it.
> Are you not content, happy? Yes, I am content, airy with a sort of
> delight every time I think of it, and the delight is constant. What
> then? Did you expect it to strike you like a thunderclap? No, but
> [the] achievement is curiously empty emotionally. I have had more
> genuine emotional feeling writing any paragraph of that book, pot
> boiler or no, than I have felt over its turning into a gold mine
> inside a few weeks.*

He had never had money, and even though commercial success was what he had set out to achieve, now he had some it didn't give him much pleasure. At face value this was perverse, but once his biography is taken into account it makes more sense.

In childhood, his status inside the family was low. He was the unlettered child, handy for sure, but never spoken of as gifted, and never celebrated. In adolescence he was the family's proletarian, considered as being good only for manual labour. His dispatch to the Agricultural Hall Cinema as an apprentice was the direct outcome of this status: being a projectionist was the only thing of which he was thought to be capable.

When the family returned to Dublin, he was left behind. He was told that this was for his benefit so he could complete his apprenticeship, but he did not believe this. Even if he was wrong about that, in life what is believed to have happened always trumps what has actually happened. He believed that he was left behind because, very simply, he wasn't regarded as worth bringing back, and that certainty never left him.

During the Camden Cinema years he had not been, he felt, exactly encouraged, and sometimes he felt that he was even actively discouraged in his struggle to turn himself into a writer.

The sum of all these experiences was, in all likelihood, a feeling, deep inside, of worthlessness, and that was what was preventing him from taking pleasure now in what he had achieved.

So why did he not connect his past with what he was feeling (or to be precise, not feeling) in the present? After all, he was capable of insight. He knew that his upbringing hadn't been healthy and had damaged him. The letter he wrote to Adolf and Rita but never posted showed that. Yet, despite the connection he made there, he was not able to understand here that the anomie, emptiness and flatness he felt on having his book accepted by an American publisher was directly connected to the kind of person that his early miseries had fashioned him into. And the reason for his inability to see that, I would think, was this:

If he were to face that truth then he would have had to acknowledge that the self he presented to the world (that of a politically enlightened, if grumpy, Bohemian intellectual) was a carefully contrived performance; he was actually someone who felt that they had no value or importance. And of course if he were to make that admission then he would have to abandon his protective shell and go about as soft, unprotected tissue – and he could no more do that than a crab could go about without its carapace.

No, the only course was to carry on being the person he'd constructed, but for that he paid a price, and the price was this feeling of inexplicable anticlimax and disconnect.

III

On Saturday 17 December 1949, negotiations completed, contracts signed, the text reconfigured as the publishers had specified, 'slightly shocked' and not in his right senses, or so he claimed, he left Sally, who was appearing in a play, and went alone to Ireland for the Christmas holidays, an event he described in his ledger as the 'Return of the local boy who has made good.'

IV

On Thursday 22 December 1949, Vincent Seymour Kelly, *Quidnunc* of *The Irish Times*, interviewed him about the impending publication of his novel in the US. Anxious about what might be written about him, he gave a cautious, wary interview. On New Year's Day 1950 the sensationalist *People* newspaper ran a piece about him with the headline 'He could be a "lion" – but chooses to go fishing':

> Ernest Gébler, who has written a potential best seller with a guaranteed sale worth £16,000 in the United States this year, could be basking as a 'literary lion' in the admiration of America's clubs at this moment. Instead he prefers to fish for pike in a County Wicklow stream.
>
> He has never been to the States and he said yesterday: 'I'm not sure that I want to go either' – although his publishers,

and half a dozen societies, are urging him to undertake a lecture tour which would be a triumph.[15]

It wasn't just the American publication and book club selection that made him interesting to journalists. Hollywood was also now involved. The Sam Jaffe agency had shown the galley proofs around Hollywood, and Metro–Goldwyn–Mayer had given notice of their intention to buy the rights, with a view to making a motion picture of the book in the spring of 1951, featuring an all-star cast headed by Spencer Tracy. There was no doubt about it, he was on the up.

V

A few days later, at about 10.30 at night, he arrived at 3 Cabra Grove (he was staying elsewhere) bearing a present for Adolf: a bottle of brandy. He now had a bit of money, so could afford the gift.

Inside, he found his father as usual in his attic eyrie – the two weirdly proportioned cells he had built in the roof space were his place of sanctuary where he drank and smoked and escaped his and Rita's unceasing arguments. My father presented his gift. Adolf took it and uncorked the bottle. He had glasses up there – well, of course he did – and he poured two measures out. They toasted one another and began to drink, and as they did so Adolf's thoughts turned to the past, to the day he returned to Dublin in August 1919, and he told the old story – or Version Two of the old story:

He disembarked from the Isle of Man boat that had carried him home from the internment camp. He didn't recognize Rita on the quayside in the half-light. It was only when she came towards him that he realized that this tiny, thin, middle-aged-looking woman was his wife. He was twenty-nine; she was thirty-seven.

---

15 *Sunday People*, 1 January 1950.

They walked back to 43 Botanic Avenue. The children were in bed in the little room at the back. Rita and Adolf went up to the room. Ada was in a single bed. My father was in a cot. Ada sprang into his arms. 'Beautiful! Beautiful! How beautiful she is,' he said, and my father screamed at the strange man to put his sister down.

Ada, Adolf now explained as he drank the brandy, and not his exhausted, shrivelled wife, Rita, was the one who helped him to make a life in Dublin when he got back from his war. However, forty years after that event, all had changed: that daughter hated him, and joined with her, and in league against him, were her two sisters, Louise and Olive, and his unhappy wife, who was sitting downstairs at that very moment in the kitchen.

39.

Leatrice

I

One of my father's closest friends, and possibly even his best friend at this time, was Desmond Mac Namara, known as Mac, an artist with left-wing leanings.

Mac was not married, but he had a girlfriend with whom he was smitten. Her name was Leatrice Gilbert. She was the daughter of the great American film star John Gilbert (1897–1936) and his wife, the actress Leatrice Joy (1893–1985), a star of the silent era whose career ended once the talkies came on account of her southern accent, which audiences apparently found unattractive.

Leatrice Gilbert was her parents' only child. She was born in September 1924 on the cusp of her parents' divorce. Over the following twenty-six years she packed a lot in: she was a child actress, an MGM contract player, a US Women's Army Corps (WAC) clerk/typist and a student of Tamara Daykarhanova, formerly of the Moscow Art Theatre at Maria Ouspenskaya's New York Acting School. She was also married three times: firstly, 1942–1943, to

Francis Joseph Carney;[16] secondly, 1944–1945, to George Arthur Hoover; and thirdly, 1946–1948, to Henry Clay Hart, by whom she had a daughter, Lori Hart.

At the end of the forties, Leatrice came to Ireland (a country that had intrigued her ever since her time as a WAC during the war), where she met Mac, and then through him she met my father, either when he came on holiday to Ireland in August 1949 after finishing *The Plymouth Adventure*, or else over Christmas 1949.

It was now the New Year, 1950. Mac had to go away, and he asked his friend, my father, who was still on holiday, to keep an eye on Leatrice, who was living in digs in Waterloo Road in Dublin, in his absence. My father agreed.

Mac went. Leatrice got jaundice and was taken to hospital. My father did what Mac had asked. He took an interest. He was a prodigious and indefatigable hypochondriac, obsessed with his body and his own health, so he was just the person to have on hand when you were ill with jaundice in a Dublin hospital. Of course, he may also already have had amorous designs on this exotic American.

II

The days passed, and then came the day when he was due to get onto the boat and sail to Wales and return to Sally and 51 Colet Gardens in London. But now that he had what he believed to be duties or concerns or interests, he did not board the ferry. It left without him, for he had decided to stay in Ireland. But he didn't write to Sally to warn her that he was delayed, perhaps temporarily, more likely permanently, or to tell her that his heart was changing. He didn't tell her anything. He didn't communicate at all. This was how he left her. He simply vanished without warning.

---

16 Yes, he shared a surname with Rita's perfidious lodger.

III

Leatrice was well enough to leave the hospital, but not well enough to return to Waterloo Road. Something was established now between them, some sort of rapport, and for her recuperation they moved in to a cottage together in Ballinabrocky near Glendalough in County Wicklow. Leatrice was still weak, he ministered to her (he really should have been a doctor), and his ministrations were efficacious. Leatrice slowly got stronger, and to pass the time as she slowly recovered they narrated their life stories to one another.

My father's was a heroic tale: he, a Wolverhampton plebeian, had by virtue of self-education and prodigious industry turned himself into a writer, and not only a writer but a writer who had actually made money.

Leatrice's story (and he had never heard its like before) was a marvellous confection of estrangement and miraculous reconnection, and with its triangular structure (tyrannical mother, ingénue daughter, noble father), it was exactly the sort of narrative that was bound to appeal to him. This was how it went; or at least this was how she spun it as he recalled it later:

Her mother and John Gilbert divorced. Leatrice Joy was bitter. She was angry. She wanted to punish her ex and, as he boozed and whored around – there was no disputing that – she determined that she would use his immorality as a pretext to prevent him from seeing their infant daughter. In this aim she largely succeeded.

But then, in 1935, while swimming in Malibu, Leatrice, now eleven, was caught by a rogue wave and tumbled in the sway. As she struggled to stay afloat she felt a pair of strong hands grasp her arms and drag her ashore. On the beach she coughed, spluttered and regained her composure, then looked to see who her saviour was. It turned out that it was her father, who very conveniently had just happened to be passing when he saw her in the sea, as he thought drowning, jumped into the ocean and dragged her out. The Gods, Leatrice realized, had gifted her a chance to reconnect with her estranged father, and it was now up to her to seize it.

Without Joy's knowledge, she had sent her lost father a letter requesting a photograph. A brief, intense relationship ignited, and it lasted till Gilbert died, aged thirty-eight, in January 1936.

Leatrice also regaled my father with long accounts of her fascinating and overweening mother ('Marry rich, then suit yourself' was Leatrice Joy's motto when it came to matrimony), her mother's relentless attempts to influence her own matrimonial choices, and her equally determined attempts to avoid her mother's control.

She also provided him with detailed accounts of her complex emotional and amorous life, and in particular her three previous marriages. He found her philosophy enlightening and her candour and lack of shame refreshing. As she had it, people met, fell in love, slept together, married possibly, fell out of love, divorced or separated, and moved on, and it was all completely rational and normal. Even with regard to her last marriage, about which she might be expected to have more complex feelings given that it produced a child, Lori, whose parents had now separated, she felt exactly the same way. It happened, and now it was done and she had moved on: at least, that's how she told it.

My father had never met anyone this modern. He was smitten. On Leatrice's side I presume she saw that he was a not-quite Irishman, successful, or nearly so, without encumbrances, and liking what she saw her feelings also ripened into affection. And from here it was only a hop and a skip to love.

IV

Around the time that my father and Leatrice were becoming acquainted, another of my father's Bohemian friends (he'd a slew of them), the artist Eamonn Costello, known as Cossie, invited him to his studio at 11 Leinster Street in Dublin for a cup of tea one afternoon. When he arrived, he found, sitting and waiting for him at the scarred, paint-encrusted table, Sally. She looked aged and ravaged.

She said little. No accusation. The conversation between the three of us was halting and about nothing. Cossie obviously thought I was scum. He'd always liked Sally. There was nothing I could say to her. Probably the most troubled meeting of my life. As I walked away along Clare Street tears were running down my face.

40.

The End of Adolf's Marriage

I

There were now paying guests in 3 Cabra Grove, mostly classical musicians, mostly middle Europeans, mostly men, all demanding. While Adolf drank and fulminated, Rita did most of the work. She was tired. She was unwell. She was miserable, and the upshot of too much work, paying guests who made too many demands and too little domestic amity was, inevitably, a sundering.

Early in 1950, Rita's eldest daughter, Ada, abetted by Louise, persuaded her mother to quit 3 Cabra Grove and to move in with her daughter, Olive, who was now Mrs Davies, having married Max Davies, a Liverpudlian Jew in the furniture business.

II

No sooner had Rita gone than ... enter stage left the Jezebel that was Marianna Blaschitz. Here she is in her own words again:

170

After some years in Dublin I decide I go home to Austria. Same time I hear about the Adolf who need woman to cook and look after house in Cabra Grove. I don't want to work for Adolf, the hours, the shambles, why would I? But Adolf is alone. He needs a woman. He needs help. So Stupid go to housekeep for Adolf.

After Marianna moved in, it suited Adolf's increasingly alienated daughters, Olive, Louise and Ada, as well as his estranged wife, to assume that she was his mistress. When my father went to visit his mother at Olive's, he heard Marianna vilified as 'a homewrecker and worse', and denigrated as a 'servant' and a 'foreigner'.

41.

The Plymouth Adventure

I

When advance copies of the American edition of *The Plymouth Adventure* arrived at the Ballinabrocky cottage, my father decided to take one around to 3 Cabra Grove to show it off.

It was night. He arrived. He was admitted by Marianna to number 3. He went upstairs to the attic space, where he found Adolf working on a music score. Pleasantries were exchanged. The book-presentation moment was upon them. He remembered that he had done this before – how could he have forgotten? – when he had presented his first novel, *He Had My Heart Scalded*. He remembered Adolf's surprise that first time at his achievement, which was seemingly so unexpected to Adolf (how had he managed to pull this off?), and from that memory there arose the thought: his first novel was just a short story really in hard covers, a light novel, nothing much, whereas *The Plymouth Adventure* had bulk and heft and substance. Would it have a much greater effect on his father for that reason, he asked himself.

There are two competing versions of what followed.

One:

My father placed the copy of the US edition of *The Plymouth Adventure* he had brought into Adolf's hands.

Adolf opened the book. He saw the excellent period maps pasted as fore and end papers on the back of the binding. He turned the pages, thick and creamy and luxurious. This was an attractive object. He came to the end, closed the book, turned it over and saw his son's face on the back of the dust jacket. He looked at the spine and at his son's name.

His eyes misted. Adolf tended to hide his feelings, at least where his son was concerned, and my father was surprised. The old man was affected, and he in turn was affected by that.

This was what he had come for, he thought, so he ought to be pleased, but he didn't feel pleased. And why wasn't he pleased, since this was what he had come for? And then the Old Adam rose up inside him and he thought to himself: I am now famous, an eminent success in the world, which is something that has escaped him all his life. He's never even succeeded in being a member of a good symphony orchestra. Those aren't tears for me in his eyes. Adolf isn't moved; he's jealous.

'They used to say there's one in every family who escapes,' said Adolf finally, and that, as far as my father was concerned, confirmed what he'd thought.

Two:

He placed the edition in his father's hands. Adolf opened the book. He admired the map at the front. Then he came to the inscription written by my father on the title page: '*I wrote this solely to make money, hoping that if I did I could pay for music lessons …*'.

II

In April he travelled to New York for the publication by Doubleday of *The Plymouth Adventure*. The official publication date was 27 April 1950, and the launch was in the ballroom of the Waldorf Astoria.

The event was in the evening. He entered the ballroom. It was filled with journalists and radio people and literary types and academics. There were scores, even hundreds of guests. He began to mingle. A man from Rutgers University sidled up and intimated to him that the manuscript of *The Plymouth Adventure* would be of great value to Rutgers. 'I haven't kept it,' my father said. This was a bravura performance, but it wasn't true. He had left it behind in the flat in Colet Gardens in London where he had lived with Sally Travers, and having abandoned her, he was unlikely to get it back.

'Really?' said the man from Rutgers.

'Really.'

The man from Rutgers was appalled. A few minutes later my father mentioned the exchange with the man from Rutgers to someone from Doubleday, and was told he could have got many 'hard dollars' for his manuscript. He had a lot to learn about the literary world, he realized.

The official part of the evening got underway. There were speeches. The book was praised. All present were recommended to read it and spread the word across the States – buy this book. It was all a bit of an ordeal, he thought. Too much talking. But it ended, mercifully, as everything does.

He left with his publisher, Lee Barker, and Lee's wife, Adeline, and went out into the street. They were going to dinner, but first his hosts said they had something to show him. They led him to a nearby Doubleday bookstore where one window was given over to a *Plymouth Adventure* display (photographs, copies of the book, maps, artefacts), and they explained that there were similarly impressive displays in hundreds of Doubleday and other bookshops right across the States. Oh yes, they were pushing this book. They had high hopes. It was going somewhere.

He knew why they had brought him to the window and what they expected, but he couldn't do it. He had no wish to enthuse. He was not even sure he knew how.

They ate dinner and then they delivered him to the Mayflower Hotel on Central Park West between 61st and 62nd Street. Where else in New York could they possibly have put him? Goodnights were said. His hosts left. He waited, and then, when he was sure that he would not bump into them outside, he slipped out and returned to the same Doubleday bookstore that the Barkers had brought him to earlier. He went up to the window. He looked at the piles of his book, the maps, the photographs and the ephemera. He knew that for weeks to come this display and others like it would be on show in bookshop windows all over America, but still he felt no exaltation, no pride, no consuming satisfaction at that knowledge, and he wondered why. Why wasn't he hopping, skipping, jumping, whoring, getting drunk, and inviting everyone he met to dinner, especially nice Sam Wannamaker, the theatre director, who, he had learnt earlier, wanted to produce *She Sits Smiling* (now called *Peter Quirke*) on the New York stage?

He returned to the Mayflower Hotel. He sat up. He puzzled over his unresponsiveness, his inability to feel delight, to feel joy, his deadness. He remembered what his mother used to say when he was a child – 'Ernie has no ambition. He'll never be anybody.' Now, he asked himself: didn't he want to be somebody? Or was he suffering some kind of sickness that meant he couldn't allow himself?

He returned for a third time to the Doubleday bookstore window. He waited for something to happen inside, to feel excitement, delight, the feelings that he knew were commensurate with what he was seeing and what was happening. But the feelings wouldn't come. He was blocked or something. All that came instead was a fantasy: he would go back to Ireland and buy a cottage in the hills. It would have its own river. He would fish for trout. He would be an unknown writer. No, not an unknown one, a less public and more private one, a writer unentangled in this commercial fandango. This whole episode appeared to be a repeat of what he had felt in London after he sold the book and he wandered about London's parks feeling restless and disgruntled, except with the difference that he now had a coping strategy, though hardly a helpful or healthy one: he would disappear; he would vanish into the hills of Wicklow. The article in the *Sunday People* had been right.

The next morning he told Doubleday that his mother was dangerously ill. She wasn't, but as her marriage had recently collapsed and she had left the marital home and moved in with her daughter Olive, this didn't feel like a lie to him, but more of a euphemism. He asked Doubleday to cancel all his radio interviews, university appearances and promotional events, and to book him a flight back to Dublin. Lee Barker was disappointed, but he acquiesced. My father went home to Ireland. Or, put another way, once again, just like he had out of Sally's life, he vanished.

42.

Marriage to Leatrice

I

In June he started living openly with Leatrice in the cottage in Ballinabrocky. The truth now had to be faced: Mac had to be told that she and my father were now together. There were angry and unpleasant exchanges between the parties, the two best friends were suddenly best enemies, and most of their Dublin friends sided with the betrayed lover, Mac, and against the usurper, my father, and perhaps against Leatrice too.

II

With the dollars repatriated from the US, my father bought a cottage in Wicklow, suitably close to Dublin, and he and Leatrice went to live there. On 4 October 1950 he got a telegram from New York. He was to come immediately to work on his play, *Peter Quirke*, which Sam Wanamaker was going to direct.

He flew to New York on 7 October, and on 22 October Leatrice followed him there. She was pregnant, she said, and his understanding was that he was the father. On 12 December 1950 he and Leatrice married in New York at a civil ceremony, and Sam Wannamaker was best man. On 16 December 1950 they sailed for France, returning to Ireland on 13 January 1951.

On 14 April 1951 he saw in *The Irish Times* that Lake Park, Roundwood, County Wicklow, 'A Lovely Little Residential Sporting Estate' on 180 acres with a Georgian lodge, was for sale by auction. The cottage was too small for the two of them as it was, and there was a baby on the way. They needed space. They needed a home, a family home, something with class.

He and Leatrice went out to Roundwood and took a look at Lake Park. Five beds, thirty minutes from Dublin, high in the hills overlooking Lough Dan, it was perfect. On 8 May 1951, with the money from Doubleday and the Literary Guild, he bought Lake Park at the Hamilton & Hamilton Auction Rooms at 17 Dawson Street, and not long after, he, and a very heavily pregnant Leatrice, moved in.

III

From my father's notes:

> *What did Adolf feel when he first entered the entrance gates of Lake Park? That jealous failed person (whose father sent him to the best music college in Europe but who did not teach his eldest son a note of music or anything else, nor send him to school).*

He liked this story so much he wrote it again, dwelling on it for longer this time:

> *On one of his first visits to Lake Park, Adolf was standing in front of the house looking down over the sweep of fields, having just arrived in the little old two-seater Fiat car. He said, quietly, hesitantly, 'You must be pleased that you ... made ... became a writer ...?'*

And I said even before I knew what I was saying, 'Yes, but only second best. I know now I should have been a musician. Written music instead of just words ... '.

Adolf kept looking down the valley and I thought I saw when glancing at him, his chin tremble for a moment and his eyes became a little glassy – with tears?

IV

On 19 July 1951, in a draughty Lake Park bedroom, Leatrice gave birth to a ten-and-a-half pound boy. My father and his first wife named this first son John Karl. Not long after the birth Leatrice's mother, Joy, visited. It was not a success. When she left she took Leatrice's daughter (by her third husband) Lori, who was in Ireland at the time, back with her to America, I think. Why Leatrice let her mother take her daughter to the US is a mystery. Perhaps it was simply that she was exhausted by the baby and did not have the energy to minister to a second child.

43.

California

I

In Hollywood, the translation of *The Plymouth Adventure* from page to screen was underway. The studio hired the lyricist and screenwriter Helen Deutsch to write the script (obviously they needed a pro to do that job). Her greatest success to date was *National Velvet* (1944), starring Elizabeth Taylor, but as a sop to my father they indicated that they were keen to have him as a historical consultant, to which he agreed.

II

On 11 February 1952, my father, Leatrice and John Karl set sail for America. They crossed the Atlantic, passed through the Panama Canal and made landfall on the west coast. For three months they lived with Leatrice's mother on her houseboat in Balboa, while my father did whatever he did for the production of *The Plymouth Adventure* in his capacity as historical consultant.

My father didn't enjoy California. He thought that all the men had hard, tanned, leathery faces, and talked a lot of asinine nonsense (he based this observation mostly on two men who garaged their cars opposite his mother-in-law's home, and on whom he eavesdropped for hours as they talked while fixing their cars), while all the women, at least the ones he saw in the drive-ins, had beautiful, sad faces because they had come west to be actresses but had discovered they would never make it to a film set, no matter how many movie loudmouths they slept with.

He didn't much care for the landscape either. He wrote of Balboa that spring:

> *Dreary place – miles & miles of that endless Pacific beach, edged with oil tar [...] And yet ... to stand on that somehow desolate apparently never ending beach ... strange, unreal, a moonscape – the little waves oozing to an end – out across the waters, a million miles away apparently, Japan. Fitting place to end the Leatrice disaster. I knew in my bones she was shedding me like an out of fashion dress – she had this rich old suitor waiting in the wings. And yet, inside, I knew, somehow, it was me shedding her, etc.*

His last sentence sounds like he wanted to persuade himself of this, and not that he believed it.

44.

A Confession

I

Leatrice hadn't enjoyed living in Lake Park (too cold, too hard, too isolated), with the awkward, moody curmudgeon that my father had turned out to be while nursing a new born, and in California the couple had long, earnest discussions about their future and where to live. Their decision in the end was to sell up in Ireland and settle in America – they would be so much happier there, where it was warm and hospitable, and Leatrice would have her mother on hand, and my father could work in Hollywood.... That, at least, was what my father thought they had agreed. On 22 May he flew out of LA airport alone (Leatrice and John Karl remaining in California), and on 23 May 1952 he arrived back in Ireland. His plan was to wind up his affairs and return to California.

On 7 June 1952 Leatrice wrote a letter and posted it by airmail to my father at Lake Park. He received it a few days later. I don't have this letter: it is lost. The gist of it, though, judging by what he and she wrote later, was this:

Long before she had ever met my father, Leatrice was involved with and was even briefly engaged to an American financier, a Mr John Fountain. When she arrived in New York in late October 1950, she confessed, she saw Mr Fountain, and that was when John Karl was conceived. However, she then agreed to marry my father because he badgered her to marry him, and she let my father believe that the child she was carrying was his. When they returned to Ireland and John Karl was born, my father continued to believe that the child was his when in fact he wasn't. It was a terrible thing that she had done, but she now wanted to rectify that mistake. To this end, she wrote, she planned to move to Reno, Nevada, where she would establish residency and in time obtain a divorce. Whether marriage in the future to Mr Fountain was floated in this letter or not I do not know.

II

My father's instinct on receiving this letter was to return immediately to California and to deal with this problem head-on and in person. But first, if he was to go back, he would have to renew his US entry visa. He left his passport with the US consul, then returned to retrieve it a day or two later. Of course, on getting the passport back, the first thing he did was to open it to check the stamp. To his surprise he found that instead of his visa being extended, his passport was now stamped 'No entry to US'. He was mystified as well as alarmed. He had a wife and child in the US – why was he barred? He vocalized his queries, but the official to whom he addressed his remarks was unable to answer. He left the building feeling angry. What was going on? This didn't make sense.

He had a friend in the Irish diplomatic service, the poet Valentin Iremonger, who was currently, and rather conveniently, given my father's problem, serving at the Irish Embassy in Washington. He sent Iremonger a telegram asking him to investigate why he had been denied entry to the US and offering to reimburse him for any costs he incurred in the course of his inquiries.

Next, he replied to Leatrice's letter. His reply, sly, careful, emollient, floated the idea that all was surely not lost and that he and Leatrice might get back together. Why not? He enclosed a photograph of John Karl taken the day before he flew out of LA. That letter is also lost, so I am simply reporting here what he said he had said in later letters.

This letter gone, he heard from Iremonger. His friend reported that the day after he flew out of LA airport, two women entered the Santa Ana office that dealt with immigration and naturalization and made a sworn deposition that he was a communist agent who shuttled between Europe and America and was bent on making mischief, which was why his visa was rescinded. Who were the women? Iremonger didn't have their names. That information was classified.

III

This story is repeated several times in his notes. It's a great story, but unfortunately the stamps in his passport don't confirm it. This is the story they tell:

Frances M. Dabell, the American Vice Consul in Dublin, issued Adolphus Ernest Gébler with immigration visa number 2039 on 6 October 1950. He travelled to the US and entered New York on 9 October. In December, now married to Leatrice, he left New York by boat and arrived at Le Havre on 22 December 1950, from where he went on to Ireland.

He then returned to the US in 1952, this time with Leatrice and his son. He entered the country at San Pedro, California on 12 March 1952. Beside the immigration and naturalization stamp that noted his admission on that day, and written with a fountain pen, were the initials 'RP' (presumably standing for Residency Permit) and a seven-digit number.

And that's all there is. That's it. There's no stamp anywhere in the passport saying that his right to enter the US was withdrawn, and in his tortuous and drawn-out correspondence with Leatrice there is nothing

Mary Watson, 1941.

Leatrice and John Karl outside the front door of Lake Park.

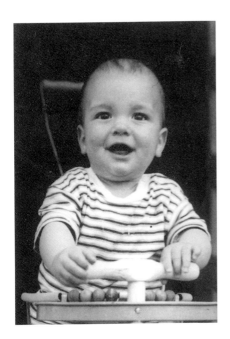

John Karl. I believe that this is the photograph that Ernest took prior to leaving for California and later sent to Leatrice, referred to on p. 184.

Ernest and Leatrice outside Ballybrocky, 1950.

Ernest Gébler in Palace Garden Terrace, Notting Hill Gate, London, 1947.

Edna O'Brien at the front door of Lake Park, May 1951.

SALLY TRAVERS

JUVENILE CHARACTER
AND LEADING PARTS

Dialects : COCKNEY, IRISH, AMERICAN
Language : FRENCH, etc.

' Clotho ' in " HAPPY AS LARRY "
—*Criterion Theatre,* 1948 ✗

' Nora ' in " THE RIGHTEOUS ARE
BOLD "—*Embassy Theatre,* 1948 ✗

' Eliza ' in " PYGMALION "
—*Dublin Gate Theatre,* 1947

' Bairbre ' in " ILL-MET BY MOONLIGHT "
—*Vaudeville Theatre,* 1947

B.B.C. & TELEVISION

2, Palace Gardens Terrace
W.8
BAYswater 6191

Height 5 feet 4 inches (1947) *John Deakin* 1947

Sally Travers's 'Spotlight' proof, 1948.

Adolf (standing) receiving a gift at the Gresham Hotel in recognition of his service to the IT-GWU Band. Marianna is seated to the right of the picture.

Irene and Jim Hendry's wedding picture, 1949. L to R: Adrian, Adrian's wife, two friends of the groom, Jim Hendry, Irene Hendry, Ernest, Louise, Rita and Olive.
Adolf and Ada are absent.

Adolf, Ernest and Marianna, repairing a car outside Lake Park, early 1950s.

The cottage at Ballybrocky, 1951.

Adolf outside 3 Cabra Grove, late 1950s.

Adolf conducting in Bray, 1940.

Adolf Gébler (front row, middle, wearing a bow tie) outside the Old Liberty Hall with the
ITGWU Band, 1949.

Rita Gébler, 1944.

Marianna Gébler (née Blaschitz), 1948.

Ernest and Leatrice at their wedding
breakfast, New York, December 1950.

Leatrice at Ballybrocky, 1950.

A publicity photograph of Ernest Gébler, 1950.

about it either, which, given what a sensational event it was (if true), and he being the sort who would be bound to make a good deal out of such an event, seems strange.

So did he make the whole this story up because it fitted with his idea of himself as the victim of the treacherous Leatrice? It's possible. On the other hand, at the end of his life, when he drafted notes for his 'Autobiog', he listed Iremonger as someone he must visit specifically to discuss this episode, though in the event he never did. Why would he want to get in touch if the story was a fabrication? Much as I'd like to be able to say categorically that it either happened or it did not happen, that Leatrice and her mother either denounced him or did not denounce him, I can't. I just don't know where the truth lies here.

45.

An Exchange of Letters

I

On Saturday 12 July 1952, Leatrice responded to his letter – the one with the photograph – and this letter I do have. It was handwritten, quite short and very emphatic:

Dear Ernest,

Since nothing seems to be gained for either of us by delaying, and prolonging the unhappy condition, I've moved to Nevada and established residence here. [...] it is a beautiful place, but filled with the usual set of hard faced, alcoholic Easterners, here for the usual reason. [...]

We will be here for the required period during which time you will be sent the necessary papers to sign. It will as painless for you as I can possibly make it. [...]

There is no use my telling you again how I feel about what I have done to you. I am not an insensitive person, and your suffering I can share only too well. This seems to be the best step to take now, to clear this wretched mess and leave us in a free position to try and re-shape our lives. And it won't be easy. But as matters stand, any other course seems wrong, futile and foolish.

II

On 16 July 1952, my father's Dublin solicitors, Fred Sutton & Co., wrote to say that they had received papers from Leatrice's Dublin solicitors.

His response to the legal process was a typewritten, single-spaced, eight-page letter to Leatrice of thirty paragraphs, each numbered. It was as savage as it was prolix, so I quote selectively:

1. *My last letter to you, in which it was implied that I hoped we might come back together again, enclosing the last picture of my son that I took before coming abroad, you have not answered nor mentioned receipt of in your present letter of 12 July written from Reno and requesting co-operation in divorce proceedings […]*
2. *I must take it then that you are proceeding to sever our lives completely […]*
3. *The difficulty here is that, unlike some of your former husbands I love my child […] (as indeed, I may add, I [did] your daughter. […] for two years you were pleased to have me accepted by her as her father, and I her as if she were my own child, until your mother took her away from me).*
4. *[…] as you have apparently decided absolutely for Mr Fountain […] I must here state my attitude.*
5. *If, besides myself, you fornicated with a dozen men from the day you arrived in New York in 1950, (with the determined intention to marry me, while also sleeping with me), you could not have conceived because you were already pregnant when I left Dublin. I flew to New York on Saturday 7 October 1950. On the Friday of the week following, 13 October, your*

menstrual period should have occurred. It did not, and you concluded, rightly, that you were pregnant.

6. *You decided to follow me to New York and there marry me; not to wait till I returned. You confided this in some detail, as to how you would very cleverly handle the situation, to a so-called friend in Dublin before you left, on the 22nd. [...]*

7. *Why you did not write the good news to me and wait till I came back, if even to avoid waste of money, I shall never know. You were never one to be thrown into a panic by an unexpected pregnancy. The result, marriage, would have come about quite naturally on my return.*

8. *The facts are quite simple. You had come to be the foundation of my life; you had talked about your desire to have more children by me. You were relying on me at that time for contraception. During a period of ten days before I left for New York there was no contraception. John Karl was conceived by my intention, as a pleasant surprise for you – if it came off – and as the first of our children.*

10. *[...] I did not tell you this about my son's conception, because I did not wish to embarrass you after you had told your small and needless lie about the child being conceived by us in New York. So I thought then. However, from your letter of 7 June 1952, in which you say you were sleeping with Mr Fountain in the same week in which you were sleeping with me, it can be gathered there may indeed have been a more than usual confusion in your mind, even to the extent of believing Mr Fountain to be the father [...]*

14. *[...] Let me recall to you that my father was taken from me for the four [sic] most important years of a child's life, which he spent in a first world war concentration camp. And when he came back to his family he was so embittered and distraught that he did not discover he had children of his own [...] until they were almost grown up. And while I worked, through twenty years, to*

raise myself from an illiterate boy to an educated man, I held a constant passionate belief that when I had children they would have from me the never-ceasing understanding, companionship and tenderness that was absent from my own childhood. [...]

20. [...] *You let us go to California together, feeding my illusions, when you knew then.* [...] *And as it came near the time for me to leave you bolstered me up with an apparently ever-growing love and affection, with your arms about my neck whispering how would you ever be able to live without me in the months ensuing and let me be quick, quick, to come back.* [...] *So you sent me abroad to sell our house and home, believing fully and happily in my return to you and children and a new life in California, knowing full well what you were about.*

24. [...] *I am a man who worked, who slaved for fifteen years, while you were riding horses in the Californian mountains and being driven to school in imported automobiles, to raise myself from nothing and secure some financial security. All the money that came to me in the year that I first met you was the result of that fifteen years work. With you at my side I spent that money to buy one of the most beautiful houses in Dublin, which was far beyond my means* [...] *It was bought because we fell in love with it. It was bought for a home. And it was bought on the understanding that you had a small income which would help to support it. You left Mac Namara with only an emotional catastrophe to deal with; you left me with both an emotional and a financial catastrophe to deal with. Your share of responsibility in our home you now also throw off without a thought. This house is now unsaleable. Nor can I live in it, where at every turn I meet a memory, expect you to walk through a door, or hear my child's cry in the empty house at night. What do you suggest I do with the sole result of my fifteen years work? Leave it to moulder, for the nettles to grow through the floors, while I set to work for another fifteen years to put some money in the bank? I made an*

investment, an emotional investment in you, your first child, and my child; and materially I made an investment for you as well as myself, in a life, a home, a way of living. And you know as well as I do that as a writer the earning of such money may never occur again in my lifetime. Consider this well. It is your problem as well as mine.

26. *[…] The evidence necessary to bring* [a] *suit for damages against Mr John Fountain is complicated, but I have been advised that it is quite ample. Certain of his letters, you may recall, fell into my possession last year; as well as your letter to me of 17 June* [sic]. *If Mr Fountain had not always been there, writing to you and enticing you from me, our marriage might still be a marriage and you and my child be with me. I regret that the evidence will not be conducive to a happy union between you and he, but then neither will any of the other facts be, and perhaps you had better get hardened to the knowledge early rather than late.*

27. *[…] I may have to oppose your suit for divorce in Reno and file suit myself for divorce from you in New York State. I do not in fact wish to do this unless forced to, because the sworn evidence I would have to bring forward from persons here regarding your moral and Communist life and views, in Dublin and London, as well as your admissions in your letter of 7 June as to your sexual promiscuity would in no wise* [sic] *be the kind of legacy I would care to leave my child. But if I have to I shall. I may never avail myself of my periods of custody, it is true, but I cannot face existence without some guarantee that in the future I will see my child and have definite rights as to his education and upbringing.*

30. *[…] I suggest finally that if you wish to secure a divorce and avoid my suit for full custody, you consider every point in this communication carefully, and propose a solution or solutions to the problems stated. Until you do I am not interested in hearing from your lawyer. And I further suggest that you file*

this document more carefully than is your usual practice; you may see it again, in more than one court.

III

What was it he hoped to achieve with this? Was it to signal his intention, rooted in his own unhappy childhood and his alienation from Adolf, to father John Karl? Was it to out Leatrice as a dissembler, who first had lured him to California and then had sent him back to Ireland, and all the while, though she had known she intended to seek a divorce, never let on, and thereby – what? – persuade her to change because of the acuteness of his criticism?

Or was it actually a declaration of terms? If she helped him financially with Lake Park then reluctantly he would grant her wish and accede to the divorce, but if she didn't he was going to be exceedingly awkward, which would lead to details of her life being made known that she would not want known.

With the way the letter was structured, with the terms coming at the end, my reading is that despite what he said about his wish to be a good father, what he hoped to achieve was an agreement. But if that was the case, this was absolutely not the way to set about securing that goal.

Or perhaps I am being too logical. Whatever he wanted was beside the point. What the letter really signalled was the struggle between his normal human instincts and his self-interest, with the latter seemingly pre-eminent.

IV

After this he wrote a second, even angrier, letter. I will quote just one passage:

Never since I first kissed you was I unfaithful to you, not unfaithful in word. Lori, your first child by another man, had her first father in me, as you have said many times to many people. You and I came together under the most trying circumstances and because of your life before I loved you I lost my best friend, your former lover, whose friendship for me turned to hatred, and I lost also [...] most of my other friends and acquaintances through the same cause. Yet I thought you might in the end prove worth it. You were nursed by me in Brocky [sic] through your sickness, which had its origin in your squalid life before I met you.

In return you have repaid me by a form of depraved treachery which even now I cannot comprehend by any rational approach because it is baseless and senseless. (Inquiring more fully in to your earlier life it appears now that this turn-about treachery is common to your later relations to men who have loved you).

V

On Saturday 30 August 1952, Leatrice lodged a complaint to secure a divorce with the office of the Second Judicial District Court of the State of Nevada in and for Washoe County, and on Tuesday 2 September 1952, Leatrice wrote to him:

Dear Ernest,

Both your letters have been received and read with alarm and sorrow. I have turned them over to my lawyer to deal with as he chooses.

Notice of the petition for divorce (Leatrice Gébler versus Adolphus Gébler) appeared in the *Reno Evening Gazette* on 5 September 1952.

46.

Divorce

I

On 20 September 1952, my father received notice of Leatrice's petition for divorce from the Clerk of the Second Judicial District Court in the State of Nevada in and for Washoe County, and about a month later the petition for divorce of Leatrice Gébler, plaintiff, against Ernest Gébler, defendant, was heard and, in the words of the DECREE OF DIVORCE subsequently issued:

> [...] the Court finding that all of the allegations of the complaint are sustained by the testimony, [...] the above named plaintiff is entitled to a decree of divorce from the defendant upon the ground of extreme cruelty, [...]
> IT IS HEREBY ORDERED, ADJUDGED AND DECREED that the bonds of matrimony heretofore and now existing between the above-named plaintiff and defendant be, and the same hereby are, dissolved and declared forever at end [...]

II

The date the divorce was granted was 24 October, a Tuesday. Nine days later, on Thursday 2 November, Leatrice wrote a letter from Virginia City in Nevada, where she was now living, to my father. Written in a jokey style, it began, 'Sweet Ernie, I'm very fond of you old cabbage.' She then continued by telling him that never, no matter what financial inducements were offered, would she, 'take back the job of being your housekeeper no matter what the circumstances, rewards or payments.' She explained that she had returned to the US looking like a forty-year-old woman who was stricken with anaemia, but now that she had had some quality R & R in Reno her looks had returned and she was 'a young woman again.'

Leatrice's post-divorce transformation was not limited to her appearance. 'I'm sorry to admit it, dear, [but] I'm really, peacefully happy now, for the first time since I've known you.' Her capacity for 'spontaneous joy' had disappeared during the summer at 'Brocky', but had now returned.

Not content with that, Leatrice had also found God, bonded with nature, and still found the time to make 'the greatest discovery I'll ever make about myself': that she too was a writer – and she had 70,000 words to prove it. Whilst she was 'over the mountain' about this, it was going more 'slowly' and 'painfully' than it had at the beginning. Her newfound writing talent she attributed to no longer having to 'spend [...] time consuming energies in home-making for a man and catering always to someone else's talent.' After remarking that she was no Jane Carlyle (to whom the success of her husband, Thomas Carlyle, was often attributed), she warmed to her theme:

> *What I want is a wife! A nice, quiet, devoted and yet distracted wife.*
> *By distracted I mean someone capable of amusing herself – reading*
> *books, developing good conversation-material, practising chess*
> *moves, when she's not preparing beautifully seasoned and perfectly*
> *cooked meals! Who will take all our clothes to the Laundromat, [go*

to the] *market, do the ironing and disappear into the wall when I don't want to see her.*

This description encapsulates, presumably, what my father had expected her to be: self-contained, intellectual, a fantastic cook, someone willing to throw herself into doing the housework with gusto, and most importantly, somebody who would vanish when their presence was unwelcome.

Up to this point the letter was handwritten (to signify its larky credentials, no doubt), but now it switched to typescript, anticipating its change in mood. The next part was serious, concerning as it did the solution to the fix in which they found themselves. The solution, obviously, was that my father should move to Virginia City:

One possible solution to […] our dilemma is that you move to Virginia City and join our chess club. You will have your own days to do what you like with, to grump about your own shaded and shuttered house or perhaps even write. Evenings you could drift up to C Street and into the Brass Rail where you could find Walter [Clark, the author] *and me playing shuffleboard and discussing Zen Buddhism. […] We would […] have a few […] beers and maybe go down Taylor Street to my house, set up the chess board or listen to records. I think I have the best collection in Virginia City. About one o'clock I throw you all out (I have to be up early with children […].*

What was not to like about such a life?

Just to be sure, though, that he did not imagine that she was hinting at a possible reconciliation, she told him about her immediate future in the next paragraph:

John Fountain arrives here next Saturday to get me to marry him and to go live in the East, which I don't want to do, not yet anyway.

The fact that he's still supporting me doesn't make it any easier. If only I had the money spent on that damn Ford van and the seven hundred dollars [...] spent on your fare to California, I would be in a better position. I'm cleaned out completely now. I haven't a dime. I don't suppose you're any better, but if you are, a small repayment of cash would strengthen my stand considerably. I don't want to get married yet! – Ernest. Help

She then reverted to letters of his to her. These, she wrote, had touched her:

Your letters make you seem much softer, a hundred times more understanding and perceptive. It is really as though you've come out of a drugged sleep. Is this true? You always had moments, even days at a time of 'yourself', but then would come the weeks and even months of elephantine gloom and surly, uncommunicative, unbearable behaviour. [...] can such a metamorphosis have occurred? The wonder of it stuns me. Are you sure that getting away from me wasn't the good thing you needed?

And then came the kernel of her message. In Lake Park, where he had been at his worst, she had never been so alone, not that he had noticed. The unhappiness he made her feel had given her the strength to go her own way, for which she would be eternally grateful to my father, and having gone her own way there was no going back: they could never be together again.

On the letter's final page she turned to the American writer Walter Clark, a habitué of the Brass Rail. She considered him, she said, to be the only great living American writer, and added that he had helped her to reconnect with her nation.

She thought they'd get on, my father and Walter, providing he eschewed the wearying anti-Americanism that had so alienated the American friends he had made when he had been staying with her and her mother in Balboa.

196

You will like him and he will probably like you, if you don't come here as the cultivated English writer, gently tolerating the American, his bread and oleo-margarine. That's what cost you the friends you made at first in California. No one likes to be constantly belittled, even if the person says it's in fun. It's not fun.

If I don't end this letter now it will go on forever.

Love, Lea.

III

Leatrice followed the letter quoted above almost immediately with a second, undated. This one was sharp and angry, its message uncompromising:

Dear Ernie,

I just wrote you a voluminous letter which wasn't really an answer to yours at all. Re-reading your letter I find all manner of items worth discussing, such as the fact, apparent to me, if not to you, that I could no more 'go back' as you put it, than fly. [...]

In speaking of your compulsion to discover and explain, you say that it comes from seeking one's way alone. Who, pray, does not make his way alone? I have not been aware of any strong, helping hand in my direction. You know my mother, you know, or should, that the way from Hollywood to reality is if anything further and steeper than the road leading from Wolverhampton to Lake Park! I suffer my own neuroses, less obvious, perhaps, because of the acquired veneer of manners and social behaviour, but no less painful than your own. You attempted to cure mine by ridicule and abuse, I failed utterly in approaching yours. Why? Who knows. [...]

The most important [thing], *however dear, is that none of us ever gets what you call, the fresh start.* [...] *The person I am* [...] *is all of my past, every moment of it. Mac Namara, the operations and sicknesses are all me. You could never have me without them. You shouldn't want to. It's unreal of you and childish. You mustn't keep looking for the 'princess perdue', the unsullied virgin who will swoon as you approach. It will destroy any relationship you begin with any mortal woman. Without every blow inflicted by and upon me, I would never have arrived at the condition of maturity and foresight, dim as they are, that I have now. I'm not sorry for any of it, because through it* [all] *there's been a slow refinement, not just for me,* [...] *but for all the people I've been concerned with. Can you say truthfully that Mac isn't better for the crisis he passed though with us? His whole life has shifted to something healthier and stronger, not because of me, but because of the growth we all went though at that time.*[17] *I learned a lot about hurting people, because of Sally and Mac. I could never have written you the letters I wrote Mac from Brocky, those cruel hard words seem to have been said a hundred years ago. I had to hurt you this summer, because it was really a matter of survival. Another year with you dearest, and I would have been dead, or so benumbed that life or death would have looked the same. For no other reason would I have inflicted the wounds, but my survival is important, again not only for me, but more for two young children who need the kind of parent I am now. I couldn't have been that parent while living with you as things were.* [...]

Another thing you ought to face squarely is why you aren't writing and haven't written in three years. You have made one excuse after another to yourself. I suspect that until you face it, [...] *you will never write, ever again. There is a blockage somewhere in your thinking*

---

17 Leatrice's footnote: *You, dear, rejected the experience, reacted negatively, so you missed growing by that incident and had it all to learn later. Read this paragraph carefully. It's very important.*

[…] You have not yet written your major work, or anywhere near it, and you know this. Are you afraid of writing pot-boilers? That's what you've criticized so ruthlessly in poor Roodums [Rudy] (how is he?) If you could even write a pot boiler now it would be good for you, even if you burned it afterwards, but bring something to completion. But Ernie, your excuses get paler and weaker every time. They can't convince even you much longer. Come out of it.

That's enough for now. I'll charge you $15.00 for the next half hour.

Love, Lea.

IV

21 November 1952.

Dearest Ernie,

Things come to such a pass! On November the tenth – just two hours before your cable was delivered – I married John Fountain in a civil ceremony in Reno …

I will answer your letters more carefully later. I'm too upset now. Keep writing – but you were right to question my real meanings. It would be disastrous were you to come here now. Perhaps later.

More soon – Love Lea

PS: Basie [John Karl] has 8 teeth, walks, climbs stairs, says a few words and kisses me!

47.

After Leatrice

I

My father believed that Adolf was a functioning alcoholic. His father certainly never went a day without drink. Wine, brandy and cider were his preferred tipples. He was also an indefatigable smoker. After a lifetime of excess, he was in poor health by the 1950s. Among other problems he had stomach ulcers, for which he was prescribed medicines.

The chemist nearest to Cabra Grove was on Cabra Road, and quite often when Adolf went to have his prescription made up this was done for him by the trainee, a girl from the west of Ireland. They became slightly acquainted, little guessing that in time he would become her father-in-law and she his daughter-in-law, for this was my mother, Edna O'Brien. At this time, however, she was just the trainee pharmacist and he was the customer with the German accent and the Homburg hat.

Thus far, all parties agree on these facts – my mother did dispense Adolf's medicines, and that is not in doubt. The next part, however, concerning the coming together of the trainee and the son of the man in Homburg, is contested.

My father's version (repeated endlessly in his Autobiog notes in numerous variants) presented him as the literary master and her as the tyro, and was as follows:

One day, when Adolf was in the chemist's and the trainee was mixing his medicines, she asked if she could borrow the books written by Adolf's famous author son. Adolf obliged and lent her the books, and then, inevitably, having read the books, she asked to meet the author of the books in order to discuss literature, and she went on asking until eventually Adolf told my father to go into the chemist's on the Cabra Road for God's sake and to speak with the girl who made him his medicine because she was driving him mad with her endless requests to meet the great author. And according to his account my father did, and in this way he met my mother for the first time.

II

However, what I've always understood is different:

Besides working in the chemist's and studying, the trainee chemist wrote a weekly column for CIÉ (the Irish Public Transport provider) under the pen name 'Sabiola' (the column was titled 'Sabiola says …'). In addition, she occasionally had pieces in Dublin papers or on Radio Éireann, and that was how she met Rudy Jones, no longer with *The Irish Times* but now with Radio Éireann working as a correspondent and presenter under the name 'John Ross'. Early in December 1952, on the day before her birthday, he invited my mother to a bar in Henry Street beside the GPO, from where Irish radio was broadcast, to meet his old friend Ernest Gébler, the author of a novel called *The Plymouth Adventure*, which had been made into a film with Spencer Tracey. My mother went and met this man, and soon realized that she knew the father – he was the man in the Homburg with the accent whose stomach medicines she mixed!

The next day my father, having picked up the previous night that it was her actual birthday, appeared at the chemist's shop at lunchtime when it was closed for an hour and she was free. He spirited her away to Grafton Street and bought her a grey astrakhan coat with a red velvet collar, and so started their relationship.

III

There were two main reasons for my father's ardour: one, he was on the rebound; two, my mother connected him to the lost happy world of his Wexford childhood, to the hills and the streams and the hedges and the country faces, and most of all to May Geraghty.

And so he fell in love.

IV

Of the next part, my mother's move into Lake Park, there is nothing in the Autobiog notes bar this one story.

One spring or summer day my father received a telegram from his friend, the writer J. P. Donleavy, who was on the Isle of Man with his wife, Valerie, staying in the large house of his mother-in-law Valerie's mother, Mrs Heron. This was what it said:

> *Mother-in-law gone India to look for God. Wine cellar, all comforts.*
> *Fly over. I need you.* Ginger Man *MS gone knotted. Help.*

My father and mother decided to go. Somehow, my father's old friend Rudy heard of their imminent departure. Things hadn't been right between my father and Rudy since *The Plymouth Adventure*. There was jealousy at play, and both sides felt unrespected by the other, though the hurt was felt more keenly by the master, now seemingly spurned. Rudy had access to the information services of *The Irish Times* and Radio Éireann. He tracked down the address of Donleavy's mother-in-law, Mrs Heron, then contacted my mother's parents in Scarriff with the news that their daughter was about to visit the Isle of Man with a divorced womanizer, and provided them with the address.

My parents flew to the Isle of Man. Donleavy met them at the airport and whisked them to the Heron home.

Back in Ireland, my maternal grandfather and others, including my mother's brother, my uncle John, conceived the following plan: hire plane at Shannon; fly to Isle of Man; teach my father a lesson; wrench my mother from danger; carry her back to Ireland. It was a sort of reverse bride snatch....

The next day. About two o'clock. The sun shone. My father was sitting in the garden. He was reading the manuscript of Donleavy's unpublished novel, *The Ginger Man* ('too long and somewhat too verbose at that stage,' in his opinion); he was making notes and identifying passages that might be cut.

Mrs Heron's garden had a door on one side that opened onto a passage that ran up and down the side of the house, and through this door my father spotted 'a tall, firm, older man' coming into the garden. The older man was my mother's father, but as my father had never met him he had no idea who he was or why he had come. Ditto the other men right behind him.

The visitors entered, and quickly made their feelings towards my father clear. They knocked him down and began to kick him quite severely. Donleavy, hearing the rumpus, bolted from the house, saw what was happening, removed his valuable wristwatch and waded in. The visitors, who had not anticipated violence, were shocked and awed. They fled without their prize, my mother, and that was the incident over.

The result of the attack, of course – and how could my mother's family have failed to work this out? – was that it drove their daughter closer to my father, which was the very thing they didn't want.

48.

Fissures

I

My mother, who was now living in Lake Park, began to receive letters from Ada, and then, one day, Ada appeared on the doorstep of Lake Park, greeted my mother affably, expressed surprise that she had cut her hair (she'd never seen my mother before, so this was a surprise), and requested fifty pounds. My father appeared and told Ada that if she did not go away he would ring for the police – they would come and they would take her, and they wouldn't be very nice about it.

Ada left.

II

Ada next visited 3 Cabra Grove. Adolf was out when she knocked on the front door; it was Marianna who answered. They had never met either. Ada explained who she was and why she was there: she had come to recover property of hers that was inside.

Following Ada's visit to Lake Park, Marianna had been warned that Ada might call at Cabra Grove and make demands and had been told that if this happened she was not to let her in.

In her idiosyncratic English, Marianna refused Ada entry.

Ada left.

III

Up to this juncture money appears to have been Ada's focus. That now changed, and rather than trying to extort she determined instead to inflict hurt. Her main target was her father, whom she detested because of his estrangement from Rita and because of her misguided belief that he was a rich man who would not give his poor daughter help. She couldn't strike Adolf directly, but she knew that she could cause damage through his housekeeper, which was what she now did.

She denounced Marianna to the state as an illegal immigrant who had no right to reside or work in Ireland. As a result of Ada's detailed and compelling testimony, a deportation order to expel Marianna was raised. Adolf went to his employer, the ITGWU for help. John O'Connell, whom Adolf had taught how to play the clarinet years earlier, was now a senior union official. He helped to coordinate Marianna's defence, and after a bruising legal tussle the deportation order was rescinded.

IV

Ada's next move in her war against her father was to attack him through Rita. She persuaded her mother to petition for divorce, firstly on grounds of cruelty and immorality (throughout the marriage Adolf the alcoholic had spent everything on drink and nothing on food), and later on the grounds of his adultery, with Marianna named as the other party.

When Rita's petition was finally heard in the High Court, Adolf, representing himself, challenged the application. They were married, and marriage was forever, he said, and he would not accede to a divorce.

This was a surprising position to take. He was not a believer. He did not believe that it was wrong in the eyes of God to sunder a marriage. Moreover, as he would not have been able to deny, the marriage had been miserable (no matter that he and Rita had six children) and now it was over. Rita lived away from the matrimonial home, and her place had been taken (certainly practically, and probably erotically) by Marianna. So why did he take the line he took?

Perhaps feelings for Rita lingered? Perhaps he didn't want Dublin's numerous gossips to be able to single her out as that great rarity: a divorcée. Perhaps he also wanted to save himself opprobrium, divorce in Ireland then being incredibly rare. But I suspect, though feelings may have played a part, that to understand why he contested the petition, one has to look at his nature and his history. He was a dogmatic man, obdurate and unyielding when required, so he was going to be inclined to say no. In addition to this inclination, and no doubt a stiffening of his resolve to oppose the petition, there was the fact that only now, after more than forty years of marital misery had been endured, just when he and Rita did not have long to live, it was to be terminated? No: to do that, or to allow it at this juncture, would have been an admission of failure. Having racked up quite a number of other failures already, he was in no mood to add one more to the list. Absolutely not.

Adolf's arguments prevailed. The judge denied Rita's petition. The costs, however, which came to hundreds of pounds, including Rita's legal bill, were awarded against Adolf. The court also ordered him to pay maintenance to Rita while she lived away from the matrimonial home.

49.

Second Marriage

I

On 3 March 1953, my father wrote to Leatrice from Lake Park with some queries. One, 'What exactly does Fountain understand about John Karl ... the matter must be cleared up.' And two, 'Have you received any divorce papers from Reno, and if so can you let me have a Photostat copy of the degree [sic] absolute or whatever?' He then extolled his current circumstances, hoping perhaps to excite her envy: 'The sun [is] shining, the trees are budding [...] and the daffodils are blazing yellow in the fields.' He was just back from London ('There is still only one Capital City in the World, London. A pity you didn't get to know more of it when you were actually living there'), where he had been for the publication of the English edition of *The Plymouth Adventure* and the English premier of the film ('The film is probably the dullest that has come out of Hollywood in many a long year'). He also reported that Mac, now resident in London and with whom he had reconciled, was married to Priscilla, known as 'Skilla', and had 'a fairy child, just a month older than J. K., which makes him fairly well pleased with life …'. He ended, 'I try not to think of you, because if I do I am unbearably sad for your lost life,' and signed off 'Love, Ernie'.

II

Leatrice replied on 8 June 1953. She hadn't got the Photostat to him yet, but she assured him that she would do so soon. She also assured him that their divorce was perfectly legal everywhere, because in order to get it she had gone to the trouble of becoming a bona fide resident of Nevada, which was what the law demanded. Her letter ended: 'I heard you were marrying again. I hope it's true and it will give you happiness and peace. You're a very good man. Love, Lea.'

III

The most revealing of my father's writings are not the Autobiog notes, which were written long after the events, but the ones in his ledger, which were contemporaneous. The last entry to which I referred was the one he made on 13 December 1949: 'Going to Dublin next Saturday for a few weeks over Xmas. Return of the local boy who has made good.'

After that he wrote nothing until 2 July 1953. This entry begins:

It is 4 ½ years since I picked up the second hand ledger in London and decided to use it as a Journal – must not every serious writer keep a journal? […] And it is 3½ years since the last entry. Am I not a serious writer then?

Young men put into writing much of the imagination and vitality for which they can find no outlet in their cramped worlds. I think I am now more interested in the actual process of living than writing it down. Still, this shall be filled in now and then and if publishable in 20 years may bring me a few shillings.

How time indeed changes one! No more do I care whether I leave anything behind me or not. (Though a journal may be pleasant and informative for one's children to read; and it is good to have children). For instance, to write with an eye on posterity seems now but a great vanity and waste of time. What I add to the biological growth of the species is the entire sum of what my life is worth. Whatever you may do to add to the growth of man in your lifetime there's small chance your books will do it after your death – life moves too quickly now for one thing. Our contributions should be self-evident in our life-time. I haven't much patience, now, for the slow pen.

What struck me when I read this were its contradictions. On the one hand he was not averse to keeping a journal that might one day find its way into print. On the other, the creation of text for publication was something in which he no longer believed. Life and the living of life were, he claimed, his current preoccupations, not publishing. I was not persuaded. The philosophy struck me as contrived, a pose constructed for the purpose of offering comfort and support and enabling him to avoid the problem, which was this:

His main ambition since adolescence, or perhaps even earlier, had been to produce works of literary value that would secure his parents', and particularly his father's, belief in him.

Unfortunately, that had not happened. Publication had changed nothing. This was bad enough, but on top of that there was the problem of how he had made sense of what had not happened, which made a bad situation very much worse.

He was enough of a critic to know that he was not a great writer: he was just an ordinary writer. There was nothing wrong with being such a writer, and given what he was he had achieved wonders and he made money. But that didn't count. At an unconscious level he believed that the poverty of his work was the reason why he hadn't secured his parents' affection, and that, in turn, stopped him writing

– inevitably. He just didn't want to go on with it once he discovered in early middle age that it wouldn't deliver what he yearned for, and that blocked him. That was why he didn't keep his own counsel and keep his journal. That was why he wrote nothing about meeting my mother or their courtship, which were huge events and, I would have thought, should have unleashed torrents of words. That was why he found it so difficult to advance *A Week in the Country*, the novel he had started. (A *roman-à-clef* about a woman who leaves her husband, taking their son, it was clearly motivated by the anger he felt towards Leatrice because of the way – as he perceived it – in which she had traduced him, and because anger is such a superb propellant of literary production it should have written itself, but didn't because of the obstruction located deep within his psyche). That was why he found it so difficult to write anything until he made these brief, allusive entries, which I quote in full because they suggest that impending parenthood (my mother and he presumably having discussed having children) had forced him back into a productive relationship with his self again, albeit temporarily:

IV

According to the Autobiog notes, the date of my conception was 28 October 1953, which he presumably included in the notes because this was the catalyst for my parents' marriage, or at least it became that.

On 7 May 1954 my father obtained a copy of his Birth and Baptismal Certificate from the Church of St Joseph, Berkeley Road (which he had to have to marry), and on 13 July 1954 he and my mother married in the Church of St Brigid, Blanchardstown. The witnesses were my mother's elder sister, Eileen O'Brien, and Valentin Iremonger, the diplomat who may or may not have discovered that Leatrice and her mother had kept him out of America by denouncing him as a communist.

V

From the ledger again:

21 August 1954
> *A son born. Karl Gébler. Edna well.*

26 August
> *Baby and Edna well. She looks very well. Baby was 7½ lbs. Asleep he is pale, delicate, very good looking.*

1 October 1954
> *Lea moved to new house September in Old Greenwich on Long Island Sound, which Fountain has bought. But she has not written for some months, and I do not know the correct address. In any case her letters might suppose that small John does not exist. She never mentions him. Having told big lies she finds it easier perhaps not to refer to him at all …*

12 October 1954
> *Karl 2 months already … A ravenous baby. Very precocious. Likes also making talking noises and carrying on grinning. A pale, actual, impatient, handsome baby.*
>
> *[…] I give one bottle to baby at night. When fed he will break into smiles and conversational noises at slightest provocation. Or will agitate with whinging, if hungry, to be taken up. Edna alarmed that baby of 7 weeks has erections. I told her it is normal in healthy boys – all through life … When his napkin is being changed he will pee straight up into the air like a fountain. Tonight he landed his water all over his face, to his dreadful surprise. We have to avoid speaking to him so as not to arouse his nervous energy.*
>
> *A very warm, dry, windy autumn after the wet summer. The hills are beginning to be coloured. The*

> *Larch is already yellowed. Sycamore first goes, then beech, then oak.*

16 January 1956

> *Sold Lake Park to Patricia Avis Murphy after long negotiation with her Boer father in Johannesburg. She and Richard Murphy* [are both] *poets. They are encased with a humourless shell of self concern. Guess they have decided to live in Ireland because they think it be will the last feudal bastion in Europe – here, peasants are poor and exploitable, at least in Wicklow. So they think.*

The tone of the last entry makes me think that, following a respite, he was back to what he had been when he lived with Leatrice: he was angry, he was bitter, he was sullen. Why did he say nothing, for instance, regarding what he felt having finally sold the house that, or so he claimed, he had been attempting to sell for years? And why was he so ferocious about these two poets who, after all, were guilty of nothing more than buying the house he was selling? I think the answer was that he ascribed to them what he was unable to abide about himself. He was the haughty, selfish, detached Olympian who was alienated from life – that was what his discoveries about his literary worthlessness had made him into – but, unable to admit that these traits were his own, he attributed them to others, at a stroke relieving himself of the burden of processing what he felt.

Projection like this was a nifty solution when a psychic load weighed him down, as was the case here, and henceforward it would be his habitual practice. Everything unwanted and everything he didn't like about himself he would attribute to others.

50.

Rita's Death

I

With the money from the sale of Lake Park my father bought 29 Garville Avenue, a red-brick house of Edwardian provenance in the south Dublin suburb of Rathgar. I have a clear memory of the day we moved in, the removal men carrying furniture into the house while I sat on the bottom step of the stairs (no doubt I was in the way) and stared transfixed at the coloured panes in the fanlight above the door. It was my first conscious experience of beauty.

II

The ledger again:

> *24 February 1956*
> *Bought a long-playing record player and semi-high facility 'bi-ample' wireless amplifier, and Dvorak and... Brahms no 1, 2, 3 and 4. Nothing I have ever bought has given me, I think, such satisfaction and pleasure.*

2 March 1956
> *Karl had his 3rd injection for diphtheria and whooping cough.*
>> *Sasha due to be born about 2nd or 3rd week in May.*

And there, for the time being, his journal in the Ledger stopped. There was no reference to my brother's birth on 25 May 1956, or to our family life in Garville Avenue, or to his ongoing relationship with Adolf and Marianna, or to his novel *A Week in the Country* (on which he was still at work), or to the declining health of his mother. However, after Rita's death he put together a letter that detailed the strange and fraught circumstances of her final months and her end. I have no idea to whom he sent it, or indeed whether he sent it to anyone at all. He might simply have written it because he needed to get the facts straight. Here it is. I have reorganized the order of the paragraphs so they are chronological, and I have made small cuts in the interests of clarity, but otherwise this was its text:

III

29 Garville Avenue,
Rathgar,
Dublin.

19 December 1956.

[…] Three months ago I asked my mother, who was then very sick and infirm and weak of heart, if she would like to go back and spend the rest of her time with her husband. She told me that that was the one thing in the world that she wanted.

I talked to my father and Marianna about it. Marianna is a quite ordinary woman, an Austrian refugee, who got caught in the swing doors between two opposing parties, and suffered because while they knew the rules she didn't even know the language the rules were written in.

Marianna was terrified that if the mother was brought home to spend her last days in Cabra Grove, that when she died – and the daughter [Ada Armstrong] *said she did not have long to live, Marianna, and my father, would be accused by Ada Armstrong of causing her death. My father knew that; we all knew that the accusation was inevitable,* [...] *But they agree*[d] [...]

About October 1956 Adolf goes to Louise's to fetch Rita back to Cabra where he lives with Marianna. This will be the last time Ada [...] *sees the mother (the day she went back to father)* [and the last time but one that Louise does]. *They felt betrayed in some way because the mother went back to the father, and they will not come to visit her at Cabra (though they would have been welcome. Despite their long and stupid vendetta against Marianna, I know quite well that they would not have been refused entry to see their mother).*

The three months she was in Cabra everyone knows that she was treated like a baby, with the utmost kindness. My father, perhaps to make up a little for the past, and of course knowing from Dr Magnier, who was attending her, that she was likely to die at any time, could not do enough for her. He used to get up in the middle of the night sometimes to make her tea; and as you know the mother was anything but an easy patient.

The mother's health had appeared to improve enormously in Cabra, her colour got good and she had been out for drives with the father. Her disposition did not improve, however, and she was constantly quarrelsome and finding fault with everything. Nevertheless [...] *the last three months of her life – those spent at Cabra Grove – she was as happy as it was possible* [given her nature] *to be. She told me many times how very good the father was to her. He took his meals with her in the bedroom to keep her company; he got up many times in the middle of the night to make her tea.*

They did not like to leave the mother alone at any time for long, so when Marianna wanted to go out for half a day or so, once a week, [and as Adolf was out as well] *Edna used to go over and stay with the mother.*

Edna was the last person the mother talked to coherently. Because the last time that Edna performed this service of staying with the mother was a few days before the mother was taken to Richmond Hospital, where she died.

Wednesday 5 December: Edna minds mother.

The mother had an obsession about getting enough food, and was eating far, far too much for an invalid. In the middle of the afternoon when Edna was with the mother, the mother asked for bacon and tomatoes. Edna tried to dissuade her from this but the mother insisted. […] *And she ate* [the] *bacon and tomatoes and a plate of toast.*

Anyhow, on that day, it was plain to Edna that she was eating too much. By the day following she had become very ill and unable to hold any food in her stomach at all because of vomiting. The day of vomiting was too great a strain upon her heart and she began to collapse. No improvement took place. The doctor called a specialist, and they decided to bring her to Richmond Hospital. On the last night there before going to the hospital [the father] *sat with her throughout the night.*

8 December: Mother has stomach attack.

11 December: is brought to hospital.

12–13 December: In semi-coma.

14 December: afternoon; she recognizes self and Edna. (Her bed is near the fire grate in which there is a blazing fire of turf day and night and she is very warm and comfortable). When we are leaving, near tea time, she asks if one of us will stay behind with her. Edna goes home, and I stay a little longer. She asked me to sit her up and give her a drink of water and I did that. A nurse asked me to go over to the office and tell them something about hospital dues and so on. When I came back she seemed to have gone to sleep so I did not try to speak to her again, and I went home. I didn't believe that she was so bad. I know now that I should have stayed there that evening.

16 December: Sunday: the father came and said he had been with the mother in the hospital, that she was no better and had not really known him. He asked if I'd like him to drive me over there to see her. I thought I ought to do that, but it being Sunday and therefore official visiting time, I felt sure that Ada and Louise would be there and that it would be best for me not to appear at the same time. [...] I did not wish [for] another scene of public abuse. And that is how it came about that mother actually died without any of her family with her. I decided to go and see her the next morning; but of course, she died that night.

She died actually as the result of a bilious attack; she would have died anyhow, perhaps in a few weeks and in her sleep. She died because she insisted [on] such food as bacon fried in butter when she had no teeth to chew with. She died just a little sooner because her violent attempts to vomit gave that extra strain to her heart. She was in hospital for a week, but she could not recover, and died in her sleep.

Mother died at 2.30 in the morning of 17 December last. She had slowly been losing consciousness for two days before, the result of straining her weak heart. She died quite peacefully in a deep sleep.

The father and Auntie Bee made arrangements for a funeral at Glasnevin and managed to get a grave in the old churchyard near the Botanical Gardens – a spot where we used to get over the wall as boys – it is very nice there under the junipers and pines and the high wall.

The father went out to tell Ada the arrangements for the funeral but she was not at home, so he left a message with Joe [her husband].

On Tuesday evening I went down to the hospital and went into the mortuary with Edna and we looked at the mother. Her face had got very small in death, fragile, like egg-shell, dead white, serene – somehow like another person with only a resemblance to what we had known. I put my hand on her forehead, and Edna did too; the skin was as soft to the touch as a baby's, and icy cold.

We walked down along the quays. The mother dead had looked like someone many hundreds of years old; and we remembered that after all she was an old woman who had had a very long life, and, as lives go in Europe, not a bad one – I mean of course comparatively.

So when we walked back down the quays after seeing her dead in the mortuary, a full moon was shining over the Liffey, and the river was a rosy colour with the fairy lights strung across the bridges, and the bells of Christ Church were practising Good King Wenceslas; so somehow it was alright, because she died in her own city and she was at home and she was a very old woman. Now, she would be buried in peace, or so we thought.

Well actually no, because what Adolf and Marianna had feared would happen if Rita spent her last months at Cabra Grove now happened. Encouraged by Ada, Louise, with whom Rita had been living before she returned to Cabra Grove, went to the police and made allegations. Her mother had not died naturally, she said, but unnaturally. Adolf and Marianna's care regime was heartless, even cruel, which caused Rita's health to decline, on top of which they had poisoned her or done something else that had finally killed her. Adolf and Marianna, according to Louise's deposition, at the very least were guilty of criminal negligence, and at the very worst were guilty of murder. Following this statement an autopsy was ordered to see if Rita had indeed been poisoned, which impacted on the funeral, following which the police interviewed the suspects. My father's account describes in detail these bewildering events:

The next day, Tuesday 18 December evening, the funeral cars with hearse, mourners etc, assembled at the hospital mortuary to bring the body to Cabra Church, where it was to lie all night, and where Mass was to be said for her the next morning prior to proceeding in procession to Glasnevin. Ada and Louise had been told of the arrangements; neither of them were there, neither was there a card from them for the coffin, or any flowers.

We were told by a plain clothed detective that the organs had been removed, that the City Coroner was at that moment holding a post-mortem. Louise alone, or with Ada, had filed charges with the police. We were not allowed to remove the body to the church. So we went back to the church and told people waiting there that the body was not coming. The next morning the undertaker was permitted to bring the body, or whatever [...] was in the coffin [...] to the church; and Mass was said for her and the offices and all else. The coffin stood on trestles at the back of the church. There was still nothing on it [from] Ada or Louise, and they were not there. We proceeded to Glasnevin. There, there was a burial service in the chapel and at the grave.

As the coffin was lowered into the grave, Ada ran out from behind some bushes (I don't know where from exactly), knocked Marie O'Brien aside, and flung something into the grave. I looked down and saw that what had been thrown into the grave and lay on top of the coffin, was a dust jacket from one of my books [He Had My Heart Scalded] with something scrawled all over it. At the same moment that my eye caught sight of what it was the grave diggers began to fill in the grave. Ada looked at me, as if she would tear the wreath from me, and I knew that her face showed not the death of her mother but the death of her inner self. My father staggered with the shock of seeing the hatred in her face, and I held his arm. Aunt Bee said, 'Jesus, Mary, and Joseph – she is mad.' Everybody who saw her knows that.

She ran away immediately, ran up the tarmac path towards the entrance gates, looking back. Further up she was joined by Louise and [her husband] Mick Breen and the three of them ran away up the main path. The grave was filled in a matter of moments, and the wreaths and flowers placed upon it (it takes some weeks to settle and is then tidied up). We went away, walking up through the double row of red-berried juniper trees. There was no sign of the three fugitive figures. Perhaps someone had stayed behind to trample on the flowers; not even that would be surprising, now. And anyhow, nothing worse could ever be done to the dead woman than had already been done.

On the day following the funeral [...] my father, grey in the face and having to play at a symphony concert, [...] was faced with an Inspector of Police in his house and another and questioned for three hours. The father had then to go to his concert and the police were to come back at two-thirty the following day [...] I heard of this and went over to Cabra the following day and waited until the police came. It appeared, at least to me, after a little while, that the officers were in possession of a very detailed if somewhat imaginary history of our family and of a very degrading nature and it seemed to me also that they did not wholly approve of my father or me. And further it appeared to me that they had no real grounds for questioning him other than that they were doing their duty following upon whatever representations or charges had been made or laid by a person or persons undisclosed whose identity was not too difficult to guess. My father was on the point of fainting with fatigue. I had in my pocket a medical certificate which stated that due to the state of his heart and blood pressure any undue excitement or emotion would be extremely dangerous to him. I advised him therefore that he should not answer any further questions until his lawyer was present. I told the officers that, and after some further persuasion back and forth, they reluctantly accepted this situation and [the] fact that they would have to wait over Christmas until our lawyers were available. They then [said that they] wished to ask some questions of Marianna Blaschitz [in the kitchen]. The father agreed to this, to see how it went. After a while – in that type of house conversation can be heard through the walls – it was apparent that Marianna was becoming emotional. My father went in and tried to advise her that she need not answer questions without a lawyer. And I advised her of that also. She then decided to follow my father's course and not answer questions until she had a lawyer. The police then left the house.

The document ends here, without a proper conclusion. Perhaps there was so much going on there was no time to write any more. However, there would be a second letter about the next stage in the saga.

51.

Rita's Inquest

I

29, Garville Avenue,
Rathgar,
Dublin.

31 January 1957

Dear Peggy [Auntie Bee's eldest daughter] *and Auntie B.,*

I am sending you my father's and my own account of the inquest as you and your whole family ought to know the conclusion of this vile and degrading affair.

    When you have all read it, kindly send me back the typewritten sheets, as I am publishing this widely and need all the copies. You may keep the newspaper report if you want it.

Yours, Ernie

II

He attached his account of the inquest, which he says he and Adolf produced, though I suspect, given how closely the document mimics a report of the inquest as it might have appeared in, say, *The Irish Times*, that he was the principal author. For all I know he may even have hoped when he wrote this that it might be published in a newspaper.

[…] *Monday 28 January, at the City Morgue, Dublin, a public inquest was held into the death of Margaret Gébler, aged 74, who died in the Richmond Hospital on 17 December 1956.*

Persons notified by Coroner to be present:
Adolf Gébler,
Louise Gébler,
Dr Magnier,
Dr Hickey (Autopsy and state Analyst Report)
Dr Counihan,
Police Officers.

We conclude that Louise Gébler was called and not Ada Armstrong because it was in Louise Gébler's name that the original statement was made to police, Ada Armstrong […] not taking such [a] *risk herself.*

It should be borne in mind that the charges brought by these women were not for the purpose of establishing suicide; no one goes to such lengths to prove that their own mother committed suicide or died by some misadventure. The suggestions made and the so-called evidence presented to the Court were for the express purpose of trying to prove that Adolf Gébler, their father, had singly or in collusion with another, so neglected his wife when she was in his charge immediately prior to her death, as to cause her death, or [had] *himself administered to the dead woman drugs or other substance*[s] *resulting in death, the lawyer of the two women even asked the doctors about possible 'blows on the head.' Such charges are not put forward and followed to the bitter end unless the person so charging hopes that they are proved. The result of such a charge being proved could only be that Adolf Gébler would spend the rest of his life in prison or be hanged. By pressing these charges thus it can only be deducted that this was the desire of the two women concerned. And it should be borne in mind that the charges so pressed by the two women were put forward with the knowledge that the said charges were false but with the hope to have them proven in law and their father suffer the penalty,* […]

Present in the court also:
   Ada Armstrong,
   Mick Breen, associate of Louise Gébler,
   A lawyer presenting the case for and representing Ada Armstrong and Louise Gébler,
   Ernest Gébler,
   Edna Gébler.

The coroner first called to the witness stand Adolf Gébler, who was questioned by the Coroner and the accusing party's lawyer about relations with his wife, food, care, how she came back to his house, if he ever administered any medicine or drugs. Adolf Gébler said that one of the reasons he brought his wife home again was that his job was ended, age forcing him to retire, that he could not therefore continue to pay his wife the same [maintenance] *money; that he asked his wife to come home and share with him from then on whatever he should have, that he arranged that Dr Magnier should attend her once a week and continue her treatments and that he did everything in his power for her etc. Neither Adolf nor Ernest Gébler considered it necessary that Adolf Gébler be represented by a lawyer at this hearing so that the only questioning from the floor of the court was done by the accusing party's lawyer, who asked various questions relative to food, drugs, nursing etc.*

Lawyer failed to prove in any way any of the accusing party's contentions.

Louise Gébler then testified under oath, and following her the lawyer requested that Ada be allowed to testify also. Various letters from the dead woman to her daughters were produced: all such letters were undated, appeared to have been tampered with. One letter with a portion torn from it was put forward as evidence that the dead woman was not only practically held prisoner [in Cabra Grove] *but that her letters were censored. These letters were the usual rambling letters written by the dead woman and contained nothing whatsoever to suggest that the dead woman was not being treated well. This 'evidence' occasioned some amusement in the body of the court; it was by then becoming obvious that there was something more than odd about the two women* [who laid the charges].

An attempt was made to show that the dead woman had been taken by force from the apartment of Louise Gébler on the occasion when she had returned to her husband. Adolf Gébler [then] *put in a letter from his wife* [to him] *asking him to come and bring her home. The other party contended that this was not a genuine letter being signed Margaret Gébler instead of Rita Gébler. Coroner pressed other side if this* [letter] *was* [in the] *dead woman's writing. Evident loss of nerve occurred; they agreed that it was their mother's writing. It was later put forward by* [the] *lawyer that said letter was in some way obtained by force by Ernest Gébler. It was put forward under oath by Ada Armstrong that* [the] *deceased was forced to go back to Cabra by her son Ernest Gébler because he was in some dire and terrible trouble concerning Adolf Gébler's housekeeper. General bewilderment. Coroner asked witnesses certain questions as to what they contended about deceased woman's care, nursing, administering of drug or other substances etc. Again, evident failure of nerve, particularly in case of Louise Gébler; the most she could be got to state explicitly was: that her mother had been wearing a hospital nightdress, that her mother, also in hospital, had not been provided with powder, that her mother did not have enough cardigans, that her mother was in good health leaving her care (subsequently disproved by Dr. Magnier) and that her mother was 'neglected' (subsequently disproved by Dr. Magnier, Ernest Gébler, Edna Gébler, and other relations and persons who visited her in Cabra Grove).*

Failure of accusing party to prove any single one of their points.

Dr. Magnier testified that he had been asked by Adolf Gébler to attend his wife regularly, that he had done so from the time of her arrival at 3 Cabra Grove to her departure to the Richmond Hospital. He testified that Mrs Gébler had been in a wasted and poor a condition of health when she came from Louise Gébler's, though she had appeared to pick up for a while, [...] *He had continued certain treatments which her previous doctor had been giving her. The only complaint she had ever made to him was that it was a little difficult at times to sleep with so many musicians in the house.*

Failure of accusing party to establish any point – it had been suggested by Louise Gébler that the deceased had left her in a fairly good state of health for such an old woman but due to neglect in Adolf Gébler's care or being given something she should not have had, wasted away and died. It should not be forgotten that this was put forward by a person who had only gone to see her mother once in Cabra [...] *that the said Louise Gébler did not go to see her mother* [in] *hospital, no more than the said Louise or Ada Armstrong* [who did not visit her mother in hospital either] *attended the chapel, funeral, graveyard,* [or] *sent* [a] *card or flowers.* [...]

Dr. Counihan, a Specialist, called in by Dr. Magnier and Adolf Gébler, to advise about Mrs Gébler, corroborated Dr. Magnier's evidence.

Dr. Hickey testified that he had made an autopsy upon the remains and presented his report of his findings. He also presented the report of the State Pathologist. No foreign substances or traces of, either vegetable or mineral, were in the remains. Dr. Hickey's report spoke of a congenital defect of the spine, and of [the] degenerated condition of kidneys, heart, liver and a long standing condition of lungs. Shrunken and granulated condition of liver and kidneys were of some standing and due to the disease from which the dead woman suffered. Death was due to natural causes. There had also been a typical shrinkage of a particular part of the brain due to the condition stated.

The lawyer for the accusing party, obviously under brilliant inspiration, asked the Doctor thus testifying, if the shrinkage he had noted could have been caused by a blow on the head or anything like that. Murmurs of either admiration or amazement from the body of the Court. Dr Hickey replied shortly and coldly in the negative.

The Coroner was then ready to sum up.

At that point Ernest Gébler stood up and asked for permission to address the Court. Dr. D. A. MacErlean gave such permission, and Ernest went to the box and was sworn.

He testified thus:

That the accusations there made [...] were false in every particular according to his certain knowledge, that he and his wife, Edna Gébler, had been constant visitors to Cabra Grove prior to his mother's death. The lawyer had asked Adolf Gébler who had cooked his wife's last meal. Edna Gébler had in fact cooked her her last meal. He testified that in his certain knowledge all that had been sworn about lack of clothing, neglect etc etc and the accusations, which the accusing part[ies] had been careful enough not to put into plain English, w[ere] not true. He testified that he had asked his father to take his mother back home, because she had expressed a wish to spend

226

whatever little time she had left with her husband, that the deceased had spent perhaps the happiest days of her later life there before her death, that Adolf Gébler, attempting to make up for the differences that had come between them latterly, was unendingly kind and affectionate to her, as was his housekeeper. That the reason Louise Gébler was not informed by her mother that she intended to leave her apartment was that the dead woman feared the daughters would make trouble about it. […] That the reason Louise Gébler and Ada Armstrong had been requested not to visit her in Cabra for at least a few months was because they made rows and disturbed her unduly. The witness had seen his mother, at his request, write letters to the daughters asking them not to call for a time. That was the basis of the accusations of the dead woman being held prisoner, and these letters, it need hardly be added, were not produced in Court by the accusing party.

The lawyer, waving the letter put in by Adolf Gébler, interrupted Ernest Gébler's statement to shout was it not true that he had put undue pressure upon the deceased to sign the letter asking the husband to take her home? To which the witness replied by asking the lawyer was he suggesting that he, the eldest son of the dead woman, had had no right to advise his own mother as to what he thought she should do? Or did he mean something else? The witness concluded his address and left the stand.

The Coroner brought in a verdict of death from natural causes. He said that most of the evidence he had heard there that evening had been irrelevant, but he had gone on with the inquest because so much unfounded rumour concerning the death of this woman had been put about etc.

Footnote: it was evident from the autopsy report that Mrs Gébler living as long as she did with such a heart was extraordinary.

III

A clipping from the *Evening Press* (probably January 29 1957):

CORONER SAYS WOMAN WAS NOT POISONED

Rumours alleging that this woman was poisoned were made without the slightest foundation.

So said Coroner Dr MacErlean at the inquest in Dublin on Mrs Margaret Gébler (74), 3, Cabra Grove, who died in Richmond hospital on 17 December. A verdict of death from natural causes was returned.

Dr Maurice Hickey, State Pathologist, said he performed a post mortem examination and found no evidence of any poison. Death was due to natural causes.

Had Bad Turn

Mr Adolf Gébler, husband, said his wife had lived with their daughters since 1950. On 2 October, she returned to his home. She had been ill, but her condition improved, and she was able to get about the house. About 8 December last she took a bad turn and on 12 December she was removed to the Richmond hospital.

Dr John Magnier said that on 3 October and each week subsequently he attended the deceased. On 3 October she was very poor, emaciated and wasted, and her heart was weak and irregular. He attended every day from 12 December when she went into hospital.

'Want me to die'

Miss Louise Gébler, 30 Victoria Road, Clontarf, said her mother was in Jervis Street Hospital for 12 weeks from May last. Later she was in four nursing homes and then was under the care of a nurse witness engaged at her home. On 2 October deceased returned to witness's father's home.

Witness had several letters from her mother, and believed that these were tampered with by someone in her father's house. In hospital her mother told witness: 'They want me to die.'

Her mother was wasted and looked neglected. She did not suggest that deceased was improperly fed or did not get medical attention.

Dr J. Counihan, Richmond Hospital, said that deceased was admitted on 12 December in an advanced state of heart failure, and was very emaciated. She died suddenly on 17 December.

52.

After the Inquest

I

Adolf, a dedicated smoker and a prolific drinker all his life, had not been well for a while. Now, on top of damage done by the fags and the booze, he had to cope with the anxiety precipitated by Rita's death, her funeral and her inquest, as well as the certain knowledge that though he was not legally guilty of anything in respect of Rita, morally and emotionally he was.

It was all too much, and sometime in the early months of 1957 he suffered a heart attack, strong, fierce and terrible in its intensity. He ought to have died, but his indomitable granite constitution wouldn't allow that. He survived his ordeal and emerged alive on the far side, but he was no longer the man he had once been, or indeed the musician. He could no longer play the clarinet (he didn't have enough puff), and his teeth had loosened to the point where he couldn't feel the mouthpiece any more.

In the past, when everything else failed, when he was broke, when he was hungover, when he felt thwarted, when he felt overwhelmed by the bitter knowledge that he had failed as a musician and never cut it with a great European orchestra but had wasted his time in Ireland footling around with pygmies and philistines, he could always make music in private, and in that way he would cheer himself up, but now he couldn't do that any more.

On its own, the loss of his ability to play might have been endured, but it came on top of so much more. His relationship with Ada had broken down irrevocably and was irretrievable. His relationship with Louise was hardly better, while his relations with the other children, the ones who still spoke to him, weren't exactly close or warm. Then, beyond the family, there was society, the people of the city where he lived. Yes, he had been exonerated by the Coroner, but he knew that there were those who, on the 'no smoke without fire' principle, believed he was in some way to blame for Rita's death. They thought he was guilty of something, and possibly something very serious. Put it all together, and the conclusion was inescapable: he might have lived in Ireland for nearly half a century, but he could stay no longer. He would have to go.

So – what to do? Well, before he did anything else he had to put his and Marianna's relationship on a sound legal footing, and so they married, according to some records on 5 April, and others on 16 April, 1957. I have a photograph taken immediately after the ceremony. Marianna wore a day dress with buttons up the front and a fur coat, and looked plump and cheerful. Adolf, on the other hand, dressed in a long black coat and a bow tie, holding a Homburg in one hand and a cigarette in the other, looked gaunt, emaciated, depressed, morose and close to death. Of course, after everything that had happened, why wouldn't he?

II

Marriage achieved, Adolf approached his sister Helen (the same Helen that Rita and the children lived with in Düsseldorf in the early 1920s), who now lived in San Francisco, with a request. Would she sponsor the application by her brother and his new wife to settle in the United States? Yes, said Helen. The forms went in.

My father heard about this. He was alarmed. He called to Cabra Grove. Adolf looked terrible. He looked hollow-cheeked, ill and drawn. He was a broken, desperate-faced, very old man, my father thought. They talked about Adolf's planned emigration. My father was opposed. Adolf had been conducting a love affair with Ireland, he said, since he was twenty. It had been the one happy thing, the one good thing in his life. Why abandon her? It was dog-in-the-manager, wilful, foolish, and it might even be dangerous, he argued. Adolf, with his various health problems, might not survive the voyage. Instead of leaving Ireland, why didn't he just leave Cabra (with its associations), my father suggested, and move to the coast, somewhere like Dun Laoghaire? Living there, in the south of the city, far from the northside and in a house from which he could see Dublin bay every day, he would, in time, forget everything bad that happened and recover his equilibrium. He might even become happy again.

Adolf demurred. After the dreadful reports of the Coroner's Court hearing in the papers, it wouldn't matter where he went in Dublin: he'd be singled out and pointed at. No, no, he couldn't go on living here. He had to go, and the only place was California.

My father tried a different tack: he told Adolf that America was a land of and for the young and the middle-aged young, and these young and middle-aged young didn't like old people because they reminded them of what was waiting at the end of their lives – decrepitude, humiliation, atrophy and death. So they ignored the old, with this inevitable result: because they were invisible the old suffered terribly from loneliness.

Adolf listened and shrugged. He'd take his chances. He wouldn't be swayed. He'd even made inquiries about shipping his piano across. Apparently, it was perfectly feasible and affordable. His meaning was unmistakable, and nothing would dissuade him.

In the autumn of 1957, word arrived: the US authorities had granted Adolf and Marianna, despite their advanced age (he was sixty-seven, she was fifty-two), the visas necessary for their emigration to the United States.

III

December, 1957. My father called to 3 Cabra Grove. He went up to Adolf's attic lair where he found his father sorting out papers and musical manuscripts to be disposed of.

They talked about Adolf's plans. God alone knew what would happen when he and Marianna got to California, he said. Perhaps he would take to it and stay. Or perhaps he wouldn't take to it, in which case he would come home. He wasn't going to sell Cabra Grove anyhow. He was leaving the house with an agent to be let in case he did return.

Adolf pulled out his gold Hunter pocket watch, the one his father gave him on graduating from the Prague Conservatory of Music. He detached the chain from his waistcoat and held it out. Would my father be so kind as to take care of it for him? He asked this, he explained, because he was worried that his pocket might be picked on his journey out.

My father wanted the watch. He always had. But at that moment, when it was his for the taking, he had a sudden vision of his father, alone and far from home, feeling for his watch chain and finding it gone. It was better, he thought, that Adolf took with him to California as much of his old life in Ireland as he could, and his watch was a part of that.

No, no, he said, it was all right. He added, remembering their corporation house, 2 Offaly Road, and the Lenin anthology he discovered in the wardrobe under his father's old shirts, along with with Marie Stopes's *Married Love* and Rita's Dutch cap, that he didn't think Adolf would stay in California. Adolf would be back, he was sure of it, he said, and when Adolf came back he could dispose of his watch then.

Adolf slipped his Hunter back into his waistcoat pocket. When exactly did he leave? asked my father. Adolf named the time and date. It was four days hence. My father said that he would see Marianna and Adolf before they left to say goodbye properly, and then he left.

The next day, which was three days before the date Adolf had given my father as the day of their departure, he and Marianna slipped out of 3 Cabra Grove without telling anyone, travelled to Cork, and on to Cobh. The electricity was down, so it was in pitch blackness they boarded their tender and went out to the ship in which they would make their crossing, the SS *America*. They were leaving Ireland under cover of darkness, quite literally. The liner glided out to sea before dawn. By the time it was noticed that Cabra Grove was empty, Adolf and Marianna were beyond reach, and it was obvious that Adolf had organized their vanishing in this way to avoid emotional scenes, which he never liked anyway, particularly as his estranged eldest daughter might have ambushed him at the last moment and caused one.

Adolf and Marianna arrived in San Francisco on 3 January 1958. They stayed initially with their American sponsor, Helen. As well as putting them up, Adolf's sister also let her brother turn a spare room in her large house into a music studio, which allowed him to start taking pupils who wanted to learn piano, clarinet or violin. Later, Adolf and Marianna bought a house, number 314, 24th Avenue. It was only a small place, and Adolf continued to teach out of his sister's house.

I have often wondered what it was like for Helen to find herself re-enmeshed with the brother she last saw in Germany just after the end of the First World War. Unfortunately, Adolf and Marianna's letters to my father, and they wrote him a fair few of these, say nothing about this. Perhaps the relationship with Helen was entirely practical and detached.

53.

Move to Morden

Leatrice had said it. When they were together my father's psyche wasn't cooperating and he wasn't writing much. He was blocked. After their rupture, and no doubt their rupture didn't help, though the root of his problem remained his relationship to his parents and particularly Adolf, this lack of productivity continued. He wrote a few talks for the radio, some bits of journalism and one or two reviews, but otherwise he published nothing. His reputation rested on a single successful book.

Then he met my mother. Happiness followed and children, but his productivity remained slight. Little appeared in print. During the early period of his second marriage the only significant work with his name on it was a production of *The Plymouth Adventure*, broadcast by the BBC Home Service on 12 April 1957. The actual script, it should be noted, was not written by him but by the production's director.

During this time, however, he was still labouring on *A Week in the Country*. He only worked on it intermittently, and the words didn't flow, but gradually, albeit the painful and frustrating compositional process, the story crept forward, the pages accumulated, and eventually, though the language and plot were heavy and leaden, he got it finished. He knew that he now needed to re-establish himself in the kingdom of letters, which he had been out of for ten years. He needed a champion, but who would that be?

The answer turned out to be Iain Hamilton, an editor from Hutchinson, the London publisher who visited Dublin around this time to scout for talent. He met my father and, after a lot of finagling and quibbling on my father's part (he had a talent for wrangling over contracts and an inexhaustible appetite for legal argument), Iain Hamilton agreed to publish *A Week in the Country*. The novel came out in September 1958, to mixed reviews.

After so many years of negligible contact with anyone in publishing, the experience of having an editor at a London publishing house was novel, and not unpleasant. It also made him think about the future. He had had an idea for a popular comic novel about the burgeoning interest in sex as a research subject entitled *The Love Investigator*. Iain Hamilton had indicated that it might be of interest to him. Things were happening, but not in Ireland it appeared, and this in turn led my father to wonder if Dublin was the right place in which to live. The conclusion he reached was that it was not. The place to be, he decided, was undoubtedly London, not only the centre of publishing in English, but the world's 'Capital City'. That was where any self-respecting writer should live, and that was where he would go and live too, taking his family with him.

II

He put 29 Garville Avenue on the market. He got a buyer. He sold it. He found 257 Cannon Hill Lane, a mock-Tudor semi-detached house overlooking a common in the London suburb of Morden. He imagined that it would be a pleasant place to live, and bought it. Early in November he went across, taking the grey Railton motorcar (Z6201, as it was called), and a day or two later, travelling by ferry and train, my mother followed, bringing my brother and me.

54.

Turbulence

I

A recap:

The love shown to him by my father's parents was wayward, fitful and conditional. In order to get it he'd had a plan – at least from adolescence through to early adulthood he had. He would publish books; he would achieve the incredible feat of becoming a writer. That would make them love him. It didn't, and it was a blow to realize that the belief system by which he had operated for years was pointless. It was also a blow to be rejected again as the adult that the child had grown up to become.

On top of his failure to secure his parents' affection came a slew of personal disasters: the failure of his relationship with Sally (with him the guilty rejecter of her), the death of his friendships with Rudi and with Mac, the collapse of his marriage to Leatrice (whose rejection had been brutal), his mother's death, Adolf's move to America, which made reconciliation with his father impossible, and finally the wide and widening differential in literary capacity with the other writer in the house.

When he met my mother my father had recently returned from the US as a successful author whose novel, *The Plymouth Adventure*, had been made into a movie. In the fifties he wrote *A Week in the Country*, and then started *The Love Investigator*, and that was about it. By the time they moved to London he had little to show in the way of of work produced since *The Plymouth Adventure*, and, worse, he knew that what he made himself grind out did not have much lift or virtue. As a result, his work was not liked by readers.

His wife, on the other hand, couldn't stop writing. The sentences were pouring out of her. She was generating stories and poems and some journalism, and before long she would start, if she had not already done so, her first novel, *The Country Girls*, and then her second novel, *The Lonely Girl* (later retitled *The Girl With Green Eyes*). And if all of that was not bad enough, he also knew that the words she fashioned were going to be liked by readers far more than the words he produced had ever been. She had something that he did not: a talent for writing what readers wanted to read.

So, newly settled in Morden, on top of his numerous personal failures, he had gnawing away at him this sense that his literary talent was deficient and his stock as an author was falling. He did not acknowledge it of course. I think he dimly recognized that to have done so might well have destroyed his psyche's equilibrium. I'm speculating, of course – I don't know.

I am on surer ground, though, with regard to what happened next, which was, as he perceived, yet another abandonment.

II

Iain Hamilton, his publisher, was also in conversation with my mother about becoming her future publisher, which he did become. On 4 December, about a month after the move to London, they were on the phone. My father listened in, and transcribed what they said into the ledger, where he kept his very occasional journal. He decided on the strength of what he had heard that they were in love, or if not in love then in cahoots against him.

His life was long story of abandonment, originating in childhood and reinforced by Leatrice's divorcing him, his mother's death and his father's move to the US. What he believed he had heard joined the list. What he didn't consider was the way in which his history had primed him to project an abandonment narrative onto situations where it didn't exist.

The move to London was meant to be the start of something. As it turned out, it marked the beginning of the end.

III

Relations in the Morden house became strained, unfriendly and fraught. The next entry in his ledger is for Christmas Eve 1958:

> *I am sick in bed with flu. Edna brings up post. There is an envelope with Leatrice's address. She comes up again: what did I get from Lea? A card, I say, saying that they are all well (which means of course that my son is well).*
>   *Ed: Aren't you going to show it to me?*
>   *E: No.*

They rowed. Then he continued:

> *I can take no more of this idiocy – not in bed with a temperature of 104. I go down to study. She [follows] me there […] I push her out and lock the door. My stomach feels perforated, my head splitting. So for her I left Lake Park. For her I came to the fog of London suburbia? How I begin to realize about Edna: I was sick in bed; she did not come up to smooth the sheets – she came up to demand her satisfaction. She must feel 'loved', 'wanted' – she wasn't concerned that it was pleasant for me to hear my son was well, that my book*

was a failure (due perhaps to Hamilton and her relationship with him), or that I had a pain in my stomach for 3 weeks. [...]

Perhaps I should stay out, gamble, go with other women, seek race tracks, spend money on pleasure, show her a more 'normal' man?

IV

Central Immigration Office,
San Francisco,
CALIF.

Dear Sir,

I understand that some while ago Security Officers questioned my father, Adolf Gébler, of 314, 24th Avenue, San Francisco, because of a letter received by you or them from Ada Armstrong (maiden name Gébler). Whether this letter was signed or not it was undoubtedly from the last named. Upon hearing of this from my father, Adolf Gébler, I did, once again, write to the said Ada Armstrong. You may be therefore interested in the enclosed carbon of the letter I wrote to her. Ada Gébler, who lives in Dublin, is my sister; and Adolf Gébler, of course, is our father. Ada Armstrong has in the past ten years or so written many many letters about her father to cause him annoyance – the Irish Minister of Justice's Office and indeed the U.S. Embassy and Emigration Office in Dublin have sheaves of them.

My sister, Ada Armstrong, is slightly mentally unbalanced. Her father, Adolf Gébler, was to us a quite ordinary father in every respect. But she had a quite common persecution complex and had turned it upon her own father and indeed the rest of her family. I myself, my wife, my children, and other members of my family have suffered from it for years.

My father, like myself, has no particular politics, and to my knowledge, and I am forty-three, has never belonged to any political party or anything of like nature in his life.

I myself am the author of what is now one of the American standard works on the founding of America, The Plymouth Adventure, *Doubleday 1950.*

Sincerely
Ernest Gébler.

V

6 January 1959

To, Mrs. Ada Armstrong,
'Maryknoll',
Sandyford Road,
Dundrum,
Co. Dublin.

You know, better than anybody else, that your father, Adolf Gébler, is a very old man who is liable at any moment to die of a particularly dangerous heart condition.

You know that he is alone in a distant land, near death, and very unhappy.

You know that you were instrumental in driving him out of Ireland by having him publicly accused of being responsible for the death of his wife and dragging him through police examination and public inquest two years ago – arising out of which he had a heart attack and is in his present condition of near death [...]

You know that he is waiting to die, with no child of his near him, and yet you still pursue him with your vile spite and vengeance: you, a woman of forty-five years of age, he an old and very ill man. And now you have written to the Emigration and Police Authorities in California, making a charge that he is a communist and should be deported from America.

This old man is suffering out the last year or so of his life. What sort of a human being are you? Is there nothing too low or too vile for you to use in this persecution of your own father? You know that your father is no more a communist than you are yourself. By devoting your life and energies to such a cruel and despicable end you have destroyed your own life and made yourself an object of ridicule and a person to be avoided like the plague. Is this what life is worth to you? Is this the best you can do with your life?

Surely it is sufficiently before your eyes daily in that private hell which you have made of your domestic life, wherein you live as does a tapeworm, consuming everything, giving nothing, and fouling and destroying the host you inhabit, that to pursue with hatred is to live always in hatred and finally to be oneself shunned and hated.

If there was some way in which I could publicly disclaim that we had the same parents, the same way that one can change a name by deed, I would do so. At the odd moments when I do remember your existence and the manner of it I am filled with disgust and shame.

I now hereby warn you that if you do not leave this very old man alone to die in peace I will come up to your house with a heavy stick and I will beat into you at least the recognition of some human decency as existing in the world.

A copy of this letter goes also to the Police Station, Dundrum, Detective Branch, Dublin Castle, The Office of the Minister for Justice, the Editorial offices of all Irish newspapers, all family relations, your known friends and acquaintances, shopkeepers in

Dundrum, and the occupiers of twenty-five neighbouring houses on either side of your house in Sandyford Road, to the emigration and Security Branches, California. My lawyer is considering what action to take in relation to your letters sent to my business associates in publishing and to other places.

Finally, I repeat, if you attempt to disturb this old man's last days again, I will visit you, with a stick. That is something you <u>will</u> understand.

Ernest Gébler

55.

A Cold Neutrality

I

My father's Autobiog notes, which he made at the end of his life, are good up to the early 1960s, but after that they are thin. This was doubtless intentional: my father knew that once he got to 1962 he had his desk diaries on which to draw, and from now on these are my principal source.

At the start of his 1962 desk diary, he wrote:

> *Smart girls like Edna marry older, kind men because they get more of everything that way: more spoiling, more care, more indulgence. They know what they are doing.*

It was how he saw himself – generous, complaisant, used. The events suggested otherwise.

In March he picked up his first novel, *He Had My Heart Scalded*. He judged it a 'strange little book' that looked to him as if it were 'obviously written by some tender female.' He decided on the strength of this insight that he would rewrite the text and re-offer it for publication under a female pseudonym, an obviously absurd scheme. By 1 April he had rewritten the text as far as page eighteen. In his diary he noted that the day was Adolf's birthday. This was wrong – Adolf was born on 2 April – but from this point on he assiduously cultivated this error. Perhaps he had forgotten his father's date of birth, or perhaps he *wanted* to believe that his father was an April Fool's baby. After all, it made for a better story, didn't it – his old man, whose life was a waste (as he was coming increasingly to believe), born on the day synonymous with foolishness?

He pushed on with the rewrites of the book he hoped to publish as a woman until flu stopped him on 16 April. His next entry was on Monday 30 April, when he noted that my mother's novel, *The Lonely Girl*, was published on that day. This was his entry:

> *Edna would sell her mother to get her picture in a newspaper – why, come to think of it she has done just that in something called* The Country Girls. *And today, would you believe it, she's selling me, under the name of Eugene Gaillard (a name I gave her from a music concert programme).*

Gaillard was the novel's male protagonist.

The next entry in his diary was made five months later, in September. There was an Irish au pair, Maureen, who had been living in the house for some months, and now, suddenly, he thought he detected a sinister plot in which she was a part:

> *Why did Edna go away, often, and for nights, and leave Maureen alone in the house with her husband? Why did she often remark to him what an attractive girl she was? Because she wished him […] to compromise himself [so] that in a divorce Edna might get custody of the children. He made a small test with the girl, which proved her quite ready.*

245

This was a strange entry to make given that there had been no separation yet, though perhaps there had been talk of it. He may have written this later and stuck it in to explain and give narrative coherence to what subsequently happened. Or he may not: it may be a contemporaneous entry that owed its existence to his prescience. But whatever its exact provenance, its meaning remains unchanged. My father was jealous. He resented his wife's growing literary success hugely. He not only didn't want his wife to be esteemed, but he believed that the praise she was receiving was actually due to him. These were impossible feelings to acknowledge openly – how small would he have seemed to himself had he shouted out his truth? So to justify and thereby explain these feelings away he gave himself all sorts of stories about her perfidious ways, and this one about her encouraging him to stray with the au pair was one of these.

The atmosphere in the house whilst this psychodrama was unfolding was anxious, fraught, even febrile. Although I didn't know what it was about I certainly knew that something was very badly wrong within my parents' interactions, and I knew that something was looming.

II

Towards the end of September 1962, his wife, my mother, received a cheque from Woodfall Films for just under £4,000 for the film rights to *The Lonely Girl*. During the evening of Sunday 23 September he demanded that she sign the back of the cheque and thereby assign it to him. There was a confrontation. She signed the cheque, put on her coat and left the matrimonial home. That was their marriage over.

My father's diary makes no mention of what happened next to my mother, nor does it suggest that he had the slightest interest, even though, as he knew, she had nowhere to go and no money. For the record, after she left the house she went first to the outpatients' department of Nelson Hospital, and then to Waterloo Station, where she spent the night sitting on a bench.

The following day she went to the office of Woodfall Films. She explained her predicament, and someone phoned Penelope Gilliatt, who was married to John Osborne and lived in the country. Could Gilliatt offer sanctuary? Yes, she said. My mother borrowed some money, probably from someone in Woodfall, removed us from school and took us down to Gilliatt and Osborne's house. In his diary my father wrote, 'Edna takes children while I am asleep in early morning.' It was the morning when our mother came, and he was probably asleep, but we were at school and not in the house as the entry suggests.

At end of the week, on Friday 28 September, my mother and father met by arrangement in Putney in the flat of a mutual friend, the playwright Ted Allan. My father was drawn, his manner cordial. He said that he was a reasonable man, that the marriage was over, and he offered terms.

My brother and I would go back to the house in Morden. That was the best thing; it was what we knew, and by being there we could continue going to school. In the meantime, my mother would get herself sorted. She would get somewhere to live and, once that had happened, they would share us – we would live in his house in Morden, and in her house, wherever it was. It would be an adult separation, amicable, intelligent and rancour-free, and more importantly, it would put the interests of the children first.

My mother, persuaded by his emollient tone as much as by his reasonable counsel, agreed. She went back to Osborne and Gilliatt's country house, and the following day, Saturday 29 September, we returned by taxi to 257 Cannon Hill Lane.

While my mother settled with the driver I hurried to the door, which was open, my father standing beside it. I went in, bolted to the stairs, which were halfway down the hall, and started to go up. A wooden battleship I'd made (unconsciously I'd acquired my father's fixation with model boats) was beside my bed in the back bedroom, and

I wanted to see it. As I climbed upwards there was a kerfuffle behind. It was my father putting on the safety chain and then opening the front door again. I stopped and turned. My mother was now being spoken to by my father through the gap. She'd deserted her children, he said, and that was that; she'd never see us again. Curiously, I can't remember where my brother, Sasha, was during this scene. Nor can I remember if I understood what had been said and if was upset by it. I suspect I opted not to grasp the implications of what had happened at the door because to do so would have required me to accept the end of the family as I knew it, and that was too dreadful an idea to countenance. So I turned, resumed my climb and hurried to my bedroom, where I was reunited with my battleship.

III

As his marriage unravelled, news of another kind of unravelling arrived from America. California had not worked out for Adolf. He did not like America. He did not like Americans. He missed Ireland. He missed the Irish. He was sick. He had heart trouble. Stomach trouble. It was obvious: he was dying. The dying was horrible, but it had one benefit: it forced the truth to the surface. Late in 1962 he came out with it. He wanted to go home, no, he had to go home to Dublin, and Cabra Grove was still his.

No definitive decision was now made, no plan set in motion. The tenants in Cabra Grove were not given notice to quit, for instance; their lease had a while to run. But the idea was out, and once it was out it could only harden into certainty. He and Marianna would return, that much was clear.

IV

But then, before anything could happen, early in 1963, Adolf became really sick. It was his heart. From this point on he was in and out of hospital pretty regularly. His Ireland plan was put on hold. He was too ill to travel. He died in hospital on 6 July 1963. Marianna sent a telegram immediately: 'Father Died Today Heart Attack – Marianna.' That was Saturday. The next day, Sunday, my father observed in his desk diary:

> *Cable from Marianna to say father died in San Francisco yesterday. Mac and Skilla to tea. Two charming sons. I suppose I'll feel it more tomorrow.*

He later wrote (the entry is undated):

> *I should be able to say that his death of alcohol and despair alone in California 'served him right' – but I feel only a kind of cold neutrality.*

I was in the house when the telegram from Marianna arrived. I was told what had happened. I was there over the following days when he made the entries quoted above. I remember his mood during the period as gloomy, morose and surly. I assumed that it was grief. I had no sense of the darker, more complex feelings that Adolf's death had stirred. That was absolutely hidden.

56.

The Helmet

I was not exactly happy at this time myself. I saw my mother only occasionally, and the regime of prohibitions imposed at 257 Cannon Hill Lane, previously endurable only because of her presence, became intolerable now that she was gone. Items that were forbidden by my father (this list is not exhaustive) included:

> War toys of any kind, especially plastic guns;
> War comics (these were small, square publications with poor-quality black-on-white illustrations – at school, in the playground, I would occasionally be loaned one of these joys, and afterwards I would invariably have smudges on my fingers that smelt intriguingly of industrial ink);
> Airfix kits (every one a glory); and
> Miniature plastic soldiers, about an inch high. These were of every conceivable type, from Greek warrior (Trojan War) to Royalist cavalryman (English Civil War) to Prussian Grenadier

(Battle of Waterloo) to artillery officer (American Civil War) to Chindit (Burma campaign, 1941–1945).

From where did these rules come? It must have started with his early experience in infancy of paternal loss. By the time he was born, Adolf was gone. They had no contact thereafter for five years, and when Adolf finally returned they probably never bonded. That experience laid down an early antagonism towards, and fear of, conflict, which was then subsequently reinforced by what he glimpsed in Germany and Ireland in the early 1920s and by what he imbibed unconsciously from Adolf, who, although never a doctrinaire pacifist, was a lifelong opponent (and a vocal one at that) of militarism in all its forms. As Adolf saw it, most wars were organized by the elite for their own benefit, but it was the poor and the weak who did the actual fighting and who suffered, and that was why militarism had to be resisted.

In addition to that, there was my father's emotional history and its peculiar woes. In childhood he had never had the affection he craved whilst his less-deserving sibling, Ada, had had love in abundance, being Adolf's favoured child – or at least that is how he saw it. In childhood, because of what happened at home, he had come to believe that chaos was imminent, which in turn ushered in his extreme conviction, which he never sloughed off, that he must always be ready to walk the world alone in a pair of well-soled boots. In adolescence and beyond he hoped by his writing and publishing to secure the affection that had so far been denied him, but that plan failed. The series of disasters in his adulthood, culminating in the collapse of his second marriage, was a heavy load to carry, and his solution was the old, time-honoured one. Telling himself that it was ethically justified, he introduced a drastic programme of control that included these prohibitions, and much more besides.

In the midst of catastrophe, these rules offered him the certainty that, in the domestic sphere at least, he was still in charge. In reality, of course, he was not.

II

At school (Hillcross Primary) around this time (I would have been eight) we did a project on the Second World War, and children were instructed to bring in martial objects of World War Two provenance. As a result of this I saw and handled such things as:

An officer's belt with a holster, both surprisingly rigid (alas, the holster contained no Webley revolver);

A gas mask (this was an incredible object – when I put it on, my mouth was filled with the taste of rubber and through the portholes, slightly steamed up, my vision was terrifyingly reduced to just what was immediately in front of me);

A gas mask bag (I think) of heavy waxed cloth, with industrial poppers to hold the flap in place that closed the top, with an intriguing system of pouches and sections inside;

A cartridge tin (I assumed it smelt of gunpowder, but the teacher said no, it was cordite);

A full battle dress (British Army, small, surprisingly small, a shade of khaki exactly like wet cardboard, made of some itchy material that was dense, stiff, and I presumed unbearably uncomfortable to wear);

A dagger in a sheath (ex-commando, and said to have seen active service in Norway, though many of us suspected it was actually from Millets camping shop on Wimbledon Broadway); and

A private soldier's helmet (British Army, metal, incredibly heavy, wide brim, spherical crown and, inside the crown, revealed when I turned this sacred object over in my hands, an intricate mesh of stained webbing with adjustable chin strap, which smelt even after so many years – oh, how evocative – of the hair oil and sweat of the unfortunate squaddie who had once had this jammed on his head as he slogged through Libya or Italy, or wherever he had the misfortune to serve).

These mass-produced objects produced in me, and I imagine in all other boys in the classroom, the same curious mixture of feelings. On the one hand these were factory-made items with no gloss or burnish, and as such they were no different from all the other objects (motorcars, school desks, window frames, everything) by which we were surrounded – they were ordinary.

At the same time, they were absolutely extraordinary, of course, because they were objects from a different world, the very idea of which made us weak and giddy and filled with longing, and this was the world of the Second World War, not as it really was but as we had all somehow come to believe it was, which was a heady confection of marvels and heroics and thrills. When we touched these objects we were connected directly to that fantasy, which was why contact with these artifacts was so psychically stirring. The one put us in touch with the other.

III

After handling these things I was filled with desire. I wanted something real from the war – anything would do just as long as it was authentic. Inevitably my yearning was spotted, and one day, in the school playground perhaps, or as I walked home along Monkleigh Road, a boy (name forgotten, like so many other details in this story) offered me a helmet (US or German, the bulbous type at any rate with the bevelled flap around the sides and back) that his father or someone had carried home in 1945. It wasn't wanted any more, he explained, and it could be mine for a small fee. I knew this was a scam, but I wilfully ignored the message surging through my system that I should stop this right now. Of course I did. I was desperate to own a numinous object connected to the war. How much? I asked. He named his figure. It was quite a sum, but not so great a sum that I couldn't scrounge, cadge and perhaps even steal it. And I did. I got the money. I don't remember how, but I know that I did.

I took the money to school, and my vendor took the money and explained that he would pass it to the helmet's owner, and then the helmet's owner would pass the helmet to him, and then he would bring the helmet to me – an arrangement that shouted buyer beware, and a warning I managed yet again to ignore. We arranged to meet somewhere. My father didn't allow us to wander about at will. We went unsupervised to the Children's Library in Morden, however, so perhaps that was where. Or perhaps my contact offered to bring the helmet to school. My understanding was that he would hand it to me behind the air-raid shelter at the bottom of the playing fields where we children traditionally finalized our financial transactions. I forget. And how was I going to smuggle the helmet into 257 Cannon Hill Lane? And where was I going to hide it once I got it in there? I forget that as well, or maybe I am still so ashamed I have suppressed those details. Whatever the case, what I know is that we did not meet on the steps of Morden Children's Library, or behind the air-raid shelters. My contact never showed up, and when I tackled him he said he had never taken money for a helmet. I was making it up, he said. But I wasn't: I'd given the cur the money! I knew that, only I was too timid to challenge him.

IV

We now get to the important part of the story, because this has to do with the writing – mine – that came later. My father discovered what I had done. He found me out. I don't know how, but I do know that he had a special talent for uncovering a wayward son's duplicity. Did I have a secret place where I kept my money, and did he check it regularly and, finding it empty one day, did he divine the sorry truth? Or did I let the story slip inadvertently? I was a boy who did prattle endlessly. Or did he see me crying silently, mooning about the house, looking depressed? I think this the most likely, though I don't actually know how he got all the details. All I know is that somehow he did, and what happened next.

I was summoned to his study. It was a warm, male space. There was a big ugly German desk, a stove full of Anthracite that whispered as it burnt, a bookcase full of Gorki and Marx and James Stephens, a

Tallboy, a strongbox where he kept our milk teeth and birth certificates, and a bay window with a view over mournful, muddy Cannon Hill Common. My father sat. I stood. He'd heard, he said, that I'd handed all my money to some imbecile for a helmet and got nothing. 'A bloody army helmet! What were you thinking?!' he continued.

He followed with questions, lots and lots of them, one after the other. He wanted to know everything, in detail. And I remember, as I stood there, first answering badly, then understanding (but in a dim, childish way, and not as clearly as I am expressing it here) that what was being sought was the truth, the unvarnished, unreconstructed truth, and then responding again, but this time giving more complex, considered and accurate replies, which appeared to please him.

And what I understood, when I reflected on this experience later, and on the numerous other similar occasions when he threw question after question at me in order to assemble a complete picture of some awful error of mine, was this. When it came to the exposition of things that had happened to me, there were all sorts of different accounts of that event (whatever it was) that I could give. I could give a sad or a funny account. I could give an account that made me look foolish or wise. But if I went further, I realized, if I dug down deeply, dug right down under all these variations, what I came to at the bottom was a sort of bedrock truth, a version of what happened that even a wily, angry sceptic like my father had to concede was what happened, because, well, it was the truth, as far as it was possible to enunciate the truth, whatever the truth was.

Now I want to be clear: this wasn't an epiphany or series of epiphanies I'm describing. This wasn't something I understood whole and complete at some point in childhood. No, it was something I vaguely ascertained during the scores of interrogations during the unhappy time when I lived with my father, and it was as a result of the agglomeration of all these that I gradually acquired not just the knowledge that it was possible to give a convincing account of what happened, but also the ability to judge the difference between what rung true and what rung false, at least as far as convincing my father went.

I also learnt something else as part of the process of learning how to be convincing: I learnt how to take people off and replicate (or parody) their talk. I later discovered that these skills could be used not only to access my own story but those of other people as well. By using parody and mimicry I found that I could give a convincing account of something that had happened to someone other than myself from inside their head, including how they thought or felt.

Thus were the skills necessary for empathy (or what looked like empathy) developed in childhood, and it is on these that most of what I've subsequently done, at least when it comes to writing, has rested.

V

At some point in 1963, after the helmet debacle, things fell into place for my mother. She got a room in a flat at 29 Deodar Road, and sometimes, when her landlady was away, she'd have us over. The kitchen smelt of chops and kidneys, half muttony, half uriniferous. At the flat's rear the windows overlooked the Thames. The water was silty grey on the surface, livid green in its depths. The river was a highway still. There were often tugs to be seen, small vessels, and streaming behind were long lines of barges heaped with coal or grain. I loved to count the barges, but no longer remember the top number I recorded.

And then things got even better. Because my mother had found the room she was able to work, and because she was able to work she started to make money. With the money she got a little house, 9 Deodar Road, and after that my brother and I started living the life that had been sketched out in Ted Allan's flat. We spent three nights a week with her, or sometimes four, and the balance of the week with our father. The nights were alternating, so we spent a lot of time shuttling between houses and schools by bus and by the Tube.

57.

Camilla

I

My father was lonely. He needed female company. Desperately. He met the popular Australian singer Shirley Abicair – blonde, lively, feminine. He was smitten. She was not. She rebuffed him.

Over the following months he met other women, there were occasional dinners, occasional encounters, nothing rewarding, nothing serious, nothing satisfying. Then he met ... I will call her Camilla. She was unattached and had a nine-year-old daughter. She lived in a rented flat in Gospel Oak, Kentish Town, north London. She also had the use of a little Suffolk cottage. Her circumstances were tricky, uncertain, and she had little money. They began an affair, and though the intimacy was 'without pleasure' he was seized by an idea that she would solve all his needs, both sexual and domestic, at a stroke. He'd dispense with Maureen, the Irish au pair who slept in the small box room, and in her place he would install Camilla, and she would look after us, and him as well. Her nine-year-old daughter would obviously come too as part of the package. She'd fit in. Of course she would. Children could slot in anywhere.

What Camilla made of his offer he didn't record, but he did note, by mid October, that he had changed his mind. Camilla was too 'difficult' for the 'job', he had decided, while the daughter was 'totally spoilt'. At the end of the month he wrote and rescinded the proposal, saying that the whole situation was 'unworkable'.

Despite the rebuff, Camilla and he continued to see each other, although, as he confided in his diary, he now believed that she was 'mad'. He doesn't say why he thought this or what she had done to warrant this judgement, though he did think that there was something about him that attracted mad women.

His ambition now was to disengage, but Camilla was not to be sloughed off so easily. On Guy Fawkes Day she rang him, needing help. She had found a 'good flat', much nicer than her current one in Gospel Oak. The trouble was that she had to pay 'key money' to secure tenure, and it was £250. Would he stump it up for her? He had no current commissions, he told her, and only £800 in the bank, so no, he could not.

Despite this second rebuff, they still saw each other again on Thursday 7 November. Camilla's conversation, he noted, was unrewarding (as opposed to Edna, who, though a monster, was 'more often than not entertaining'). The sex was joyless, just as he remembered it having been 'with Bunny' (the only admission in his papers of this) years earlier.

The next day, Friday, she rang. Camilla had a question, *the* question. What if she were pregnant? Impossible, he responded. They'd only done it properly twice, and each time with the benefit of her 'horrible Dutch cap and preserves to boot,' and not even at 'a dangerous time' in her cycle. Then Camilla popped her next question. Would he give her £120 for an abortion should she need it? No, he said, he preferred to have the child. The conversation was over. The phone went onto the cradle, and he began to ponder. Was this a ruse? Was this what Camilla did, make love and then ask for money for a termination? Was this her schtick?

The following week (this was her idea) they met for a drink somewhere on Tottenham Court Road at 9.30. Camilla had her daughter with her, which was odd given the child's age and the time of night. Perhaps Camilla thought that having the child would strengthen her hand.

Speaking carefully, she raised it again. If she had to have an abortion, she needed money. Would he give her that money? They talked around the subject for an hour. My father decided that she was not pregnant but that she wanted him to believe she was so that she could extort money from him. This he would not let happen, of course. Nor was he going to have anything more to do with her, he decided. They 'parted coldly'.

On Sunday 17 November he noted: 'Didn't ring C since.' The Camilla interlude was seemingly finished.

II

At the end of December 1963, a letter arrived from Leatrice. It had been written on Christmas Day at 5.30 in the afternoon. The letter talked first of Bobby (as she was now calling their son, John Karl) and his experience of Christmas Day, then of the death of John F. Kennedy, and only finally of its real subject, which was him:

> *I re-read your sad letter of last June. You were on your way to Ireland alone, and described Edna's mental aberrations, which I can only judge through your eyes. [...] The old cry of persecution sounded fairly familiar, having lived with you under some strain. [...] I felt you persecuted me too. [...] You just don't know any other way of treating people. Probably because no one treated you any differently when you were living through your lonely childhood.*
> *[...] I continue to worry about us, because out of all the many, interwoven relationships I have had in my nearly forty years, yours is the only one, of the ones that meant anything, that remains unresolved, impossible to deal with on an honest level because of the issue of Bobby [...] My guilt in leading you into the initial*

259

deception is one I will carry to my grave, Ernie, but your persistence in continuing the illusion, even to yourself, is the purest folly that can only be painful to you now and in the unhappy eventuality of your confronting the poor boy, murderously destructive to him. He's fiercely proud of being his father's son.

Her letter closed with family news. She had had a card from Marianna in San Francisco ('She feels a total foreigner in a strange land, poor soul') and she had heard that Irene, my father's favourite sister, was living in New Zealand and was adopting.

III

In his diary he wrote: 'Long letter from Lea – in a sudden panic – am I going to "confront" Bobby. What set off the panic? Not guilt or conscience, I'm sure.' Curiously, neither here nor anywhere else does he make reference to one way of solving the problem – a paternity test. Perhaps he thought that Leatrice would never agree. Or perhaps he preferred it like this, the situation never resolving and just running on and on....

He replied to Leatrice not long after he wrote the above. He began by insisting that he was Bobby's father. He then continued:

I met Edna in the year following your marriage to Fountain. The first six years with Edna were very happy years. [...] So happy that I often suspected the Gods were waiting to drop the gate on me. There were two children, so beautiful, that I used to be filled with astonishment that I was their father. One day I gave Edna a book about Scott Fitzgerald. She became haunted by the idea of Zelda. People have premonitions about themselves. She is Zelda Fitzgerald. Our relationship didn't fail because of any of the nice normal complexes, such as my 'sad' childhood, or even her [...] really frightened childhood. It stopped because the gate fell on me one day out of nowhere. It stopped for the same reason that Fitzgerald's life with Zelda stopped, because of a gene inherited from a long line. Most of Edna's father's family have it. From father to father to father disaster stretches away into the past of Ireland's dark windy western seaboard, for their family.

He named the condition as schizophrenia.

IV

A couple of days later, on 3 January 1964, Camilla rang. She needed help moving things from her old flat to the new one she had just got. She also needed £5 because she was absolutely broke. He drove up to north London to see her. The new place was small, pleasant, newly painted white. He assumed that her family had stumped up the key money. He transported the furniture that needed moving in his car. When the work was done, she asked for the loan of a tenner. She had two lovers, she added, but he was welcome to stay. He declined her invitation and did not lend her any money.

A few days later, due to an act of 'compulsion', he rang Camilla. He accused her of being unfair to her daughter. She accused him of bringing out the worst in her. Afterwards, he confided in his diary: 'Sometimes at night I get a deep pain in my chest from a sort of accumulation of injustice and loneliness.'

On 5 January 1964, Leatrice replied to his letter, the one with the memorable phrase about the Gods waiting to drop the gate on him:

At the very least what I did to you and to me and to Bobby was as cruel a selfishness as any human being can imagine. I 'told you it was yours and entered into a false marriage,' half believing that I could live with that kind of a lie. And this ghastly truth, that I slept with John, conceived his child and left him for another man, is the horror that someday I must tell this boy, this child I love more than life.

[…] *What I did was almost unforgivable. How John* [Fountain, her husband] *ever has I will never know. It took a long time. The young judge even harder. What he will think of me, I shudder at. But I can't change it to make it any prettier. Not for you, or for him. What is, is, and no amount of repentance or rationalizing or psychiatric claptrap can make it any different. We will simply have to live with an unbearable situation as best we can. God help us all.*
Lea

V

His diary says nothing about this letter, but makes plenty of references to other grievances. Adolf was back in his sights ('weak, unhappy, self-obsessed, ignored us, cut us out of his life […] because our mother claimed the children to "her side" '), as well as my brother and me. Victims of our mother's 'empty ambition to be famous and mix with famous people' and corrupted when 'down at Putney, with presents, entertainments, any kind of rubbishy television,' we had turned into 'parasites' who were 'selfish to such a degree that they won't wash up a cup after them or pick up an orange peel they drop on the floor.'

On the same day he wrote these observations he got a letter from the solicitor in Dublin who was handling Adolf's estate. His belief had always been that 3 Cabra Grove had been bought outright by Adolf. In that, he was wrong – Adolf hadn't owned the freehold; he had it on a long lease. This, and the fact that Adolf had not made a will, the solicitor explained, meant that Marianna couldn't live in the house. It would have to be sold and the money divided, with all the children getting a cut, including Ada.

In his diary my father wrote: 'It means in fact he left Marianna with nothing but the mortgaged house in San Francisco – 6,000 miles from Europe. What a selfish bastard he was.'

He weakened again and rang Camilla. A man answered, with a 'sort of bus conductor voice. Said she'd gone out for while. I didn't ring again.'

58.

Phyllis 'Jane' Innot

I

In the spring of 1964 there were two events of significance. One, my mother bought a larger house in Deodar Road, number 87, with a garden that ran down to the Thames, and this provoked such a spasm of jealousy that he actually wrote in his diary: 'Must control my detestation of her.' Two, having had numerous fruitless encounters since Christmas with various women, he joined a dating agency and began to place advertisements in the hope of finding love.

II

His copy caught the eye of Phyllis 'Jane' Innot. This was her account of what happened:

March 1964
I was twenty-six, living in a small bed-sitter in Sydenham – rent £2. 15s. a week. Teaching in Catford and sadly and abortively conducting a six-year-long love affair with a very married man.

*There was a lonely hearts column in some left-wing paper –
Private Eye? New Statesman?*

*I saw an intriguing one of 'A middle-aged man of foreign
extraction, wealthy, good conversationalist, able to put people at
their ease.' I wrote to the box no. enclosing a photo and forgot about
it. A week or so later a letter came from a Wimbledon address. I
could not quite decide what the flamboyant signature said, but the
enclosed photo showed a lean, vigorous looking man standing on
a white sandy beach. 'I am not as pugnacious as I look,' said the
writer', and he gave a phone no.*

*I rang and the voice that answered was light and, I thought,
transatlantic. We arranged to meet on 13 April at the Trattoria
in the Earls Court Road. 'I will be wearing my face,' the voice
solemnly promised. I said I would be wearing a brown coat with a
round fur collar.*

*I walked into the Trattoria and knew him immediately. A
rather haggard, shaven-headed man sitting at a table. He did not
recognize me from my photo but took my cold paw in a large,
warm, dry handshake that I instantly felt was 'Right'. We ordered
steak for him and lamb's kidneys for me. We talked, mostly about
me and my background, and his large, kind, brown eyes twinkled
most engagingly and I felt ridiculously pleased when he laughed
loudly at my wry jokes about myself. I learned almost nothing
about him, except that he had had 'a few catastrophes'. A youth
played a guitar; we drank gallons of black coffee and were about
the last to leave the restaurant.*

*Across the road was a long-nosed grey vintage car and it snarled
along beautifully as he waved his hands and talked all the way to
Sydenham.*

*He insisted he must come in and have a cup of tea before he
began the long trek back to Wimbledon.*

*He made the tea himself, talking all the while. I saw him
properly now, tall, long legs, elegant movements, an animated,*

handsome face that somehow seemed familiar. I liked him. Cheekily I asked him if he would like to come with me to the Red Lion Square meeting which was to establish CND's 'Committee of 100'. [He came and] *Laurens Otter (the anarchist) was on the platform along with the more radical element of CND. Celia with baby Fiona sat with us. She opined that Ernie looked 'rather nice'. Huge praise from her. We left before the end and Ernie took me to the Salisbury in Drury Lane where we drank Bushmills Black Label before going to Santi Romanos in Soho for a meal.*

    He did not come into my Sydenham room that evening but kissed me quickly on the mouth; then pushed the door open as I was closing it and said, 'That was nice. Another dose please.' Then he ran back down the stairs. We had arranged to go to a Sibelius concert at the Festival Hall in early May (1964) and we met at the Eleanor Cross in front of the Charing Cross station. No car this time, we walked over Hungerford Bridge laughing hysterically at a graffiti, 'Nigs get off our wimmin', on a hoarding. We were late into the Festival Hall and had to stand for the opening overture (to Kavelia Suite). E had his hand in the nape of my neck. This was to be our last meeting for three weeks as I was going on a school journey to Dorset with forty eleven-year-olds, and another member of staff. Ernie gave me a copy of A Week in the Country *to take with me. He rode on the underground with me to our changing point at Earls Court. His breath was sweet as he kissed me smackingly and publicly as we parted.*

    I phoned him on my return and was greeted with great warmth. We arranged to meet at Morden Station. I had never been to this part of the world before. He was parked outside the underground in a huge, shining, black, open-top car. He had a blue bush jacket and blue jeans on and looked tanned and handsome. He hugged me and said I looked blooming. I could feel him constantly turning to look at me as we drove up to Wimbledon Common. We walked with our arms round each other and he unembarrassedly sang 'Mountain Dew', 'Johnny I Hardly Knew You' etc, [in] a lovely tuneful tenor. Then he asked me if I'd ever been kissed on Wimbledon Common… Then he took me back to his house for tea. A pretty house on the outside but rather Spartan and shabby inside. It smelled rather exotic (I could not identify the aroma of Lapsang Souchong tea then).

He had prepared a large casserole of braised steak, can't remember what else. We ate perched on stools in the kitchen. After the meal we went into his study and he played records and talked. Then he put on Mahler's 4th symphony and I sat on the settee and put on a listening face while he faced me astride a hard chair, hands on the curved mahogany wood of its back and he stared fixedly at me. The music was wonderful but the inspection was unnerving. Suddenly it was gone midnight and he said it was too late to drive me home, he was frightened out [in] the dark. 'I've got a new toothbrush, haven't even licked it.'

III

They went up. His bedroom was directly above the study. The bed was a small double and came from Cabra Grove. It had once been Adolf and Rita's bed, and had passed, somehow, to my father. They got in. There was no sex; Jane had her period. They moulded and went to sleep.

Jane left the next day. He noted her period in code in his diary – a box encircled by a wavy line. Once they had become intimate, which was not long after this, he always noted when they'd had intercourse too – the code for that was the number '8'. Thereafter, he noted all their intimate details – not only when they had sex, but what kind of sex, what kind of contraception (initially a reusable sheath, later the pill), what kind of creams were used, and whether he ejaculated. When I encountered his system, and then unravelled its meaning (this took a while), my feelings were not of surprise. On the contrary, it seemed to me that his punctilious record of his and Jane's intimacies was only to be expected. Machinery had always been a fascination, but I believe that by middle age he didn't distinguish between the machine and the body. To his way of thinking then, the body was like a piece of machinery and record-keeping necessarily had to be part of a proper maintenance regime intended to keep the mechanism running smoothly. His note-taking was also part of a programme of control.

IV

His diary:

> *Friday 12 June 1964*
> *Jane was not feeling well. I said, 'You should be like me. I never get sick. I'm just sick all the time.' She fell off the kitchen stool laughing.*

> *Tuesday 16 June 1964*
> *Went to local cinema to see* Lonely Girl *(entitled* Girl with Green Eyes *on film). A slight little woman's magazine type film […] Full screen credit title 'Script by Edna O'Brien from her own novel'. Nothing has been added – everything in the film has come out of the original script. They even used my idea of having a lot of oboe music.*

> *Thursday 18 June 1964*
> *Joyful evening with J. Lay in bed looking out at the dark summer rain falling on the green trees and grass* [of Cannon Hill Common].

Monday 22 June 1964
Rudy phoned and came out and occupied ½ my day. The same old
Rudy – very aged and tired looking. Had written thriller. Collins
rejected it. Could I do anything?

Long story about a young girl Colette who he sent to Paris
alone to have an abortion and who came back hating him. Lives
apart now from all his family.

Awful derivative thriller.

V

At the end of June he began to write the story outline of a play for television, *Why Aren't You Famous?* This told the story of Willie Toppet, a serious-minded but struggling English north country artist, and Eileen O'Roon, a fresh-faced Irish ingénue who arrives from Ireland in the English city where Willie lives. She's homeless. Willie takes her in to his squalid gaff. Having got in, she starts. She tidies, straightens, sorts and organizes everything, the place, the man, the artist's whole life. For a while it looks as if she will be his making. But this, in fable form, is the marriage to my mother as my father saw it, so ultimately she is less interested in helping him and more interested in helping herself, and by the end that's exactly what transpires. Willie is eclipsed and Eileen is triumphant. He's left at home minding their baby and not painting, while she, having achieved success as a pop artist (with a collage of red socks), is swanning around in London.

She, a fake artist, is the toast of the art world.

He, the real artist, is forgotten.

In his diary for Sunday 5 July he described the piece:

Facetious. The kind of thing like The Love Investigator *that I can do off the top of my head, almost without thinking. A pleasant way to pay the rent.*

He and Jane had a holiday in Ireland in August, where she had never been. They returned on the first day of September, and the next day he confided in his diary: 'It was the best holiday I ever had in my life. Mostly due to Jane.'

On the day following their return there arrived a letter from Leatrice addressed to my mother, care of Random House in New York, which the publisher had mistakenly forwarded to 257 Cannon Hill Lane, not knowing of course that my mother did not live there any longer. In this letter, which my father did not hesitate to open and read, Leatrice asked my mother if she could find out what my father's plans for Bobby were – did he intend to tell Bobby that he was his father? His response, inevitably, was to write a letter in my mother's voice, which sharply criticized Leatrice's character and behaviour, and forged my mother's signature at the end. This he then dispatched to Random House for forwarding on. After this (as he saw it) lovely bit of mischief (his second wife excoriating his first on his behalf), he went back to *Why Aren't You Famous?*, though it was 'Boringly difficult to get in to [it] again.'

On Monday 21 September he received Leatrice's reply, which was addressed to my mother. It said simply 'Nuts'. He wrote in his diary:

> *She has accepted it as a letter from Edna. I still seem to have the stylistic touch. [Leatrice's] writing seems a trifle shaky. Perhaps I've shaken her this time. Something will follow. She won't in time be satisfied with that inarticulate howl of rage.*

Two days later, Mac phoned, and from his friend's questions he realized that Leatrice actually didn't think the letter was genuine and had tasked Mac to find out. Four days later, Mac rang again. He had:

> *Met Edna at a literary party and asked her why she hurt 'poor Lea' so. She denied all knowledge and got Lea's address from him to write to Mrs Fountain.*

So that was that. His trick was found out, though neither he nor Mac said anything about it.

VI

His diary:

Sunday 4 October 1964
To Richmond Park with Jane. A golden, misty Renoir day. Lion-coloured grass and orange leaved trees. The air utterly still. Shining through the haze an orange sun. One of those unreal, as-seen-in-a-dream days. We walked slowly, talking, and sat by centre ponds. Came home, went to bed. Got up and had dinner. No more ideal companion than Jane can I imagine.

Tuesday 13 October 1964
Sat in garden at midday. Hazy hot sun low in clear sky. Many foraging wasps and large brown hover flies.
    5.30 Dear Jane comes in out of a cool misty evening, from Crystal Palace.

Tuesday 24 November 1964
Finished Why Aren't You Famous? *A lightweight romance for the young.*

Friday 4 December 1964
Bought a copy of the monstrous Girls in their Married Bliss *(a title stiff with lesbian archness). And now that I look at it in a calmer frame* [of mind] *it hits you in the face – the lesbian jealousy of men and the hatred of them.*

59.

Custody

I

At the start of 1965, *Why Aren't You Famous?* went off to the BBC and Rediffusion and he turned to another piece for the BBC, *Life Ever Lasting*, a morality play about extreme longevity. Being gifted with an extended lifespan, he wrote in his diary on 7 January:

> *Would make cowards of us all. Who, if he had extended life, even if only for three or four hundred years would dive into a rough sea to save an ordinary mortal child's life?*

Unfortunately, he couldn't get the plot of this play to gel, so he abandoned it and started trying to hash out the plot of a play called *The Beats*, but got no further with it either. On 15 January he wrote:

> *Once I deliberately made money with a commercial novel so that I could write as inner self desired. I didn't. But now is the time I want to – to write without reference to who will buy it and read*

it, [but] *the money is gone and I have to try to pay the rent with TV plays.*

For years now the part of his unconscious from where the work sprung had been incredibly uncooperative, but that was changing (the change was already in train, though it was far from complete) and the catalyst was economic. He needed to earn money, and his psyche, presented with an ultimatum to this effect, had been persuaded to cooperate. This change, of course, would be a struggle, and along the way he would experience many episodes of failure, and indeed he was about to experience one of these now.

He couldn't get on with *The Beats* any better than he'd been able to get on with the longevity project, so he abandoned it and turned to a third television play, *Where Shall I Find What Will Change My Life?*, and here he made much better progress because, unlike the previous two ideas, this one mixed his own difficult experience and wish-fulfilment.

Where Shall I Find What Will Change My Life? told the story of Sidney Lucas, the pessimistic and manic-depressive author of a single, and slated, novel, who has produced nothing for years, even though the greatest sex novel in the history of publishing is locked inside his head. Only his paragon wife, Tessa, who exhorts, entreats and coerces (at one point she locks him in the kitchen to write) is on hand to help, and in the end, for this is a fairy tale, success catches up with Sidney, though not at all in the way he expects. The story, obviously, sprung from my father's own writer's block, and offers his fantasy answer to his problem: the good wife who saves her author husband, which was what he never had, and for which this would compensate somehow.

By Sunday 24 January he had the plot organized, and he was now able to start writing in earnest. But his marital resentments were ever present, always simmering, perpetually aggravating. On 29 January he wrote:

sunshine all day.

19 WEDNESDAY   WEEK 16 · 109-256

Hay fever. with a cold.
Unable to sleep at night.

Made a air. filter to take
pollen out of air in study
or bedroom

Metal tube 8ins diametro. Small
induction motor fan. Fine mesh
chicken wire screen to keep in place
industrial wire wool, teased out
lightly and soaked in liquid paraffin.

Pollen gets trapped in the oily
wire wool. I leave it on in
bedroom all night. It serves also
to circulate air, as windows
are kept closed. This is
the worst time for pollen

	MARCH						APRIL				
S ·	5	12	19	26	·	S ·	2	9	16	23	30
M ·	6	13	20	27	·	M ·	3	10	17	24	·
T ·	7	14	21	28	·	T ·	4	11	18	25	·
W 1	8	15	22	29	·	W ·	5	12	19	26	·
T 2	9	16	23	30	·	T ·	6	13	20	27	·
F 3	10	17	24	31	·	F ·	7	14	21	28	·
S 4	11	18	25	·	·	S ·	8	15	22	29	·

Ernest Gébler's diary entry containing an illustration of his pollen extractor.

Edna O'Brien, early 1960s.

Adolf in attic lair, 3 Cabra Grove, 1950s.

Jane, 1967.

Ernest and Jane after their first holiday together, July 1964.

Adolf and Marianna, San Francisco, 1960.

Family photograph (posed), June 1961.

Ernest with the Emmy award, November 1968.

Ernest at the time of his Emmy win, 1968.

Adolf and Marianna
on the day of their wedding.

Ernest at the time of his move to London, 1968.

Carlo, Sasha, Ernest and Jane, *Cnoc Aluin*, early 1980s.

Carlo and Sasha at Cannon Hill Lane, October 1964.

Ernest Gébler, December 1986.
This was taken six months after Jane absconded.

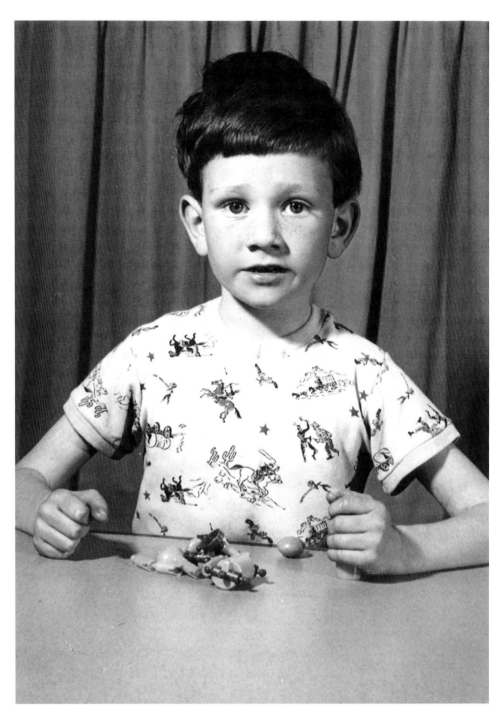

Carlo Gébler at Hillcross School, 1961.

As a writer: write a novel eight times over. Take endless pains over your craft: be a perfectionist [just as you would] *adjust your car engine. But concerning my life I am apparently careless. I take pot luck. I take an Edna O'Brien into my life carelessly. And suffer ten years.*

II

In early February, a letter addressed to my mother arrived from Howard B. Gotlieb, director of special collections at the Mugar Memorial Library, Boston University, requesting manuscript material from her. Here was another opportunity to cause pain with a letter, an experience he had enjoyed once already. In reply, he:

Forged a letter to Howard B. Gotlieb of Boston Universities Libraries [sic] *– as if from Edna O'Brien pleading she is too modest to contribute to* [a] *reference library!* [Instead] *I had her recommend me and my works for the library.*

This piece of epistolary mischief-making then gave him the idea for another stroke – one that would punish Leatrice this time. He wrote to her 'saying am depositing all correspondence on her and me for use of students' and then asked if she had 'any final letter or comment on her infamous conduct re her son's parenthood which she might like to have included'? Naturally, he did not mention the university; he didn't want her writing to them.

Not long after, he got yet another opportunity for this kind of troublemaking. He received a letter from a London theatre producer addressed to my mother indicating the company's interest in making her novel *The Lonely Girl* into a musical. Styling himself Edward Cresset of The Authors' Representation Company, he wrote back, regretting that the novel was unavailable, but suggesting that Ernest Gébler's novel *The Love Investigator* would make a much better musical. Deep down in his psyche he knew that his forgeries were wrong, so to soothe his conscience he told himself that they were justifiable acts of retribution. As he wrote in his diary, his justification for these actions was that 'The unscrupulous deserve to be treated unscrupulously.'

By Sunday 7 February, he noted, he had 'Heard nothing from BBC or Rediffusion yet about [*Why Aren't You Famous?*],' and was 'On page 30 of [*Where Shall I Find What Will Change My Life?*].' By late March, *Where Shall I Find What Will Change My Life?* was done, and went off to Granada in Manchester. On the last Sunday of the month he went for a tramp, as he put it, after dark on Cannon Hill Common, because at this time the the pale green feathers of the budding chestnut trees were 'seen more easily … by the light of the green sodium street lighting' than in daylight.

He was worried about money ('Have only four hundred pounds left in cash'), but this did not prevent him from going to the Royal Festival Hall on the South Bank on 1 April to hear the London Philharmonic under Christoph von Dohnányi play Mahler's Fifth Symphony. It was a 'moving, rich and vital performance,' but he was saddened by the realization as he listened that Mahler 'could not seem to sort it all out, could not weed out all the worthless bits and pieces.'

As spring rolled on, hay fever descended, and his left ear, damaged when he won the half-mile swimming race in Bray before the war, required syringing. Thereafter, nearly all the entries for several months concerned first the afflictions of hay fever (a new affliction, it would dog him for the rest of his life, and he would fill his diaries with notes about it), and then the bronchitis and catarrh that followed.

At the end of May he was still waiting for decisions on *Why Aren't You Famous?* and *Where Shall I Find What Will Change My Life?* This uncertainty roused his ancient resentments, or perhaps his way to cope was to vent these. On 14 June he wrote:

Bernard Shaw & Lenin both had cultivated mothers who played the piano. I had a mother who spent her energies 'fighting for her rights' for herself, usually by yelling. Did Shaw or Lenin's mother ever yell about their 'rights'? They are the two men I hold in the highest respect.

In June he went to Ireland with Jane for a camping holiday, and on 24 June they visited Church Villa, the house where he lived as a boy in Tramore. He and Jane got into the crumbling old house (it was owned by a Waterford solicitor who used it for summer holidays), and 'From the middle upper window we watched the churchyard for ghosts.' Seeing the old house left him 'sad for days,' he wrote.

III

He came back from holiday at the end of July. *August is a Wicked Month* (styled *August is a Pissy Month* in his diary) was already out in the US and was enjoying pre-publication publicity in the British papers in anticipation of its publication in Britain in October. He collected some US reviews as well as some pieces from the British press, and stuck these in the diary (he did so love to collect materials that would rouse his ire) and tried to push on with a novel (this was Jane's idea) about his second marriage.

As summer edged into autumn he was banging out treatments for television plays at £25 a time, and his bitterness was rising. His diary entry for Friday 1 October was typical:

> *Sash ill in Putney. Carlo phoned – neither had been to school – so I do not see them from Wednesday to Monday, unless I go down and face unpleasantness.*

He did indeed go to Putney to visit:

> *Carlo plainly lying. Neither are sick. A dog has been got. Carlo wearing expensive teenage pointed fashionable shoes, in which he looks silly. The campaign to subvert them, to claim them entirely and make them punch-bags for her sick, empty loveless life*

continue[s]. *What can I do to stop them being turned into mother smothered homosexuals? Her relentless brainwashing on them is having its result – I am the enemy. They obviously accept that I am to be circumvented, lied to. (Children she didn't want, children she fought against having. Children she hardly ever changed a napkin* [for] *or fed. For three months after Carlo was born she wouldn't hold the child in her arms. And she hated Sasha too – until they grew up a bit, became 'little men', became something to love her.)*

At the start of October, Granada bought *Where Shall I Find What Will Change My Life?* for £600 for inclusion in the season they were planning, *Scenes of Married Life*, which would examine modern marriage, but the pleasure of this success was negated by *August is a Wicked Month*, which he read shortly after and which, predictably, appalled him. On 12 October he wrote:

Her novel August *etc: there seems to be nothing left in her slobbering mind to write about. Rather than give up she is ready to debase and befoul herself in public. The picture is as horrifying as a moronic woman screeching for attention in a market place and failing to get attention, raising her skirts and exhibiting her diseased sexual quarters. The raging vanity is turning into raging rage.*

These appalling feelings were so powerful that confiding he had them in his diary was not enough. He needed to purge them, and he now did so in a lengthy letter that he wrote to my mother shortly thereafter. This document traced the trajectory of their relationship from start to finish. This material was hurtful, but not so novel. He was the long-suffering dupe and she was the malign traducer, which was how he'd always seen things. On top of that, though (and as he argued the inevitable consequence of what he had seen), were the new rules for his sons when they were with her in Putney that he demanded she would henceforth observe. For instance, we were not to be driven around in any car by anyone. We were not to be bathed by anyone. And we were not to be in her study when she was writing – or as he put it, his sons were to be 'preserved from the Krafft-Ebing taint of her perverted writing by permanent exclusion from the room where she wrote.' Even by my father's standards this last was a strange assertion. Richard von Krafft-Ebing (1840–1902) was renowned for his explorations of sexual difference, particularly homosexuality, which was presumably why my father, certain that my brother and I would be made homosexual by our mother's regime, threw his name in. However, Krafft-Ebing thought that homosexuality originated during the foetal stage of gestation; nowhere in his work does he suggest that proximity to a writer could have a similar effect, so this conceit makes no sense. But then, accuracy was not the ambition here; compliance was his goal. He wanted his new rules to be obeyed. And if they were not, he concluded, then he would abort the informal custody arrangement whereby we alternated between their houses and he would take us to New Zealand and she would never see us again. Ever.

IV

My mother took legal advice. On 26 October he received papers from her solicitor giving notice of her intention to seek full custody at a hearing in November and then to petition for divorce. This should surely not have surprised him, yet his response was bafflement shot through with self-pity. On Friday 12 November he wrote:

> *In the midst of this Custody Court – Divorce Court madness. Getting statements from* [the boys'] *headmasters. Dealing with this sick, sickening book. So, for those years of ministering to her, for those long-suffering years, for educating her, writing the books that made her a name, treating her gently and with care, she proceeds*

to mean for him High Court costs that can leave him homeless and charge[s] him with being 'a man of violent ungoverned and unstable temper who has dominated over your petitioner' etc. [...] And those boys? Have I wasted my substance on them too? Already they show signs of her witless compulsive deceit.

On Wednesday 17 November, my brother and I were in his house in Morden. Rather in the manner of King Lear, he determined to test us, demanding that we each write a letter confirming if we wished to live with him or with her.

I wrote:

To my dear DAD,
I must admit I prefere [sic] living in Putney at the moment. But in years to come I will probly [sic] have a different attitude. I just don't know.
    Signed your loving son, Carlos xxx

My brother wrote a cleaner, leaner, braver letter:

Dear Dad,
If I had the choice I would rather for now live with mother in Putney.
    Your son, Mark (Sasha)

Undeterred, he pushed on, gathering materials he could use to contest custody. On Monday 22 November he wrote:

Have done no work since divorce and custody petition served on me. Getting affidavits signed etc., building up my defence against her claim for full custody. The nervous and emotional strain is great. The children are subverted by what she gives them anyway – endless TV in their bedroom, sweets, toys etc.

— and Sash looks at me with resentment. So why not let them go to her? Because if she goes out of her squalid little mind and damages what little chance they have of a normal life, I should be to blame. Can you sacrifice your own children for a peaceful life?

Eventually, the answer he gave himself, or seemed to give himself, perhaps because of the letters written by my brother and me, was yes – he could, as he saw it, sacrifice us. On the night before the custody hearing he pushed a note through the door of 87 Deodar Road. In this he said he couldn't be bothered fighting her any more. He would not be in court the following day. She could have us; we were hers to destroy. But the following day, when my mother went to court, there he was with counsel ready to contest custody. So why had he put the note through her letterbox the night before? To wrong-foot her? It looks like it.

In court, my father proposed (and this is just a summary) that she was only seeking custody because of her default antagonism to men, which meant that she must oppose anything done by any man. Her petition was not rooted in real feeling, it was a gesture, and should it succeed, which he hoped it wouldn't, the arrangement had no chance of lasting. It must collapse inevitably by her abandoning us. He also alleged she'd turn my brother and me into homosexuals, and as evidence of her pathology he invited the judge to take a look at her latest novel, *August is a Wicked Month*. The judge glanced at a few pages, noted that the text was unlikely to be of interest to children of nine and eleven, and after my mother had spoken briefly from the floor of the court, he made his ruling. He awarded her full custody.

V

On 3 January 1966, my father wrote a letter to his Dublin friends and sometime neighbours from Garville Avenue (they lived at 13, we had lived at 29), the novelist Val Mulkerns and her husband, Maurice

Kennedy, which detailed, as he saw it, what had happened in court and the sense he made of it.

The judge in his opinion was hopeless and biased, and of course he had done what judges in English courts in such cases habitually did: he had awarded custody to the mother. Consequently, he had lost, but (which was his letter's import, and a way to snatch success from the jaws of defeat), he had now come to see how that was actually for the best:

> *The children are completely bought over. Total freedom to do what they like down there* [in Putney], *roam the streets, pounds of chocolates in the bedroom, TV in their bedroom on all day, never lift a finger or have to tie a shoelace; taught by her to lie about every smallest thing* [...]
>
> *So what was I fighting for? To have unwilling lumpy boys coming here to suffer out their days of imprisonment? So that in a year or so they will turn Edna faces upon me and tell me they have never had anything from me but neglect and cruelty? (They said they wanted to live with their mother because it was nicer. Sasha, at school around the corner, for a solid fortnight while living with his mother, did not bother once to walk around the corner to see his father.) Like her they have that piece missing from their mentality that has to do with faith, conscience, family affection. They are shot through with O'Brien two-faced cunning. She deserves them to fill her empty life and it looks as if they deserve her. They are as far from my father and mother and family, our kind of feelings and inner life, as parrots or lizards.*

Finally, he told his friends, affecting stoicism shot through with forced insouciance as if to say 'Such is life, what can you do?' he had given up on his children until the divorce was heard, and his intention now was to use the time that had suddenly become available to write what he ought to have been writing for the past ten years. He ended the letter:

I am working, writing, and learning to live down that horrible mistake in my life. Perhaps I wasn't meant to have a family. Well, who knows?

VI

To maintain paternal contact, my mother insisted that my brother and I must visit our father for a couple hours at least once a week on a Tuesday or Thursday evening after school. Though he might not have wanted it, he got us anyway.

60.

J. R. Ackerley

I

On Deodar Road one of our neighbours was the English writer Nell Dunn, famous for *Up the Junction* (1963), a semi-fictionalized account of working-class life in Battersea. My mother and Nell became friends, while my brother and I became friends with one of her sons (in age he was between my brother and me), and as a result our two families started to spend a great deal of time together.

Deodar Road was a U-shaped loop off the Putney Bridge Road, and at the top of one of the legs (where Deodar Road hits the Putney Bridge Road) there was a parade of shops. Sometimes Nell would call for my mother or vice versa and they'd stroll up together, dragging the children along, which was how one afternoon, around this time, I found myself standing with them outside the greengrocer's. The mothers were talking (I've no recollection of what about), when suddenly one of them, Nell I think, pointed in the direction of Putney High Street and expressed alarm.

I looked and saw an old man hurtling towards us along the pavement. This was a man on mission – of that there was no doubt. He wore a raincoat. The buttons were undone, so as he moved his coat rose on either side, which added to the sense of velocity. I'd never seen him before, but I now gathered that this was J. R. Ackerley (1896–1967), a writer who lived on the other side of Putney High Street. He was a drunk, he could well be drunk now, he would certainly want to talk, and his talk would be interminable. Evasive action had to be taken at once.

<h1 style="text-align:center">II</h1>

We fled into the greengrocer's. The mothers went to the rear and turned their backs to the front window. I didn't. I had a talent for spying, eavesdropping and gathering information without drawing attention to myself (one of the fruits of never having been able to act openly with my father), and I wanted to see more of this man who'd produced such a reaction, so I hovered by the door, feigning interest in some fruit or vegetable, and waited. Ackerley shot into view in profile. There wasn't much time, but I saw enough. His face was sharp, or so it seemed to me. He had a thin, wiry physique, and didn't look at all well. He carried two shopping bags of the heavy-duty industrial plastic type with reinforced handles, the variety favoured by working-class women as opposed to the raffia or straw jobs decorated with Italian rustic scenes that we used, and his bags were filled with empty soda siphons. I could see the levers of several sticking out. I intuited, or it was subsequently explained, that J. R. Ackerley was taking these to the off-licence farther along Putney Bridge Road, and with the deposit that would be returned to him for the siphons, he intended to buy booze. This was not such an unusual practice in those days, so it is not impossible that I worked this out for myself.

Next thing, the man who'd caused the mothers such consternation was gone, normal practice could resume, and this moment should have slipped from my memory. But it didn't. It hasn't, because there was an addendum that kept it alive. Nell often lent me books that she thought I'd like (Maupassant, Chekhov, that sort of thing), and because of this incident (though not necessarily immediately; this next bit could easily have happened a year or two later) she showed me Ackerley's *Hindoo Holiday* (1932), an account of his hilarious experiences as private secretary to an Indian maharajah, and she gave me Ackerley's *My Dog Tulip* (1956) to read, and I did. I'd never read anything like it.

My parents were both writers – of fiction. Nell was a writer – of fiction. Most of the writers with whom my mother and father mixed were writers – of fiction. The house of literature had many splendid rooms, but the most splendid of all was the room of fiction. This was the majority opinion of all the writers I knew.

But *My Dog Tulip* was different. Yes, the book used dialogue (the dialogue was brilliant), and many other devices with which I was familiar from novels. Yes, it was full of personal facts and feelings, just like in novels. And yes, this story was saturated with loneliness, something that I typically associated with the novel. Only it wasn't a novel. Everything in *My Dog Tulip* had happened. It was true.

Not only that, but this person of whom I was in awe, a writer of fiction, Nell (and others like Frances Wyndham, who came to my mother's house later and with whom I remember talking about Ackerley), and everyone else spoke of Ackerley's non-fiction as having as much importance and value as any novel. This revelation made a far greater impression than my discovery at about the same time that Ackerley was 'queer', which was the word used then. I already knew, in theory at any rate, about what would now be called cottaging and what went on in public toilets and London parks, so this didn't shock or surprise, though that is not to say I didn't find it interesting. Of course I did. But it was Ackerley's literary practice and the respect he enjoyed among writers I admired that made the greater impact. Reading Ackerley I discovered that there was another room in the house of literature, hitherto unknown until this moment, the non-fiction room, and once I'd found it I couldn't keep out of it. I started to go there regularly to borrow and read whatever I could find.

And so, inevitably, because how could this not happen after that scene at the greengrocer's, sometime during adolescence I read Ackerley's best known work, his posthumously published *My Father and Myself* (1968). The book was notable, I thought, for two reasons:

One, its focus. It included a large cast of characters and spanned many years, but everything it contained connected back to the title and contributed either to his or his father's story. Him and his father; that's what it was about.

Two, its forensic exposure and exploration of the difference between how things seemed and how they really were.

Ackerley's father, Roger, an executive at Elders and Fyffes, the banana importers, seemed like a model of bourgeois rectitude, whereas in fact he was anything but. In early manhood he was entwined in a homosexual milieu, and throughout his adult 'married' life he maintained a second secret family consisting of a mistress and three children. This fact was unknown to Ackerley and his mother until after Roger Ackerley's death. As well as by Ackerley *fils*, Roger Ackerley's story was also later narrated by one of the children of the other family, Diana Petre, in *The Secret Orchard of Roger Ackerley*, a book I also read and admired.

What I didn't know when I was reading these books was the priming work they were doing. They were getting me ready to write personal narratives in the distant future.

61.

Hoffman

I

At the very beginning of 1966 he sold *Why Aren't You Famous?* to the BBC for the Wednesday Play slot. It was a good beginning. Then on St Valentine's Day he started *Call Me Daddy* for ABC Television, his version of *Beauty and the Beast*, re-set in the twentieth century. The play tells the story of a lonely, middle-aged and not especially attractive businessman, Benjamin Hoffman, who blackmails one of his company's typists, the lovely Miss Janet Smith, into spending a weekend at his flat on the eve of her marriage to a dispatch clerk at Mr Hoffman's company. Instead of making love to Miss Smith, Hoffman introduces her to the pleasures of fine living, and as a result she falls in love with him of her own free will and becomes his lover. This narrative, of course, was a coded version of his and Jane's coming together, my father being Hoffman, cultured, willful, complicated, and Jane being Miss Smith, timorous, innocent, willing.

Why Aren't You Famous? was transmitted on Wednesday 23 February at 9 p.m. in The Wednesday Play slot. In his diary he noted:

£600 for entertaining an audience of twelve million –
something like £50 per million. [...] The critics didn't like
it much which doesn't mean anything. [...] Still the main
outline got through and those who knew saw the joke was
on Edna. What a rare pleasure to play out one's private joke
and yes, legitimate revenge through the medium of a twelve
million audience. [...] Edna's fury watching it, as it slowly
dawned on her just what it was, would have been a splendid
sight to see. And when it dawned on her that O'Roon's 'art'
stood for Edna's writing, well!

In March, his hay fever began. He attempted to fight if off using auto-suggestion. He finished *Call Me Daddy* on Saturday 19 March and posted it off. The following Monday it was dry and sunny, and he took CDF22, one of the two Railton motorcars that he now owned, for a celebratory spin with the hood down and admired the way it 'softly purrs along, like a great floating black beetle.' The next day, Tuesday 22, he:

Tuned striker on grandfather clock and oiled mechanism.
What dogging obsession has always driven me to make every
mechanical device work as near perfectly as possible? An easy
obsession? Outside there are two motorcars, large cars. Both
are in near perfect mechanical condition. Both have been put
into and kept in that condition by me. I oil door locks, hinges,
clocks – adjust, repair and oil everything. Somewhere in youth
I got the obsession that I could make anything mechanical
work true.

People and feelings had always been his problem. As he had discovered early on, people let you down or they changed their minds or they wouldn't do what you wanted or they were emotionally unavailable, and the consequences of these failed human transactions were painful feelings of hurt and loss. Maturation typically involves the development of resilience, the virtue that enables suffering not only to be endured and understood, but to be valued aand, sometimes, even transcended. But in my father's case, instead of developing the emotional capacity to cope with the problems of living, he went to the mechanical world, where he could exercise absolute control, and where, as a result, there were no failures and no pain, only bliss. Having embarked on this practice, it became his habit, and having become his habit it became impossible to derogate from folding himself into the mechanical, which became his default. It was what he always did because it gave him control, the absence of which elsewhere in his life had caused him so much pain.

On Friday 13 May he went to Manchester for the recording of *Where Shall I Find What Will Change My Life?* Thereafter, he spent his days fighting his hay fever, worrying about his health and pottering in his garage and his garden, and that was it. He wasn't reading or writing. It was a life of stasis, paralysis, and it worried Jane. On Monday 16 May, she told him: 'You are the best comic writer in England today not writing.'

II

On Thursday 2 June, my brother and I appeared at 257 Cannon Hill Lane for our weekly visit. The welcome from our father was subdued, even sullen. Jane was nervy. Something was coming. He had something to say to us, he said, so we'd better come into his study so he could say it. We trooped in. We sat.

It was a summer evening. On the other side of the leaded windows stretched Cannon Hill Common. A father and his children were playing French cricket on the grass, and occasionally I heard the wallop of the bat on the tennis ball they were using and the players' voices calling out the score.

He had made notes of what he wanted to say on two square sheets of cream-coloured letter paper. He had drafted his notes in blue Biro, and then corrected them in red and black Biro. As he spoke he occasionally referred to his sheets.

Summarized, his argument ran as follows:

We had never ever expressed a moment of regret about the end of the marriage, his separation from our mother, or the judge's granting full custody to her. And we had never telephoned to ask him how he was even once over the previous six months, while we had been living wholly in Putney. This behaviour showed that our true natures were callous, indifferent and selfish.

Our coming for the hour or two we came every week with our closed faces, and so very obviously under instruction not to mention our lives in Putney or our mother, was degrading and humiliating, and he wasn't prepared to endure it any longer.

Therefore, it appeared to him that by not coming we would save ourselves an hour or two every week in which to watch television and so on, and also, simultaneously, relieve him from being reminded weekly how the children on whom he had once founded his life had become cold, cruel and unfeeling.

His voice throughout was cool, clear, almost monotonous. I wondered if he'd rehearsed his speech, and felt certain that at least he had been over it in his head.

After we left he wrote in his diary for Thursday 2 June:

They have the same mental deficiency that she has [...] they are unable to 'feel' anything for anyone.

III

On 31 August, *Why Aren't You Famous?* was repeated on the BBC. Two days later, on Friday 2 September, ABC agreed to buy *Call Me Daddy* for £600 for the Armchair Theatre slot. The following week, the ITV programme guide ran a pre-transmission publicity piece on *Where Shall I Find What Will Change My Life?*:

The author Ernest Gébler found success with The Plymouth Adventure *— the story of the Pilgrim Fathers' voyage to America in the* Mayflower.

> *'It destroyed me,' said Ernest, whose output promptly plummeted. 'Instead of it bringing me about £500, which I thought was an enormous sum and which I could live on for about two years in a cottage in the mountains outside Dublin, it made me a great deal more. And I spent the next five years doing nothing.'*

At the end of November, Marianna, en route from Los Angeles to a holiday in Vienna, stopped off in London and came out to Morden to stay. She brought photographs of Adolf at the end of his life. When he looked at these my father felt strongly that Adolf's was a ruined and wasted life. When he had left the Prague Conservatoire his father was supposed to have had a career as a soloist and even a conductor. Instead, he'd spent his life playing in cinemas and working as a musical director for a trade union, then had died alienated from some of his children in a country where he didn't want to be. Given where he'd started, Adolf really couldn't be said to have flourished.

Because Marianna was a living link to our dead grandfather, my brother and I were summoned to see her, and when we appeared we gathered that what we were told in June no longer applied and that our weekly visits should resume. Marianna only stayed for two nights, which was two too many as far as my father was concerned. 'A greedy, stupid woman,' he wrote in his diary on Thursday 1 December after he had dropped her to Euston Station.

> *Perhaps I should have let Ada deport her after all! From what she says I gather Father deliberately killed himself with alcohol in California. Her mindless anti-Semitism. Wish not to see her again.*

A fortnight later he received notice from my mother of her intention to seek a divorce. The *Daily Telegraph* reported this on 16 December under the heading 'Edna O'Brien seeks divorce'. Jane cut this out of the paper, dated it in her looping writing, and put it in his diary. He, however, wrote nothing about this.

IV

Call Me Daddy, with Judy Cornwell as Janet and Donald Pleasence as Benjamin, was taped at the ABC studios in Teddington on 19 January 1967. The weekend after, he posted a copy of the Irish Constitution to my mother with this line in Article 41 marked for her attention: 'No person who has made a lawful marriage may marry in Ireland while the partner to said marriage is alive.' His inference was that he was still married to Leatrice, so therefore he and my mother weren't married, so therefore they couldn't be divorced. Much wrangling followed. My mother eventually agreed to withdraw her petition and to allow him to petition instead for divorce on grounds of desertion: hers of him.

Call Me Daddy went out at 10.30 on Saturday 8 April on ATV. It caused a stir, was liked, and was thought to have further commercial potential. After the broadcast several producers were in touch, and there was talk of remaking it as a film. My father thought it should be a stage play first, and got to work immediately. As he wrote, and the words came easily for a change, pollen levels soared. In March he had been to the Ideal Home Exhibition to look at electric air cleaners that sucked pollen out of the air, but baulked at the cost: they were £120. But his symptoms were now so extreme that he decided to make one. His machine to filter pollen from the air was a metal tube, eight inches in diameter, with an induction motor fan inside and a plug of liquid-paraffin-soaked wire wool, which trapped any pollen as the air was passed through. He tried it out overnight on Wednesday 19 April, and reported the following day: 'Good night's sleep. The air cleaner is effective.'

On 12 April he was granted a decree nisi because of my mother's desertion, which she did not contest. As was agreed in advance, there was no order as to costs, each party paying their own. There was no order for maintenance either; that had also been agreed.

He got the stage version of *Call Me Daddy* finished at the start of June, and sent it out.

V

On Friday 7 July, Jane learnt that she had to go to hospital to remove a varicose vein from her leg. She was a haemophiliac, which although not unknown, was unusual in women, so this would not be a simple procedure.

The operation was performed on 11 July. He went to visit her afterwards, bringing some cooked steak. 'The sight of the whole upper part of her leg' in its post-operative condition stopped his breathing. He was shocked by the 'horrendous yellow [...] scar [...] where the varicose vein had been taken out.'

After the visit, he talked to a nurse in the corridor. She was 'fine, strong, handsome,' and he had no doubt that she 'would have come if I'd asked her out that night.' We will have to take his word for that. In any case, he didn't. The horror of Jane's 'outraged [...] leg' was too vivid in his mind, and he felt conflicted:

> *Should I run, run from that leg in the bed? We would never be able to have a child, or rather, want to. Could I abandon that thin, pale woman in the hospital bed that I had met so lately? [...] what would the pain and distress of that do to her? Could you abandon her to loneliness in later life if, say, she was going mad? There are certain things you cannot do. Or you pay dear.*

Three days later he wrote that her hospitalization had 'depressed' him and left him 'nervous and apprehensive.' Jane returned to 257 Cannon Hill Lane on 24 July. Her recovery was slow, and she was still sore on 17 August when his decree absolute came through.

His next task was to write the novel of *Call Me Daddy*, which would be called *Shall I Eat You Now?* so that in the event of a film he'd be paid for the book *and* the script. He spent the rest of the year writing it. It wasn't easy. He was held up, as he wrote on 31 October, by 'the silliness of the plot,' and found it 'extremely difficult to keep it going with only two people.' He also opened negotiations about the novel with publishers including Lee Barker at Doubleday, who'd published *The Plymouth Adventure*. He and Jane spent Christmas in Blackrock in Dublin with Rudy and Bunny, who were now reunited.

VI

He finished *Shall I Eat You Now?* at the end of January. He had it typed (surely a provocation?) by my mother's typist, Mrs Hughes, who lived opposite her in Deodar Road, and then he sent bound copies to prospective publishers in London and New York. In March he was commissioned by ABC to write for the series *The Sex Game*. His play, *Women Can Be Monsters*, told the story of Edwin, who, just as he is embarking on his second marriage to Liz, is lent by her to his first wife, Louisa, who claims to be terminally ill and in desperate need of her ex-husband's attentions before death. Simultaneously, LWT asked him to write another play, *A Little Milk of Human Kindness*.

April was a golden month. *Call Me Daddy* won the 1968 American Academy of Arts and Science Award, the Emmy, for the best entertainment programme in the International Division. His stock rose. Doubleday in New York and Macmillan in London bought *Shall I Eat You Now?* (the Americans paying $6,000, which was good money), and he spent the rest of the year writing the plays he'd been commissioned to write, talking to producers and advancing the film version of *Call Me Daddy*, which would be called *Hoffman*. There were only two spoilers: his sons never visited (as he complained endlessly in his diary), and he learnt that his estranged sister, Ada, intended to sue both him and my mother for libel. Ada claimed that several works by each of them had maligned her. In an interview with the *Sunday Express* on 19 May he described himself as 'flabbergasted' by this news. Ada's case, as he gleefully noted in his diary, never came to court, because his sister was unable to deposit money against costs, as plaintiffs in libel cases were required to do before proceeding.

Women Can Be Monsters, with Eileen Atkins and Siân Phillips as the sparring wives, was broadcast on 27 November 1968. By the end of the year, *Hoffman* had a producer, Ben Arbeid, a director, Alvin Rakoff (who'd directed the TV version of *Call Me Daddy*), and a putative production company, Columbia Pictures. Even he was impressed. As he wrote on Saturday 7 December, 'In 1968 I was at the top.'

But 1969 exceeded these heights, at least initially. Peter Sellers agreed to play Hoffman. With a star in place, the film was guaranteed. On 29 January he was offered £21,000 for the *Hoffman* rights and script, a huge sum (though Sellers, as he noted peevishly, was getting £200,000). The novel *Shall I Eat You Now?* came out in Britain on 20 February. On 24 February he wrote:

> *Very good reviews coming now. Film sale ready. It seems I have written a popular success – which was the aim.*

He started the *Hoffman* script, and at the end of March the first cheque for £9,000 came. He sold his grey Railton, Z6201, to a J. O. Dyson for £450, and bought a Ford Transit Dormobile Caravan from a dealer in Staines for £1,160. My brother and I were now away at Bedales, a boarding school in Hampshire, but we were home for the Easter holidays, came to lunch on Sunday 30 March, and after we left he sat and composed a letter:

> *Letter to my sons:*

> *My mother taught me to hate my father and to be against him just as subtly and meanmindedly as your mother fostered your attitude.*
> *There is really only one thing I really regret in my life – the day I met your mother, Edna. That was the worst thing that ever happened to me.*
> *But perhaps I should be a little thankful – after all you might have gone on living here but for Edna, and I lavished on you the*

normal human affection of father to son, only to later discover that I was saddled with a pair of unfeeling, soulless zombies [only] after what they could get – Edna all over again.

Most people get what they deserve in this world. In a way, it is a kind of justice that you should become victims of the English public school system. With your peasant origins it will turn you into phoney class snobs with unpleasant fake accents [...] You may remember that I warned you that when you became a nuisance she'd pack you off to boarding school. The natural people for children to be with are their parents – and the most natural and valuable other human being for a son to be with is his father. Your mother's gift to you was not to start you off in life with your father's abilities but with a fake accent and an ill-nourished body. And serve you bloody well right. Your conduct has proved that you have inherited the O'Brien false-hearted meanmindedness.

Other than this letter, which he did not send, he wrote nothing but the *Hoffman* script, first alone, then in conjunction with the director and producer ('never again. Next time hand it in finished'), and then alone again. Throughout, he was stricken with hay fever (his pollen extractor was no longer producing the same results), and he duly noted his symptoms and other details regarding his health in his diary.

Shall I Eat You Now? came out in the US in April ('jacket is horrifically crude, crass back street porno shop design. Goodbye Doubleday'), and on 23 May he finished the first draft of *Hoffman*, and on 18 July the final draft. This went to Sellers, and two days later, on the day of the moon landings ('American cowboys landed on the moon today and planted the stars and stripes. Everything full of it. What a bore'), the actor phoned my father. He thought that the screenplay was one of the best he'd ever read, and he was anxious to start. Sellers had seen 'how to do it' too. 'He said, "It is really you, isn't it?" ' His plan was to do Hoffman as my father, do him 'the way I speak.'

At this point Columbia baulked, and the script (this was my father's idea) went to Bryan Forbes, who had just assumed control at EMI. He agreed to do it. There was now a distributor, and Sellers had approved, and as Judy Cornwell, Janet in the TV version, wasn't going to be cast, an actress had to be found. He identified Sinéad Cusack, daughter of the actor Cyril, whom he claimed he had known when she was a child, as perfect for the role, and on 7 August, despite considerable competition, including Jane Asher, he got his way.

The ocean was traversed; the harbour was in sight. All that remained was to make the film. What's not to like? Well, yes. But at this point my father's indefatigable capacity for feuding and fault-finding and disparagement and criticizing others, in particular the director and the producer, led to his exclusion from the set throughout the whole rehearsal and filming period (Monday 8 September to Friday 14 November), and other than when he spoke by phone with Sinéad Cusack, which he did once, he had no contact with anyone involved in the making of the film at all, which is all the more remarkable when you consider that some of it was shot in Wimbledon only a few miles from his home. His diary entries written at this time were disgruntled, as one would expect, but also, here and there, he adopted a pose of forced indifference. 'I have learnt not to mourn too long for lost children,' he wrote on 6 October, 'or friends lost to pride or cupidity,' and this disaster, his exclusion from the set, was no different. He would cope. He was struggling physically, however, his body perhaps expressing what he wouldn't allow himself to feel. He was bleeding from his anus (all details were carefully noted). The gods, however, were still smiling, or the one in charge of cinema was at any rate. Not long after the start of the *Hoffman* standoff, Sir William Piggott-Brown commissioned him to write *A Day of Freedom* on pretty good terms: £3,000 on delivery of first draft, £2,000 on completion and £2,500 on the first day of principal photography. On the day he received his contract confirming these terms, Wednesday 26 November, as he noted moodily, he was 'still bleeding at the lav.'

62.

The 1970s

I

His Cannon Hill Lane neighbours, the Fannings, had departed, and there was a 'Sold' sign outside their house. On 29 January 1970 he noticed a couple, Alan and Denise George, looking 'sadly at the empty house.' He went out and told them that his house might be for sale. He ushered them into 257 Cannon Hill Lane and showed them around. Alan, who was something in the police, and his wife pronounced themselves delighted and said that they wanted to buy it. Yes, he said, just like that – he would sell it to them.

He was not a man given to sudden impetuous decisions, so why had he agreed to sell to the first couple who had viewed and without first having had the house valued? It was a mixture of things. It was partly what happened with *Hoffman*. He had been excluded during filming, and judging by the absence of any reference to the film in his diary since the end of shooting, he hadn't been to the cutting room either. Not being wanted had bruised him, and now he was going to pay back the director and the producer and the stars who had ignored him by showing them that he didn't want or need them either, and the way he was going to show them that was by folding his tent and quitting the country. To go now, though, was not wise. Yes, he may have felt insufficiently valued by the *Hoffman* team, but it was a movie, and when it came out it would have his name attached, and that wouldn't do him any harm. He was also doing well, and had an outstanding commission, with more surely to come. If ever there was a time not to leave, it was now, but bolting when success loomed was something he did. He had form in this department. He'd fled New York when *The Plymouth Adventure* was published and he ought to have stayed, and to leave London at this point was to repeat that pattern. Deep down in his unconscious he simply was not able to believe that he deserved or was entitled to success, a driver that had deep roots in his childhood. And that was why he always went. It was that simple.

But as he saw it, at the time, he wasn't fleeing because of something in his personality. On the contrary, he was doing something intelligent, he was acting in his self-interest, and this was indicated by his destination. He was going to Dublin, city of his young manhood, where he intended to 'see if the no tax on book earnings,' as he called the artists' tax exemption scheme, was 'true.' He also felt that it was the right time:

> *To return and see if it is possible to live* [in the] *south* [...] *and grow potatoes free of DDT & chemicals etc. and calmly write.*

One week after his agreement to sell, on Thursday 5 February he finished *A Day of Freedom*, and on the following day he noted that the Georges had already measured the house for carpets and draft contracts were underway.

Two weeks later, on Saturday 21 February, he came home after seeing *Sleuth* and decided that he was 'a lunatic to give up this house [...] which cost but £100 a year to keep' and 'was such a warm, bright, comfortable little home.' But the deal was done; he couldn't back out now.

A month later, having put the black Railton CDF 22 in storage in Coleraine, Northern Ireland, where his sister, Irene, and her husband, Jim, were living, and all the furniture from 257 Cannon Hill Lane in a depository in Wimbledon, he and Jane packed the Dormobile and drove to Swansea, where they boarded the ferry for Ireland. They arrived in Dublin early in the morning of Friday 20 March and took a room in a hotel at 52 Lansdowne Road.

Their primary need was to find somewhere to live. Halfway through April he and Jane viewed '*Cnoc Aluin*', 92 Coliemore Road, in Dalkey outside Dublin. This was, as he noted, 'A nice old house from outside, a slum inside.' On the next day, 16 April, he attended the auction at which *Cnoc Aluin* was to be sold and 'surprised self & Jane by buying … for £10,150. Now I shall have to rebuild it inside. Why do I do these things?'

He got to work straight away, knocking down walls and chipping off damp plaster. A month later, on Friday 22 May, he and Jane moved in, though the house was more building site than home. Thereafter he worked on, digging the garden, knocking rooms through, tearing down old lathes and plaster, and a week later he wondered why he had landed himself 'with endless work – once again! – in this old house, charming though it is.'

It kept him busy though – so busy that he didn't note *Hoffman*'s opening in Britain on 15 July or get down to work on a new play, *A Cry for Help*, until the start of September. On 5 October, a month later, he reported:

Nothing much of […] written yet – the usual resistance deep in the self to start, to put to test, give one's existence to something.

By the end of 1970, his mood was morose. On 1 December he wrote:

Once I seemed to know what I was doing in the world as where going. But now, no […] Sitting in the kitchen of this mouldering

299

old house in dead Dalkey – working like a labourer all day building garage, mending roof – what on earth do I think I'm doing with my life? Too long the habit of letting this one & only existence go by default. All I know now is I want to be freed […] of motorcars, of possessions – be free to come and go, travel, mingle with other people, write, write, and somehow do something for other human beings.

II

It was not just his domestic circumstances that produced his mood; it was also the place. Being back inevitably stirred memories of all those dark and mournful events of his Irish past. He'd had nothing to do with Ada really since the late 1950s, but his coming back precipitated memories of his estranged sister. He wrote, not long after settling in:

Not so far from Ada – but know will never see her again. I would always mourn her somewhat – like someone lost in the Titanic.

Being back in his city also reconnected him with old ventures, old projects, old stories. For instance, Bob Ferran (Roibeard Ó Faracháin) told him the true story of his play, *She Sits Smiling*, when the Abbey had it. The Abbey management liked it, he told my father, but:

Lennox Robinson blocked its production, saying that the Abbey already had its 'Russian' play, which was his own play, Drama at Inish, *and* She Sits Smiling *would only be produced over his dead body.*

The Abbey management's solution to this problem was to keep the play for eight years, thinking that old Lennox would 'retire any day or keel over or have to do a stretch in the John of God Hospital to dry out,' but he soldiered on. By 1949 the board realized that the case was hopeless, old Lennox would never leave or die, my father's play would never go on, and so they returned the script to him.

Although this story was more than likely untrue, my father loved it, he absolutely loved it, because it confirmed, once again, the story that he was increasingly coming to see was the story of his life: he was a man of literary talent, but at every turn he was stymied and thwarted, his progress blocked by pygmies, in this case by Lennox Robinson.

III

His diary for 1971 contained just one entry of note. On 24 April, in the Academy Cinema, which was previously the Ancient Concert Rooms where his father had played before the First World War, he saw *Hoffman*.

> *The film has been recut by studio and lengthened to nearly 2 hours. Quite passable now – not even Rakoff could kill it. Peter fair. Sinead very hammy & amateur – obviously received no help from 'director'.*

Over the year that followed he finished *A Cry for Help*, and he rewrote *Why Aren't You Famous?* as a musical with Irish songs for production in Germany in German during the 1974 Munich Olympics. At the year's end he offered a bleak summary:

> *End of a wasteful year – wasted on repairing this home out of sheer habit. Wrote two plays only – and one of those a rewrite which for me, with my manic facility, is disgraceful. More and more I feel like a man locked in a room miles from anywhere.*

His 1972 diary was emptier and sparser still. On the title page he wrote:

> *17 Nov 1965* [the day he made us write letters saying where we wished to live] *Carlo & Sasha elected to go and live wholly with*

*Edna wherewith their visits to me dwindled to an hour or less a
week with a taxi booked to call for them. So I told them to go to
hell around 1969 and returned to Ireland 1970.*

Thereafter, other than brief references to the weather, his health and
what he was doing to the house, he made only three meaningful entries
during the rest of 1972. The first, on 14 June, described the depression
he felt on account of his self-absorption, which was so overwhelming
that he sometimes found it impossible to talk to Jane. The second, on
23 June, concerned Ada, who had died the day before in the Richmond
Hospital following an operation to remove a growth, after which her
heart had collapsed:

*So after a life of petty hatreds she dies aged 60 of misadventure, like
being run over on the roads. I have not seen her since just before she
hounded her father out of Dublin. A life unrealized in every way.
I remember her when young as a selfish, vain girl. My mother said,
'Her jealousy will be her downfall.'*

And the third, on 9 July, concerned Jane and her inherited traits.
Her father, he opined, was, 'small, given to airs, pettish & partly
homosexual – unknown to himself,' and therefore wholly ineffective
as a man, while her mother, to whom Jane's father failed to stand up
of course because of his supposed sexual orientation, was 'a bully,
a niggling fault-finder & righteous nag.' These characteristics came
doubly to Jane: she inherited them and she learned them as a child
'when modelling herself on her mother,' with the result that she was
now an adult who marred married life with her 'bitter, indeed petty
fault-finding and complaints.' They discussed this many times, he
said, yet very often Jane fell back into those patterns established in her
early life, and he saw little chance of improvement 'because people
revert more as they grow older – as if giving up, failing to be what
they tried to be.'

And then silence. Nothing. Not another word. Something had stopped.

IV

When I cleared *Cnoc Aluin* I found no desk dairies for the years 1973, 1974, 1975 and 1976. I don't know if he kept any. If he had they would make melancholy reading, for as described on scraps scattered through his papers (and which were substitutes perhaps for his diaries), these years were one long round of reversals and defeats and mortal warnings.

He had always had very good teeth, and always took care of them, but despite a lifetime's careful husbandry his teeth now began to go. Fillings crumbled. Abscesses flared. Tooth pain became a constant. His bite on life was going, literally. He took action, of course. He was at the dentist all the time, nearly every month, sometimes more. But as fast as he got one tooth fixed, another required repair. It was never-ending.

Where his teeth were leading, his body was following. His legs were unsteady. They were no longer up to snuff. He tottered, he tumbled, spraining wrists and turning ankles in the process. His bones ached. He had arthritis everywhere, but especially in his back. He self-diagnosed ankylosing spondylitis (an inflammatory arthritis of the spine, characterized by inflammation and ossification of the intervertebral discs and ligaments), and noted grimly that he had inherited 'poker back' as it was popularly known from his mother, who was also a sufferer. It couldn't be cured, it could only be managed, and he did endless exercises to maintain suppleness and mobility, but it was a losing battle. He was calcifying up.

Pollen was an ancient adversary of his, and his annual bouts of hay fever, now referred to as his 'June purgatory', with its awful symptoms, all of which he noted – streaming eyes, running nose, itching throat and a general debilitating sense of being uncomfortable in his skin – continued as before. However, during the mid 1970s, these symptoms began to occur out of the pollen season, and worse, in addition to the symptoms familiar from hay fever, new allergic reactions began to afflict him, His chest roared, his organs creaked, and his skin became inflamed. These rashes were all over his body, but the particularly affected parts were his tongue, the insides of his cheeks, behind his eyelids, and around his foreskin, the last being the worst, endlessly flaring up and weeping, and no amount of medication and attention would make these skin eruptions go away. Clearly, pollen had been joined by a new line of irritants. He kept a close record of symptoms, diet and lifestyle, and discovered that besides pollen he was now allergic to milk, eggs, shop bread, a wide range of ascorbic and green vegetables, Dublin mains water, tea (of which he drank an immense amount), all sugars, alcohol, cigarette smoke, aspirin, petrol, an array of household cleaning agents and fluids, paints and sunshine.

And the problems with his auto-immune system didn't end there. It wasn't only overactive, it was also compromised. It didn't work properly any more. The gashes, cuts and bruises he inevitably sustained as he worked on the house or fell because his legs were no longer reliable wouldn't heal like they had when he was younger. They lingered and they worsened, sometimes becoming septic.

He had always believed in the adage 'You are what you eat' – indeed, he wrote this phrase many times on bits of paper during this period – and in order to help himself he overhauled his diet. He grew organic vegetables, he sourced organic foods, he switched to hormone-free meat, he drank distilled water. All these dietary practices helped, but he was fighting a war that it was not possible to win. His body was out of kilter. The clockwork mechanism was running down.

His apprehension of decline depressed him, and this in turn led to him becoming ever more testy and irritable, and correspondingly much less able and inclined to tolerate and accommodate other people and their ways. He resented his neighbours' noisy children and barking dogs, and he did not keep his opinions to himself. He let them show. He feuded over party walls and boundaries and trees. He became a serial complainer, usually by letter. He also developed an unhealthy obsession with the night-time antics of raucous, belligerent and incontinent revellers from the nearby Dalkey Island Hotel when they made their way home past *Cnoc Aluin* at night. Now they were noisy, it was true, and as they passed they would always shout and sing, which disturbed him and Jane. They also sometimes liked to pop into his garden and use it as a toilet. He made detailed notes worthy of a policeman, and he joined with other residents of Coliemore Road, who took the hotel's licensee to court to try to get the hotel's opening hours restricted. It was an ugly, protracted, frustrating business, and though changes were ordered, the nuisance caused by the hotel's patrons never entirely went away, and his nights went on being blighted, albeit only occasionally now, by their misbehaviour. As with his teeth and his body and his house, here was yet one more example of the awful truth. It was all downhill everywhere. The speed of descent could be slowed, but it could never be stopped.

Of course, writing, had he had this outlet, would have helped, if only because it would have provided him with something other than his problems to focus on, and as result he might have been that bit less intolerant and obsessive and that bit more open and outward looking. But he didn't have this outlet. He wasn't writing at anything like the pace he'd been writing at just before he left London. He did a bit of work on a stage version of *Call Me Daddy*, and the play was produced at the Project Arts Centre in Dublin in 1974. He got *A Cry for Help* finished, and it was produced on the Peacock Stage at The Abbey Theatre in 1975. He did a few reviews as well, but otherwise all his time and energy was devoted to those practices and activities that had always absorbed him. He observed his health and made detailed notes, he refined his diet in the hope of curing himself of everything, and he worked on *Cnoc Aluin*, the repair and renovation of which was an enormous, gigantic, colossal, back-breaking, debilitating, and worst of all, unending job. No sooner was one problem solved than another appeared. And then, as if *Cnoc Aluin* weren't enough, and it still wasn't finished, on 26 April 1977 he bought at auction 5 Leslie Avenue, Dalkey, a cottage in need of renovation, for £16,250 as an investment, and at a stroke he doubled his workload. It need not of course have been like that; the unending programme of building works he was snarled up in was his own doing. Had he got builders in to help and not insisted on doing the work himself he might have got his properties finished, as far as properties can ever be said to be finished. But he wouldn't. He couldn't. One, he was constitutionally unable to pay anyone else to help him; he had to be completely self-sufficient. That *idée fixe* had been established in childhood and couldn't be changed. Two, the endless labouring allowed him to withdraw from social interaction and avoid the difficult practice of writing. Jane, who had found work as a teacher at a small, private, non-denominational, co-educational school, Sandford Park, was concerned, particularly by his literary inactivity. She regularly reminded him that he was one of the best writers around who wasn't writing. But her cajoling and her joshing didn't work. He went on repairing and renovating and gardening and fretting about his health. Something else would have to bring him to the typewriter.

V

Sometime in the later summer of 1976 he bumped into Micheál Mac Liammóir. 'I'm finished, Ernie,' the old actor murmured. He was so shocked by this that on 28 September he wrote Mac Liammóir a thank-you letter.

> *I, and my generation, owe you and Hilton a debt. Nothing can pay it off.* [...] *For you and Hilton fed our imaginations in the theatre in very dark days. Whether by accident or design is immaterial: you were there, and we were and are better for it.*
>
> *And something else – when I think of you (and you'd be surprised how often that is in this familiar Dublin of my young manhood), it is of you at your best* [...] *I am fond of you, Micheál, and the Micheál that goes a long way back.*

Mac Liammóir replied on 19 October 1976. He was happy to have had the letter, though he thought my father had perhaps exaggerated his and Hilton's achievement. It was a good reply, genuinely grateful, gently self-mocking, a little rueful and above all graceful.

Maureen Cusack, whom of course he'd met at the Gate, died just before Christmas 1977, and the following year, on 6 March 1978, Mac Liammóir died. So much of his early manhood was bound up with the Gate, and now these figures he identified with the theatre were gone. He began to ponder. There was a message here, a warning. He had entered his final act. All he had to look forward to were the funerals of all those people who were once so important to him. Then his own funeral would happen. He didn't like this – not any of it. It chastened him. It frightened him. But it also made him realize that once you were gone, you were gone. That was it. You couldn't do anything when you were under the sod. But he was not gone, not yet. He was still above the sod. In which case, in the time remaining, he must just do it. He must seize the day. He must get writing.

VI

In the weeks after Mac Liammóir's death, my father's plans began to take shape. In his mind, plans evolved for four books: one, an autobiography, *Grateful for Life* (so titled because, as he noted, 'I am increasingly and always have been'), which, he and Jane agreed, owing to the research that would be required and the secretarial support that would be necessary, they would write together and which, between themselves, because it was shorter, they called the Autobiog; two, a self-help text, *The ABC Handbook of Allergy*; three, an exposition of his philosophy, *The World Explained*; and four, a novel, eventually called *Not The End Of The World*. He had actually first begun to think about this novel in 1974, and since the material had had plenty of time to ferment in his imagination over the intervening years, he knew that was what he must write first. So he went to the typewriter and wrote a plot outline:

It is 1946. Unhappily married Annie Hythe lives in a grimy mill town south of York with her children and cold-hearted husband, John. While

John works away in Liverpool (he's an engineer), she has a part-time job as a waitress in a York tea shop. One day in York she meets Christian Pettarde, a student who is in the city doing six months of training at a stained-glass factory. They become first friends and then lovers. Annie gets pregnant. Christian, unaware of this, returns to London, and Annie has the baby, Grace, which husband John assumes is his.

Leap forward twenty years. It is 1966. Annie is terminally ill. She writes a letter to Grace explaining that her father is actually a London stained-glass artist, Christian Pettarde, and gives this to her friend Betty to pass on after her death. Immediately after the funeral Betty gives Grace the letter. Grace is not entirely surprised by its contents. She has always intuited that there was something different about her – she wasn't from the same stock as her siblings, she wasn't her father's daughter.

Grace decides that she will find her father and introduce herself to him as his daughter. She goes to London and tracks him down. It's easy to find a stained-glass artist called Pettarde. However, having made contact and discovering that he is unhappily married to frumpy Margery and has children, and also that she desires him romantically and sexually, Grace decides not tell him that she is his daughter and to pretend instead that she is an art student looking for work. Christian, who is instantly attracted to Grace and assumes that she is what she says, is happy to help. He sees a potential girlfriend, and she, obviously, given what she wants, is happy to be seen as such.

For Grace, of course, there is no incest taboo. Though Christian might be her biological father, he has never actually been a father to her, so why should she treat him as one, she thinks. At the same time, Grace has her cake as well as eating it, so to speak – she believes that the reason they *must* be intimate is precisely because she is 'such a part of him.' As for the truth coming out, she assumes that if it ever did it wouldn't matter to him. Indeed, as an unhappily married broad-minded chap who drinks too much, Christian not only would not mind her deception, but in fact would be grateful. After all, sex is sex, and it is what men like. And so they become lovers.

Meanwhile, Grace's elder sister, Addie, full name Adelaide, a character clearly modelled on my father's despised elder sister, having had sight of her dead mother's letter to Grace, and so knowing the truth about Grace's paternity, comes to London, tracks Grace down and makes a proposition.

She and Grace will tell Christian that he has been having sexual relations with his daughter, which carries a mandatory four-year sentence, and that they will shop him to the police unless he pays them off. Grace is appalled by this scheme. She loves Christian. She tries but fails to kill her sister, and then, knowing that she cannot stay in London near Christian, she returns north to York to work as a housekeeper for George Thompson, an L. S. Lowry-like outsider artist who only paints scenes from working-class life. Grace has known George since childhood. Indeed, he has been the real father that her biological father, John, never was, and for that reason, unlike with Christian, there's no question of a sexual relationship. With George, the incest taboo is in operation. The novel ends with Grace in George's squalid terraced house, happy and content with her new lot as the helpmate and handmaiden of his talent.

By 1 May, despite an inflamed bronchial tube, anal bleeding, pain in his upper right incisor, hay fever, a worrisome slowing pulse, heat flushes, various rashes, a weeping foreskin and an angina-like pain in the left breast now and then, he was '3/4 through detailed synopsis' of *Not The End Of The World*, and sometime during the summer that followed he got it done. Now all he had to do was write it.

VII

On 1 January 1979, my father wrote in his new Boots Desk Diary:

Sixty-four today. See Beatles' song. In twenties, after a year of 1st [allergic] attacks thought would do well to see 47. Think now, despite clown legs going bad, will do well to see 87. Great desire to complete 'Not the End' & 'The World Explained' & autobiography.

On 5 March he conceded that this novel was a grind to write, especially as he was heavy with allergies, which made him weary. By 23 May he had 35,500 words written, and had reached the point at which Grace, having come to London, met Christian. The pace was now bound to increase, he thought, but he was wrong. Rather than getting easier, the writing got harder. In an uncharacteristically extended entry on 10 June he analysed why he found it so hard to write. It really didn't have anything to do with his allergies; that was just his excuse. It was to do with him and his:

> *Unconscious fear of failure* [...] *For how could it be otherwise? No schooling whatsoever, no proving of self when young, no reassurance from anyone, at any time, of an ability to do anything – but plenty of arrows from Ada and her like that Ernie was stupid, unable to do anything.*

At the end of the entry he wrote that he 'did not mean this note to develop into this,' but there it was, it had.

> *And the fact remains that my difficulty about sitting down to write has to do with family background, that lack of encouragement ever, to do anything. So it's about time I recognize it and climb over it once and for all.*

But he never did climb over it. On the contrary, he clung steadfastly to the belief that all he had done he had done *despite* the discouragement offered by his family, and as time passed the incredible resentment and rage he felt because of what he believed about his early life, which was inaccurate, as it happened, got bigger and deeper, stronger and darker.

63.

The Early 1980s

I

On 1 January 1980 he looked over the 45,500 words of *Not The End Of The World* he had written, realized 'what a good story it was,' and got back to work. On 20 April 1980 he began to experience severe pain ascending through the bladder and into his abdomen, colon, and small intestine. 'To pee was like fire and agony. The intestines like iron. Went into shock, losing life in fingers after tingling in tips.' The symptoms persisted, and his weight dropped from eleven stone (his weight for about forty years) to ten stone three pounds. A kidney stone was suspected. On 28 April he was taken by ambulance to St Vincent's Hospital. Dye was injected and X-rays taken, but no stone was found. He went home in a taxi. He was still in pain, and he stayed in pain. By mid May he was down to nine stone six pounds.

He went back to *Not The End Of The World*, but wrote little. His younger sister, Louise, died on 24 June. Peter Sellers died in London on 23 July. He was nine stone now. He was practising the

Coué method in the hope of reversing his decline.[18] It didn't work. He wrote on 2 September:

> *What a purgatory of a life, to have enough to eat in a starving world & to be poisoned, as it were, by food. Which is what auto-immune disease in the form of combined ankylosing spondylitis & extreme food allergy bring about.*

He started Nalcrom (sodium cromoglycate), a type of medicine used to relieve the symptoms of allergies, and felt better, stilled. His mood rose and stayed elevated, for at the year's end on 17 December he ventured that:

> *Jane is a great success as head of the Preps* [sic] *School in Sandford Park* [...] *which is good for Jane & has given her considerable confidence. She is quite happy mostly. (And very loving to me.) We've been together now coming on seventeen years.*

He was grateful, but also, lurking at the back of his mind, guilty. He felt that he didn't deserve her.

His feelings lasted. On 4 December 1981, a whole year later, he wrote another paean in praise of Jane. She grew Golden Wonder potatoes for him, and speciality Jerusalem Artichokes, garden peas, carrots, shallots and parsley – his staple diet. This was love, he was sure of it. Yes, she was waspish (no woman was ever perfect), but she was a 'sterling character' who was also 'an attractive woman.' He ended, 'One is very lucky to love someone. I am.' It was always around Christmas he wrote such things. Perhaps something of the season stirred him despite himself.

---

18 A self-hypnosis programme devised by Émile Coué that seeks to effect improvement by the endless repetition of a mantra-like conscious autosuggestion. Coué's was 'Every day, in every way, I'm getting better and better,' and this was probably what my father was reciting also.

And the warmth lingered to the far side of Christmas. On New Year's Day 1982 he wrote:

Birthday – 67 years old. As a child there was always a cake with 'Coffee icing' and walnuts – standard for any birthday. [...] Mammy always rose to the occasion, somehow or other.

Nowhere else in his considerable papers did he write as positively about his mother as he did here.

II

Over Christmas, his sister, Irene, who now lived in New Zealand, was in touch to say that she had been contacted by Mary Watson, who coincidentally now also lived in that country, and that she wanted to be get back in touch with my father. But as one figure from his history reappeared, another slipped away. On 26 January 1982, a nun from the Maypark Nursing Home in Tramore, County Waterford, rang to tell him that his father's brother, his uncle Hermann, had died. His entry in his diary was terse:

If father was alive he'd be 92 so Hermann must be 96 or so today. That would seem to be the last of father's brothers and sisters.

Yes, he was right, he was the last sibling, and also the last living link to Adolf's life in middle Europe before the Great War, as well as the period when the family lived in Tramore in the 1920s. Hermann was a witness he could ill afford to lose for the autobiography, which he was thinking about even if he had not yet got to it. And perhaps it was because of Hermann's death that he now got in contact, despite the complicated feelings he aroused, with Rudy Jones, with whom relations had been restored (he and Jane had spent Christmas with the Joneses a few years earlier, after all), and to whom he now wrote, as he put it, 'just to ask dates.'

Rudy was delighted (after all, their muddled history went back over forty years), and he phoned. What about meeting? he said, but somehow my father 'evaded meeting him,' which was curious because that would surely have been a better way than correspondence to get the information he needed. It would also have been human contact at a time when he was feeling, as he confessed in his diary, very solitary, isolated, and 'like a shipwrecked survivor.' But then his and Rudy's history was a complex one, and there were things he hadn't forgotten, which was why he demurred.

> [Rudy] *decried* [The Plymouth Adventure] *when it was ½ done –
> said it wd* [sic] *have to be 'recast', too boring, dull.* [...] *Knowing what
> a huckster he was I said 'rubbish' politely.* [...] *he was very jealous and
> backbiting after* [...] *publication.* [And yes, Rudy] *told the O'Brien
> family when Edna and self went to Isle of Man. He doesn't know I'm
> aware of that.*

He needed Rudy, but hadn't actually forgiven him – a difficult combination. But Rudy didn't know any of this; he just thought that things were back to what they should be, which was why, on 19 June, Rudy rang my father to tell him that his youngest son, Will, whom my father remembered as a five-year-old in the cottage in the Wicklow mountains, recently married and the father of a small child, had died the day before of a heart attack, aged forty-two. My father's diary note, even by his standards, was laconic to the point of being brutal: 'Rudy sounded as if he was acting the part. Funeral? R said, "As you are part of the family you [thought] shd [sic] know." Nasty lad. Send note Bunny?'

On 10 September, Sheila Iremonger, wife of Valentin, the poet diplomat who had discovered my father had been blacklisted as a communist in the US (or so my father believed), telephoned and asked if she could call out to *Cnoc Aluin*. She arrived, 'still fat and full of chat,' but without her husband.

> *Sheila said, when I asked that Val had had an accident [...] fell in the [...] bathroom and struck his head which resulted [...] in brain damage – operation on the brain, etc And apparently has not recovered.*

As Val's mother was 'a bit odd', and his father 'some kind of invalid', my father wondered if the problem with his erstwhile friend wasn't actually congenital.

III

On 19 November 1982, Hilton Edwards died. This was both good and bad. On the plus side, now that both of the founders of the Gate were gone he felt released and free. He could say what he liked with impunity, and out the words tumbled, sharp and sly, caustic and critical:

> *Hilton would have been a success in any profession that provided a complete set of guidelines* [that he could follow, such as] *the law, banking, carpentry, et cetera. He had little originality, intelligence or intuition,* [but] *he was a great learner, he possessed incredible stamina, he had patience and memory. Hilton learnt* [early how] *to be seemingly intelligent. As an actor he rather quickly bored you with his bag of tricks – as did Micheál to almost the same degree.*
>
> *As Micheál progressed into middle age his mannerisms on stage and off sometimes curled your hair. Micheál had some originality and some innate intelligence and would have developed* [much further] *had he 'not', as someone must have said, been born with*

his balls twisted. Behind Micheál's soft smiling mask there was a heartless villain, a natural born exploiter of other people – Hilton was his chosen handyman. Micheál was a totally self indulgent creature. That said, they gave Dublin its first permanent European theatre. If I describe them as they were, it is not to devalue what they gave Dublin. Though it's fair to remember that they came to be somewhat handsomely paid for their cultural service to Dublin.

On the other side, however, whatever his personal opinion, the deaths of Micheál Mac Liammóir and Hilton Edwards before he'd had the couple of hours in their company reminiscing while he had the tape recorder running was yet another blow to the Autobiog. The tide was turning. One after another, his witnesses were crossing the bar. This realization was chastening, sobering, and it made him face it. He had avoided this meeting, but could not postpone it any longer. He had to meet the most important living source for his Autobiog, so he phoned Rudy and suggested that they meet in a pub, most likely in the Dalkey Island Hotel.

Rudy, he noticed with grim satisfaction as they settled into their seats with their beverages in hand (Rudy's alcoholic, his not), had changed for the worse. He was heavy, he was bloated and he was in pain. When my father asked about the cause of this, Rudy explained that he had been troubled by a grumbling appendix for years, and finally, when he was about seventy years old, he was obliged to submit himself to the knife. The operation was 'botched', that was the word he used, and that was the word my father wrote down with relish, *botched*, and it had left Rudy with a permanent and inoperable hernia. Despite this, he was still at work, still trying to write: he was, after all, 'one of life's natural grafters' and an indefatigable scribbler. He had a novel, Rudy said, but he couldn't get the plot right. My father indicated that he was no Freddie MacDonald, Rudy's friend of the 1940s who helped him with *The Moccasin Men* and his other thrillers, and therefore no, he didn't want to help with the plot of this book.

Rudy persisted. Why wouldn't his writer friend of forty years and more give him a hand with the plot of a book he was trying to write when, after all, he had done the same for my father?

All right, said my father, post me an outline and I'll think about it.

No, no, Rudy said, he didn't want to write something out and post it to my father for him to deliberate on and pass judgement on and send back to him with scribbles in red biro all over it. No; he, Rudy, was not an apprentice. He was a writer, a proper writer, and had written a lot and published many books (more than Ernest Gébler, as it happened). What Rudy wanted was to talk it through, now, writer to writer, peer to peer, equal to equal.

My father countered. He suspected, he said, that Rudy had no plot worked out, and that was why he didn't want to write a treatment and post it to him. He was on a roll now, and there was no holding him back. He told Rudy that his head was empty. He told Rudy that he knew exactly what his game was. Rudy thought, he said, that by talking and endlessly mulling over his 'ideas', the plot of the book would come to him without his having to do any work. Well, my father said, he had news for him. It wouldn't work, and my father wasn't up for it. He wasn't going to help him with his tired old book. Of course my father was on the same jag, he was looking for dates and reminiscences for the Autobiog, although in the heat of the moment he had predictably forgotten what he wanted and the reason why he was there. So, he concluded, if Rudy really wanted help then he would have to type it out, whatever it was, whatever he had, and then he would have to post it to him. Of course, a policy of mutual cooperation would have been the better plan, but my father never thought to suggest that.

IV

One might think that that would have been the end of the matter, but it wasn't. These old friend-enemies went on talking and wrangling on the phone for the next few weeks, possibly months. But inevitably (and

317

how could it not, given their history?), it ended in rupture. There are two different accounts of this.

One:

Rudy rang my father and suggested a drink. My father declined. He claimed that his physical condition made it impossible for him to enter any pub. Pubs made him sick. It was the cigarette smoke. He was allergic to it. Rudy mentioned the recent death of his son, Will. That's why he wanted to meet. He was sad, and craved consolation. Didn't my father get that? Yes, my father said, and yes, he was still saying no. Rudy denounced my father as an ingrate, and he rebuked him for letting an old friend down and not reaching out the hand of friendship when he most needed it. Rudy also threatened to hang up. He didn't, but the conversation ended so sourly that the two men never spoke again.

Two:

Rudy again asked for help with the plot of the novel he was failing to write, and my father took this opportunity to tell Rudy one or two home truths.

He reminded Rudy of the time in 1948 when he returned to Dublin with the first half of *The Plymouth Adventure* and Rudy read it and they met on the steps of the Mansion House, where Rudy told him that it dragged and would have to be rewritten, and that they would do a job on it together. He was shaken by this, he said to Rudy, badly shaken, but he went back to London and wrote the second half of the novel exactly as he had always planned. He hadn't changed a single thing in the light of Rudy's strictures, and then *The Plymouth Adventure* was published and sold four million copies.

The inference of my father's speech was that he didn't follow Rudy's advice and so his book was a success, but had he followed Rudy's advice he wouldn't have sold the number of books he did. In other words, Rudy could have destroyed him. Finally, he told Rudy that he never wanted to hear from him ever again and banged the phone down.

In the silence that followed he brooded on the Isle of Man incident: he wondered why Rudy did it. 'The *Mayflower* – was it more than he could stomach? I've never told him that I knew what he did. What point? I haven't.'

My father never did get any dates or memories out of Rudy. They never spoke again.

V

Early in January 1983, following his birthday on New Year's Day, he wrote: 'Being 68 has immense compensations – the future no longer uncertain, the past rich with people, places, disasters to be turned into literature.'

The Autobiog was in his sights, but first he had to finish *Not The End Of The World*. The old impediments obstructing composition – his health, his hypochondria and his insatiable appetite for fixing and mending – were still as strong as ever, but now there was a new problem: him and Jane. Their schedules had never synchronized. He had always liked to work at night and to sleep in the morning. Jane had always slept at night and gone to work in the morning. However, early in 1983, not long after he had written in praise of being sixty-eight, Jane moved out of their bedroom, which overlooked the back garden, and into a front bedroom with a view of the sea. Her pretext was that he woke her coming to bed late – and it was true, he did – but her departure was also a symptom (which he missed, naturally). She had become, over the preceding years (which he missed again, naturally), lonely and unhappy and homesick. My father, *Cnoc Aluin*, the marriage, Ireland, Dalkey, the job, everything comprising her life – none of it was working for her any more.

Over the months following her move from their bedroom to a room of her own, without him noticing what was happening until it had happened, all meaningful contact and even conversation stopped as Jane withdrew into a life that was actually just like the life they had always led, one of parallel schedules, only more so. It went like this:

On weekdays he was asleep when she left for school about 7.40 a.m. When she came back from work he was in his study. She might garden or she might sit in the kitchen listening to the radio through headphones while doing the crossword in *The Irish Times*. She ate early and alone, and watched television when she did. She put his meal out at about 9.00 p.m., and at 9.30 p.m. she went to bed, where she read and listened to the radio. She put her light out at about 10.30 p.m. At weekends and during school holidays, though she was at home, the schedule, with its lack of significant contact, remained unchanged. The diaries give no indication of the history of the drift apart and the gradual incremental hardening of their separate schedules, but certainly by 1 May 1983 things had got so bad that he had noticed, and was moved to write: 'Sometimes I am very, very lonely in the world.'

VI

Within six months, estrangement and a disinclination to communicate had hardened into outright hostility – her to him, anyway – at least that is how he has it in the entry he made on 26 January 1984. Jane, he wrote, pitifully thin (hers was a 'Belsen body'), haggard, short-tempered and impatient with him, now hated everything – the house, the city of Dublin, the country of Ireland. How or why this might be was not something he cared to think about. His preoccupations, as usual, were personal. He was still struggling to finish *Not The End Of The World*, still plagued by his irregular heartbeat, and now a new health problem was looming. For the first time ever he had to fight depression, which he put down to not having the 'time or opportunity to see anyone other than Jane from week to week.'

Up to this point their war had mainly been conducted in sullen silence. This now changed, and they started to row. On 13 March, during one of their arguments, Jane told him that she 'hated every minute' she had spent in *Cnoc Aluin*. This baffled him, and the next day he noted: 'Most people think it is a beautiful home in a pleasant

situation (Killiney Hill around the corner). You don't "hate" a house.'
He then wondered if what she really meant was that she was unhappy
because of him. But in the next sentence he dropped this revolutionary
idea and reverted to his more usual explanation – it was all down to
maternal indoctrination and a compulsion to lie:

> *As has been mentioned before, her mother was, as mine was, a*
> *bully through agitation. Perhaps Jane's emotions (towards the other*
> *sex) were somewhat maimed in childhood. [...] She has invented*
> *lately a myth about my bad temper. Well, if it helps her rationalize*
> *something – Every cripple creeps his own way.*

VII

Mary Watson, his first love, returned from New Zealand, where she was
living, to Ireland for a holiday, and came out to Dalkey to visit him. He
got her story.

She went to England at the same time as he went to London with
Sally Travers. After being in England for a year or two she got a job
as a doctor's receptionist. Her doctor employer was a New Zealander:
bookish, dictatorial, unattractive, and twice as old as she was. They
married. There were no children. He retired and returned to New
Zealand, taking her with him. Years passed, and he died. A widow
with no children, she was now free. She had taken to travelling, which
was why she was in Dublin, and found herself sitting in *Cnoc Aluin*,
drinking tea and looking out the window at this garden.

My father was bored by Mary. He couldn't stand the way she held
her teacup with her little finger extended. He thought her 'rigid, with
stupid gentility and ignorant of most subjects,' as well as possessed of
'a sort of dread of saying the wrong thing.' He decided that she had
an inferiority complex, and was puzzled that he had never noticed this
before. When they were young he had thought that their relationship
was easy, natural, but now they were getting on in years, it was

fraught, at least on his side. Mercifully, he kept his feelings hidden, or perhaps she didn't notice if he did let them show, because when she came back to Ireland for a second visit she yet again made the pilgrimage to *Cnoc Aluin* to see my father. About this second visit he was even more scathing, describing her as 'Deadening, boring [...] blinkered [...] uptight and limited.' But the most surprising part of their reconnection so late in life was that when Mary died (in New Zealand) she left him several thousand pounds. Why? Did this mean that she didn't see what others saw, his difficult, awkward, truculent nature? Or did she see something others never saw, something good and wholesome and even golden? It was a mystery, but for some reason she wanted to leave him money, and she did.

64.

A Rupture

I

By August 1984 my father's marital life had become blacker still, more rancorous and more acrimonious. He and Jane had passed through the rowing stage and were now not speaking at all unless they absolutely had to. He believed that she absolutely hated him. He cast around for an explanation, and on 22 September he found it:

> Jane is all too obviously passing through or entering on the menopause – 47 to 57 is usual […] She gets agitated about trifles, her face flushes, [she is] short-tempered, can't bear anything being explained to her – looks at me with a kind of hatred if I do.

A new source of friction between them was the novel he was writing, *Not The End Of The World*, to which Jane's reaction was 'antagonistic'. It did not occur to my father that at least he should try to uncover why her reaction was so negative. No, this was beyond him. All he could think about was getting it finished. And on 2 February 1985 the glad moment finally came, which he noted in his increasingly strange syntax:

> *Just finished last page corrections of* Not The End Of The World. *Final last 16 pages will take to Eliza* [the typist] *tomorrow, Sunday.*

The finished typed up MS came back a few days later. Jane read it. She had already expressed her opposition to this book over the course of the composition period, but now she had a full text she was able to offer a complete and unequivocal judgement. She absolutely hated the book. It was the character of Grace and what Grace did that was the problem. Grace looked like her, talked like her, dressed like her, thought like her. That was obvious. Grace, indeed, was her. But she was not Grace. Unlike Grace, she had never slept with her father, wanted to sleep with her father or been his mistress. But what did it say that she was the model for a character in a novel who did do this? She was greatly troubled. Was that what my father thought she wanted? Was that how he saw her? When they argued about it my father used the usual novelist's defence that novelists trot out when their models cavil at the use to which they've been put in works of fiction. Writers are cannibals, he said. They take elements from people and use those in their fiction, but no judgement is implied, and no criticism should be inferred. That he would use her in his novel as the basis of a character with incestuous tendencies did not mean that he thought Jane harboured undisclosed incestuous feelings for her father; she was just a human source that he had plundered. Jane didn't agree, couldn't agree. It might be a novel, it might be all made up, but she knew that anyone who knew her would recognize her on the page if they read it, and from that they would jump to the obvious conclusion: deep down in the kernel of her being she had incestuous tendencies and had always wanted or perhaps actually had slept with her father. The idea that anyone would think that hurt, disgusted and appalled her, but what was worse to her way of thinking was that he had stuck her into his book in the way in which he had without thinking it through, without considering the misery and distress it would cause her. And why had he done that? Well, obviously he didn't love her, did he? As far as he was concerned she was just a resource to be used. It was devastating to discover this, but now she knew the truth she was not going to be taken advantage of any more. Oh no, he could forget any idea that she was going to help him with his Autobiog. The agreement they had was now voided. Of course it was. His novel had violated her, and henceforward she wanted nothing to do with his writing or his wider literary life.

It was winter when this disagreement erupted and they were trapped inside *Cnoc Aluin* and unable to escape each other. The atmosphere in the house now got weirder and fiercer. Jane spent all her time when she wasn't in bed or at work in the kitchen with the headphones on doing crosswords. He wasn't encouraged to enter her space, and he stayed out of her way and said little. As he wrote on 17 February: 'Have to be careful what I say, because for her now small things become large and a frown of blame comes on her face.'

II

By late February 1985 he noted that the MS of *Not The End Of The World*, though not totally to his satisfaction, was certainly ready to be shown to the world. It took him most of the following month to get the photocopies made – he was slowing up and finding it harder and harder to plan and then execute his decisions, there was no doubt about it – and on 28 March he posted one copy to Christine Green, a London agent who represented many Irish writers including Maeve Binchy, and who he hoped would represent him, and another to Doubleday, his US publisher who had published *The Plymouth Adventure* and *Shall I Eat You Now?*

On 9 April the Doubleday-bound parcel was returned to him by the Dublin postal sorting office, its packaging torn, its contents battered. His book had 'Never Got Out Of Dublin,' but he got no sympathy from Jane, who was still seething with 'quiet hatred about writing a book about romantic incest.'

325

He got the manuscript off to Doubleday for the second time on 1 May, and by 8 July he had rejection letters from both agent and publisher, 'much to my relief,' he noted, though the defiance seems forced rather than credible.

On 23 July his favourite sibling, Irene, died, and a gloomy lassitude took hold. On 12 August he reported of his novel: 'Have not sent it elsewhere yet.' On the same day but in a different diary (one that I suspect he hid so Jane could not read it) he wrote: 'J indulging her so called menopause has taken to secret drinking in bed at night.'

Four weeks later on 12 September he wrote that Jane 'went back devotedly to Sandford Park School today rather than help me write Auto.' He had long resented her preferring school to home, and her children to him, but that resentment was now mixed up with another deeper grudge against her for having reneged on the plan to do the Autobiog together. As he saw it, she had made an undertaking. She had promised to help, and she couldn't derogate from that; it was simply not allowed. That he had traduced her in *Not The End Of The World* was nothing to do with anything. When you made a promise you kept it, and when you broke a promise, just as she had, then you became a betrayer to whom the normal protocols no longer applied, the right to privacy, for instance. He now began, regularly, to read Jane's day books, in which she wrote down what had happened to her and what she was thinking. On 22 September he wrote this assessment about what he'd been reading:

> *I thought her continual fault finding in her Day Book (but never aloud to me) was 'the change'. Not so. The repeated references to me – Ernie in bad temper – Ernie morose and complaining – or bitter – or whatever – I now understand they are to offset, for herself, her reneging on the agreement to be at home & help me with the huge task of the Autobiog.* Not The End *lies on the sideboard upstairs, bound* [and] *ready for a publisher for the past six months. She disliked the subject & had never spoken again about it since it was finished and she read it. Every day she sees*

it lying there (the best novel I have ever written) [...] *but never says 'Why?' or 'When?'*

Eight days later, on 30 September, he was particularly incensed. Jane was still 'doing her self-justificatory mad notes in the day book diary,' whilst simultaneously she had the effrontery actually to say to him: 'Where is your old self – you used to be such a laughing person?'

It was his opinion that publicly she loved to present herself as friendly, while privately, in her day books, which he had now decided she must know he was reading, and indeed wanted him to read because that gave her a way to hurt him, she showed her true self with her repeated savaging of him by means of her '"secret" bits of nastiness.' He actually wanted her to write about him in a different way – and gave examples. For instance, 'Ernie, at 70, is having painful attacks of spasm, rheumatic spasm in back, shoulder blades & chest' was a sentence, he said, that he would have been happy to read. But of course there was nothing of this kind in her day books. Instead, all he found in them were endless reiterations of her unhappiness, repeated denunciations of his 'quarrelsome', 'petty', 'nagging' nature, and numerous assertions of her desire 'to go and live in Spain or France with her sister Mavis.' To cheer himself up he offered himself this idea at the end of the entry for 30 September: 'People are not what they say but what they do.' Whatever Jane said about what she wanted to do, she was still in *Cnoc Aluin*, and they were still together.

Two weeks later, on 14 October, he had, he noted, a hard day 'cementing the kitchen chimney leak,' which involved him standing at the top of a ladder for three hours for the sixth day in a row. His shoulders ached at the day's end, and Jane, he grudgingly acknowledged, did 'massage the painful shoulder blade tendons.' But then, typically, 'she disappeared to her pleasant bedchamber and whiskey at 9.30 p.m.' while he went to his study to write at the same time. The entry that followed was full of complaints. Over the fifteen years he had lived in *Cnoc Aluin*, Jane had never allowed any of his friends to eat at their table 'more than ½ a dozen times.' Jane endlessly complained that she was the sole earner, but that was another lie. He had just received an 'in gratitude' payment from Marianna of nearly £5,000, had just 'earned £800 re insurance on cottage fire,' and there was rent coming from the cottage as well. On top of that, they and she lived rent-free in a house that he had bought with the *Hoffman* money, and she had never paid a penny towards its upkeep. The garden provided 60 per cent of his food, and she got a free lunch at Sandford Park on weekdays during term time. Yet despite all this she had to 'carp & record untruths' about him and *Not The End Of The World*. Why? The answer, he thought, was that 'her mother was a bitch and a bully.'

On 29 October he noted that Jane had written in her day book that he was intensely irritable, losing his memory and going mad.

Why does she have to write these untruths? It must be, I thought, a sort of guilt about abandoning our arrangement to write autobiography together.

III

He had been keeping a close eye on Jane's alcohol store (it was in the bottom of the wardrobe in her bedroom), noting with grim satisfaction (he loved this sort of detail) that she took her empties to school and disposed of them there. But he and Jane had never actually had an open conversation about what he perceived as her alcoholism, but which she emphatically did not, until the last Sunday in March 1986. As he had it, in his entry of 3 April:

She said she would go off it immediately. But despite her 'good response' the entries in her Day Book are just as rancorous about me as before – and about this 'morgue' and this country.

If I didn't feel there was something emotional and mental about her I'd suggest she go back to her beloved early surrounds in England and stay there. Perhaps I'll be driven to it?

Jane's drinking didn't stop, and now while she drank in bed at night he would sometimes stand at her door and listen, then burst in and rebuke her. Sometimes he would have words in the morning when he judged that, being sober, she would be more likely to be reasonable. But his attempts to stop her drinking did no good. She was unhappy because he was changing – darkening, retreating, hardening, becoming angrier, bitterer, sourer, more hypochondriacal, more curmudgeonly. Alternatively, he was becoming what he was always inevitably going to become, only more so, and alcohol was her only solace. Jane's drinking appalled him of course (that she couldn't control herself was bad, but that he couldn't control her was intolerable), and was a further source of conflict. On 10 April 1986 he confided that he thought she would never forgive him for knowing about it. After that observation he added, in parentheses, that she was leaving him and that his spying on her was the reason why.

His snooping hurt Jane, but it wasn't *the* problem. That was something much bigger. It was the way he was, which was difficult, withdrawn, irrational and emotionally unavailable. He made her miserable, and she had been miserable for years. She had to get out. The shock would perhaps force him to change, and if he didn't, well, she would have saved herself, because if she stayed she would go under. She resigned her post at Sandford Park and secured a position at a school in Highgate, London. She bought her ferry ticket and told him the date on which she would be leaving.

IV

Sometime in early May, as Jane advanced her plans, Mac phoned from London. Sally Travers, he told my father, after a three-year fight, had succumbed to cancer and had been buried the day before. My father demurred. His understanding, he said, was that she had married years before, had two children and gone to New Zealand. No, Mac countered, gleefully in my father's account, he was wrong. She had never married or had children. She had died alone.

After he put the phone down he 'felt empty, ashamed, desolated in an odd still way for the rest of the day.' Sally had been one of 'the most valiant, "straight" and faithful persons' he had ever known, and he had traduced her. These feelings of coruscating shame, once aroused, wouldn't go. At another point (the entry is undated) he wrote:

How could I have just abandoned her – come to Dublin. 'To see parents etc' and let the months pass. Not only that but I knew I was going to 'leave' her beforehand, that living with your 'sister' was no longer possible. And that terrible meeting with her in Cossie's studio. She appears not to have after that, though a young woman, lived with anyone else until her death at about age of 62 (cancer).

V

It was a Monday in July, the start of the week in which Jane was leaving, approaching midnight. Jane was in bed. He was up doing something, and that was when it occurred to him that Jane had done something – she had pulled a stroke.

He went to his study, opened the small yellow trunk where he kept all important documents, retrieved their bank deposit book (it was in their joint names), opened it and saw that over the preceding months, in measured amounts, between £15,000 and £20,000 had been withdrawn.

He sat up all night. Morning came. It was Tuesday 22 July. Jane got up. He asked her if she had taken the money. According to his account, 'she looked stony. She refused to answer, to speak at all.'

She was sailing on Wednesday. According to him, that is what she had told him. He took a sedative and went and lay down, believing that there was a day to go before she left. He dozed for an hour, maybe more, and when he woke he thought the house sounded unusually quiet. He got up and went down to the kitchen in the basement, where he found a note from Jane on the table. He read it. '*I am going a day earlier.'* He assumed that she had called a taxi while he was sleeping. He went back upstairs and into her bedroom, the one by the front door that overlooked the sea. He saw that she had taken only her small case, nothing else. He opened her wardrobe and looked at her shoes and neatly folded jerseys and all her other clothes that she had left behind. Either she was very cold, he decided, or mad.

He went back out to the hall, opened the front door and stepped out onto the top step. In the distance, out in Dublin Bay, he saw what he assumed was the Dun Laoghaire boat sailing eastwards towards Holyhead and Wales, with Jane on board.

He went back inside and closed the door. He appeared indifferent and inured at that moment to what had happened, but within a few days he was in turmoil:

> *And she waits until I am 71 and losing my memory and struggling to write the best book (the Auto) I have ever written, to sneak away, abandon home, garden, me – to be in her beloved England (that she's been happy out of for 16 years). How do I get them? This one is going mad too. Mean mad.*

When he asked 'How do I get them?' he meant mad women of course, for that, he had increasingly come to believe, was his fate.

Over the weeks and months after she left, Jane wrote to him at least three times to tell him where she was and how she was. He replied to none of these letters.

VI

Alone in *Cnoc Aluin*, he began to write. His subject was Jane. Why had she done what she had done? He half-thought that he could start the Autobiog, when finally he got to it, with this material.

His first notion was that Jane's behaviour was all history and hereditary. Her father was a homosexual, small, pretty, repressed and ineffective. First he deprived Jane of a father figure by being away for the duration of the war, and then when he returned he was unable to function effectively as a father because he was despised and bullied by his wife. Coming from such stock was it any wonder she would run, taking their money with her?

Five weeks on, at the end of August, a new thesis emerged. Disease, obviously incurable, both physiological and psychological, was to blame. This was what had made her skeletal as well as causing her 'depressive recession into [her] self.'

Within a few days of this he had a new idea. Jane's deficiencies, her inability, for instance, to make a fire from sticks and coal, to saw or split wood, to hammer a nail, to break coal, to unscrew a house fuse, to climb a ladder (even the first step of a stepladder), to mount even a low wall, to skip, to swim, to drive a car, to dance, to play a musical instrument, to hold a melody, to sing a song, to draw and to feel for people (to name but a few), were also the deficiencies of his second wife, my mother. It amazed him that he had never noticed this before, he wrote, but it also gratified him. The inference was obvious. Wives with these deficiencies were always bolters because such deficiencies rendered them unable to sustain a marriage. If only he had been more alert when he met Jane. If he had noticed her similarity to my mother he would not have got involved, and thereby he would have saved himself much heartache.

Having got my mother implicated in the Jane debacle, he next implicated Adolf. If his father had given him music, he wrote in early September, he would have floated through life on a cloud. If he'd had music he would never have met Jane, and if he had never met her then it followed that aged seventy-two he would never have had to experience the pain of her desertion. Adolf had a lot to explain and to answer for.

On 23 September, he refined his thesis further. Jane had had a mental breakdown years earlier, and that was why she drank, that was why she left Sandford Park, and that was why she threw away twenty-two years of happiness with him, ransacked their account and fled to England in the cold and calculated manner in which she had. He looked up schizophrenia in his *Encyclopædia Britannica*, 'and yes, there it was – Jane was your classic case.'

Taxonomy of this kind was a long-established practice, and it was a comfort to him to be able to impugn the other as having some sort of psychological impairment. This way of categorizing was also intimately connected to his mechanical obsession and the habitual way in which he saw and interacted with the world. The machine, which was what he found so attractive about it, could only follow its predetermined course, and in the same way someone like Phyllis, in this case, could only slavishly follow the path their condition determined, though he should have known of course that there was a chasm between a machine running predictably and a psyche predictably going awry. But he didn't. He didn't want to, and there was a reason for that. From his point of view the brilliance of seeing people as automata was that not only did it provide an unassailable explanation for why others behaved as they did (they were mad, they couldn't help themselves), but it also exonerated him. They had conditions. Something was wrong in their heads. That's why they followed the courses they followed. That he might have had anything to do with what anyone else experienced, with what Jane, in this instance, was experiencing – well, that was clearly impossible. It was the condition's doing and nothing to do with him.

So his taxonomical thinking was a perfect bulwark against accusations that he might be in any way culpable of anything. It got him off every hook and it made him invincible. But there was a price to pay. His bad faith, his tendency to treat subjects as objects, also applied to himself. He had, as a result of this way of thinking, never been able to grasp what was occurring in his own psyche, which in turn hobbled his development. The way to cope with the uncomfortable fact that every other human being was free to do whatever they liked (a terrifying vista) was to accept that uncertainty was part of the fabric of life, but that required the psyche to make an accommodation, as most people do. Had he done that he would then have learnt how not to be so fearful of the capacity of others to hurt, which in turn would have led to him liking people and people liking him. But because this didn't happen, by the time he came to the end of his life, he didn't like anybody or anything. On the contrary, he pretty much disliked everyone and everything. That was the cost. He might have put himself beyond hurt, but in the process he deprived himself of the comfort of proper relationships. He may have thought he gained by the transaction, but actually he lost – he lost contact, *human* contact with *people*.

On the same day as he diagnosed Jane as a schizophrenic, she wrote to him from her lodgings at Whittingham School in London on her new electric typewriter. It was a letter of intense warmth and kindness. She began by thanking him for his 'thoughtful forbearing silence,' then assured him that no matter what had happened at *Cnoc Aluin* in her absence, whether her clothes and possessions were destroyed, her photographs torn up, her cupboards changed, and her role as his special helpmate usurped by his niece, Isolde, and her husband, John (who were now living in the cottage in Leslie Avenue), she was certain that his essential essence had not changed. Or so she hoped, she said, although the only way to find out was to come back.

She continued:

> *Often I want to come back so badly, to rub your head, to ease your aches, to garden and cook and polish and bake and mend (literally & metaphorically!) that I just want to pick up my Building Society book, my electric typer* [sic] *and head for Euston Station.*

If she were to return, of course, she would sneakily have to:

> *Run out on this life here* [...] *because the pressures NOT to do such a 'mad' thing that would come from friends and the school would be unbearable to face.*

But she was ready for that. The truth was that she wanted to return, she wanted 'to slide back in and gradually re-establish myself with you alone and uninterfered with,' but only on the condition that he really wanted her. So, did he? The decision was his. She assured him that she was calm. She was not depressed. Should he say no, she would survive. Should he say yes, she would not expect him to do anything to help her leave London and return to Dublin. That was her problem, 'however arduous and expensive that might turn out to be.' She ended: 'My love to you, whether you want it or not.'

He wrote back in September to tell her that he would never live with another woman and followed this with two further horrible letters that simultaneously demanded news and rolled out his thesis regarding her mental instability.

This was Jane's reply to these three. Dated simply 'Sunday 8 p.m.' it was probably written in early November 1986:

> *Dear Ernie,*
>
> *I am answering your urgent appeal for news at the earliest opportunity.* […]
>
> *I suppose I should be angry that, after four solid months of stony silence on your part, when it now seems clear that you believed me to be suffering from diverse mental afflictions, you chose to do & say nothing – all that long agonizing time – when I wrote to you – from Nora's, from Julia's, from Mavis's – you knew where I was, why were you not writing to me then of your anxiety & concern? As far as I could ascertain, you had abandoned this poor broken wreck that had drifted away to other shores – no rescue attempt then on your part – why now? Why do you ask me to write & tell you where I am, what I am doing? You know where I am, you know what I am doing. I am living and teaching in a lovely old-fashioned school in Highgate, atop the most glorious wooded hills high over London Town. I have a lovely cosy bedsitter, separate bath/shower room, lavatory and kitchen, on the top floor of the 3ʳᵈ of the 4 houses that*

comprise Whittingham School. [...] My own classroom is one floor down and one across – so I can never be late for school! The old headmistress and her middle-aged daughter, who own and run the school, regard me as 'a gift from God'. [...]

Now, that is my news – but can you believe it? You believe me to be a 'psychotic', 'schizophrenic' AND 'cataleptic' (I'd check again on that one if I were you!) I left in the middle of July, a wasted, broken & despairing wreck – you said & did nothing (other than doubtless to wax full of self-righteous outrage and indignation), then, at the end of September one horrid letter from you finally arrives bitchily (?) addressed to Gébler/Inott – knowing this would cause gossip (?) Actually the Head knows I am separated from my 'husband' but she and the tax office know me as Jane Gébler. The letter berated me for destroying my home & my school but then went on to inform me that I am psychotic & therefore not even aware that I am mad. Well, if you knew I was 'mad' and incapable of recognizing it per se, [...] why did you not do something practical before it was too late? Why did you not catch me & hold me & save me & comfort me before [I left] instead of dragging me out of bed to harangue me (July 16th) & to read me a hurtful extract from your autobiography? – is that the way to treat a psychotic – Doctor man? Your two November letters (all I got after the September blast) then pinned labels of 'schizophrenia' & 'catalepsy' on me (yes, I have a diploma in psychology – most English trained teachers have). [...]

You in your letter, that broke the July to September period of silence, said, 'I will never live with you or anyone else permanently again – the penalties are too great.' I think you are totally right there, – I agree you are totally right there. Let's leave it at that for a while, shall we?

I see little point in any of this time I have spent in writing all of this to you, when you label me psychotic – it is worthless isn't it? However, my employer, my pupils and my friends seem to find me quite normal – I think they even like me. [...]

Look after yourself; of course I worry about you, it has been a habit of literally half of my lifetime.
I have told you all I can. Let's leave it there. [...]

Thanks, Jane.

His verdict was as follows:

Long, self-justifying letter from Jane about being in a [sic] *London with a job in a posh school and how happy she is. Will I ever understand people? Finally displays an [...]*

The entry continued on the next page, but how it continued is unknown as he tore out the page at some point. Perhaps what he wrote was so vituperative and vile that in a rare moment of insight he realized that it mustn't be allowed to stand – and destroyed it.

VII

Jane might have gone, but that was no reason not to push on with the Autobiog. He had a story worth telling, a life worth recording. Also, he needed to impugn those who he believed had hindered or hurt him: the list of malfeasants included his parents, his siblings, his wives, his children (or the two with whom he had any meaningful contact), and nearly everyone he had worked with in publishing, in the theatre and in the film industry. Finally, and this was possibly the strongest spur of all, he knew that something was happening in his head, and it wasn't good. He had to get cracking before he lost the capacity to write altogether. A helpmate would have been ideal. So big a task. It would have been so much easier if two could face it, but there weren't two any more. There had been, but she was gone, lost to him forever. Now there was only one, and so he would have to do it alone.

In the autumn of 1986, between the cranky letters to Jane and his analysis of her, and having adjusted partially to Jane's absence, he made a start on the Autobiog. He began to make telephone calls. He began to write down conversations. He wrote letters soliciting information. He looked through books on the social history of Ireland in general, and Dublin in particular. He started gathering together papers and diaries and other materials. He was a hoarder who kept everything: letters, photographs, school reports, old passports, journals written in the 1940s and his desk diaries going back to 1962, so there was plenty to pull together. Once he'd assembled this papery substance he reread the journal in his ledger and the desk diaries and he annotated the entries in red Biro. He also attached connected materials, and as a result the ledger and the desk diaries were so swollen by additional papers they ended up looking like bloated bellows.

Next he wrote down the facts that weren't already written. He wrote hundreds of pages of notes covering his whole life, and to these pages he also attached letters, clippings, photographs and so on that he thought relevant.

Clearly, what he was attempting was the construction of an archive with a clear chronological trajectory from which he could construct a written text. But unfortunately, as he worked, Alzheimer's was settling in, disrupting his capacity to perform complex linguistic tasks. He wrote the same things, the same stories, again and again and again, because every time he finished something he forgot having written it. The results of his efforts were the reverse of his ambition. Instead of making something tidy, coherent and literate, what he generated was something unruly, confused and almost impossible to read. It was an awful mess he made, but he couldn't help it.

65.

Marianna

I

Late in 1986 or early in 1987 he gave in to Marianna's pleading and went to see her in Graz, where she lived. She was sick and weak, had an irregular pacemaker (or so he claimed), gammy legs, fluid on her left lung and difficulties breathing. She was near death, or so he thought, and he loved her, or so he claimed, 'for what she was, and for what she had done for my father.' He got her to agree to go to hospital (he may even have taken her there), and he agreed that she could come to *Cnoc Aluin*.

On 23 January, by which time he was back in Dalkey, Marianna phoned him. She had recovered, and she was coming. 'Will I survive?' he wrote. On 4 February he wrote to tell her that the house was too cold for her just yet and that she had to wait till May. With this letter written and waiting on the table in the hall to be taken to the post box he had a premonition: 'Jane had reached a decision […] to come back and I'll probably be fool enough to agree.'

On 10 February he received from Marianna a money order for £2,600. He realized what this meant: she wanted to be with him when she died. 'All right,' he wrote, 'I'll try and give her that comfort.' Then he remembered his premonition: 'If Jane had any thought in her mad mind of returning, the knowledge of Marianna being here would kill it.' He lodged the money order in his account and calculated that he might keep Marianna for £40 a week.

II

The plan that now emerged was that Marianna would leave Graz, where she now lived, and come to Ireland and live in *Cnoc Aluin* in Dalkey with her stepson, now alone, now deserted, and he would look after her and she would look after him, and they would be a comfort to one another as they slowly glided towards the end.

There were many letters. A typical example was the one of 18 March 1987, which Marianna wrote from Graz:

> *I am anxious about what you were writing about Jane. I hope not that she* [Jane] *comes back to you, because in that case I can't come to you.*

Beside this my father wrote in red biro: 'No, no, Jane not coming back. I will not have it. You are coming.'

In her letter Marianna went on to tell her stepson that she had lost weight, was down to fifty-two kilos and was shortly going to a sanatorium, and he could write to her there. 'I hope I get better because in this condition I am not able to go to Ireland.' She continued: 'Have you installed the shower? Because a shower is necessary for me.' This was annotated, in black biro, not red (suggesting that he made it at a different time), 'She thinks I have installed a shower for her […]!'

By the time he made this second annotation, he had changed his mind completely. Where once he was attracted to the idea of Marianna's residency in *Cnoc Aluin*, he was now appalled and stricken with panic by the thought of it, regarding her as 'Loud mouthed, crass' and 'A born Nazi':

> *She was a Nazi collaborator – that was why Marianna had to leave Austria after the war (she couldn't get into England or America as*

Nazi sympathizer) — imagine Adolf's mind when he found this out. And having to live with such a coarse stupid woman! But if he kicked her out [he would have to start] *with another housekeeper* [and he hadn't] *the heart.*

He was also certain that she had added to the wretchedness and misery of his father's final years in the Californian wilderness by being domineering and overweening and philistine, exactly like Rita before her, and he couldn't forgive her for that. That he had no evidence for any of the above was beside the point: it was what he believed.

III

In order to put Marianna off, he now began to fill his letters with off-putting details about the place she wanted to come to, telling her that his Dalkey house was cold and damp, there was no central heating, he could not install a shower because the configuration of his old Irish plumbing wouldn't allow it, he only had a bathtub, which was huge and antique, and there was never enough water to fill it more than a couple of inches, and all manner of other things besides. These factors, he told her, whenall put together, had one meaning: after the comforts and conveniences to which she had grown accustomed living in the US and Austria, she would find his house cheerless and insupportable.

She counter-petitioned. No plumbing, even of the Irish variety, was beyond improvement. Surely a shower could be installed. She had money. She would pay, she said, whatever was necessary.

But her every assertion was met with a rebuttal, her every offer declined.

IV

As the letters went back and forth, and there were many letters, his animosity towards his stepmother rose. He confided in his Autobiog notes that Marianna was 'a broad faced wholly unattractive Austrian peasant,' and added:

Since Marianna's self-invited visit to me I've had new 'insights' into
what it must have been like for poor Adolf to find himself dependent
on such a crass, bone-stupid, not simply wholly uneducated about
everything but boringly self-assertive about everything person.

  [...] *No wonder Adolf drank himself to death as rapidly as he*
could finding himself in the hell-hole of Los Angeles [sic – it was
actually San Francisco], *California, married in his near senile*
period to Marianna. (She has skin all over which is tough like
rubber on the outside but a little coarse to the touch.)

Though he tried to keep his feelings about her hidden, Marianna
eventually saw that she disgusted him and that the simple truth was
that he didn't want her – his father's second wife, the love of Adolf's life,
now old and lonely, broken and desperate and at the end of her own
life, and wanting nothing more than to spend her final days with her
husband's eldest son. Once she realized that she had been spurned she
became angry, and played her trump card.

If her stepson wouldn't have her, well then, she would leave him
nothing. Not a penny, not a cent. She would cut him out of her will.
He received this news blithely, insouciantly. This is 'Not [too] dear a
price to pay for escaping such an awful fate,' he wrote.

V

Meanwhile, as he wrangled with Marianna, letters went back and forth
between him and Jane over the spring. Judging by his diary, his were
pugnacious and unkind, hers hot and angry. In mid April, claiming that
he still felt some sort of responsibility towards her, he wrote suggesting that
she write once a month, just a note to update him on her well-being and
whereabouts. Why did he do this? The answer, perhaps, was prescience.
Something had started, or perhaps it is more accurate to say that he had
noticed this thing that had started, and on 13 May he wrote it down:

'I go upstairs to get something and when I get there I have forgotten what. The dreaded Alzheimer's disease?' A cold shiver of desolation swept through him. What was he do? Get on with something, he thought, and spend less time in the kitchen – but get on with what? The best thing to do of course, given what was coming, was to take Jane back.

On 17 May he had a letter from Jane ('She obviously is suffering loss, loneliness now'), and at the start of June, despite his having striven to prevent this, Marianna arrived to stay. Within days he had forgotten (that is, if he even remembered at this stage) anything of what he had felt in Graz, where he'd visited her, and he was instead in thrall to feelings of hate and rage. Marianna, he wrote, was a 'self-centred and crass "old" woman [...] wholly and coarsely self-concerned.' What annoyed him initially was the way in which she spent her days in the kitchen of his niece, Isolde, complaining that he had taken her money and was now treating her badly. In order to put a stop to that he returned £1,600 to Marianna and promised that the balance would follow. In other words, she would have to pay for nothing, the notion of a £40 contribution by her per week now being discounted. This new dispensation was supposed to mollify Marianna, and for all I know it did, but its effect on my father was the reverse because (although this was his doing) he now knew that he would be supporting her entirely, and he hated that.

Relations eventually got so fraught that a move was orchestrated, though whose idea this was I don't know, and Marianna decamped to the home of John O'Carroll, Adolf's star clarinet pupil in the late forties and early fifties, and an ally in the bad times following Rita's inquest. Once the move was effected, Marianna and my father did not meet as far as I can tell, not once. She then returned to Austria. Thereafter, as my father noted bluntly, 'No more communication with me. She died I heard a year or so later.'

66.

A Turn

I

Jane received reports in London from her old Dalkey neighbours. He wasn't coping. He was frail. He wasn't well. I think he may also have written, though I have no evidence for this, and made wild promises that everything would be better. The combination of her neighbours' reports, his letters, and the fact that she had been away and felt better led to her decision. On 19 July, a Sunday, he noted that she had phoned him a few days before, when she told him that she would give up her teaching post in Highgate (she had done an academic year, so presumably that was easy) and was returning. At the end of a laconic account of what was an extraordinary phone call, he added, 'Suddenly, I am very happy.' Three months later, on 21 November 1987, he wrote directly underneath, 'And am still happy.'

II

Jane returned to Sandford Park, where she had previously worked as a teacher, but this time as matron. The job required that she live in to minister to the boarders, but as the school was close to *Cnoc Aluin* she was able to visit my father in term time every day and discharge the chores and the duties that came with being a wife. She cleaned. She dusted. She vacuumed. She cooked. She shopped. She laundered. She weeded the beds. She trimmed the hedges. She harvested the vegetables. During holidays she was at home all the time.

After Jane returned my father made no diary entries until 31 July 1988:

All well. Jane seems happy in her house and garden (and with Ernie). A summer of dark skies and rain. But we have our fond peaceful life.

III

Some years earlier, and despite everything she had done for him, he had refused to marry Jane. Her solution to the problem was to change her name to Jane Gébler by deed poll. Everyone thereafter concluded that they were married, but she always knew the truth. Now, two years after her return from London, redress of this ancient grievance was in sight. On 1 May 1989 he noted cryptically that 'though my will [is] signed, sealed and delivered leaving everything to her,' she would feel more secure if she were married, and so he had finally agreed that he would no longer evade that duty. No date had been agreed upon, only that this would happen. They would marry, she for the first time and he for the third.

IV

5 May 1989 was a Friday. Jane came over from school. The grass at the front of *Cnoc Aluin* needed cutting. She located the ancient push-mower (which had no engine – my father, averse to throwing anything

out, took delight in sharpening its blades himself) and got to work. The ground was steep. The work was hard. The sound made by the rotation of the blades started and stopped as Jane pushed the mower backwards and forwards over the rebellious grass. Then the sound went off, and it was off for some time. My father was in the house. Why hadn't Jane come in? He expected Jane to come in. That was what always happened when she finished in the garden: she came in. But she hadn't come in, and there was nothing but an ominous quiet.

He went out to investigate, and found her lying on a bank at the front, the mower lying nearby. He called her name. Nothing. He tried to rouse her. Nothing. He fetched a neighbour (either by phone or in person, I'm not sure), and the neighbour came and phoned for an ambulance. When it arrived, the ambulance men put Jane onto a stretcher and they put the stretcher into their ambulance. He got in too and rode with Jane to the hospital in Dun Laoghaire.

Jane was in a coma. The doctors in the hospital diagnosed a brain haemorrhage and put Jane onto a life-support machine. They then explained to my father that her brain had been damaged by the aneurysm and that the machine would need to be switched off so that she could be allowed to die.

He kissed her 'sleeping face' and left the hospital, crying. The machine was turned off. She died on Saturday 6 May 1989. According to the death certificate the cause of death was a brain haemorrhage. Jane was fifty-two.

V

On 11 or 12 May, he wasn't certain of the day, he 'attended in chapel the last rites, and saw coffin automatically slid gently in through the doors of the crematorium.' He realized at that moment, as he noted later in his diary, that he was seeing two things: he was watching the end of a woman who 'had adapted herself wholly' to him, and he was watching the end of his 'own life'.

Twelve days later, he wrote:

A waking dream. Sometimes come to with a twitch – She's not here. Will never be here again. [...] *Hasn't been for ages. Won't be ever. Gone, passed away from me. Not here. So much not here* [it is] *as if she had never been.* [...]

Fourteen days later he wrote: 'It is as much as I can do to get through the day. Now I know how much she meant to me.'

Twenty-one days later he wrote: 'And nothing that you can think or say or do at all abates the pain of loss throughout the ever present day.'

67.

The Book he Wanted to Write

I

He still went to his desk. That instinct was still there. He would always go to the desk because he had always gone to the desk. He had not forgotten that he was supposed to write his Autobiog. And then when he was at the desk he saw the pages of notes he had made, the lists he had drawn up, the papers (letters, photographs, documents) he had assembled, mostly during the time when Jane was away, though he kept forgetting when that was, just as he now kept forgetting when Jane had died. He could still read, so he looked through his words. Sometimes when he read what he had written at an earlier point he remembered that there was more he needed to find out. He started to annotate the Autobiog papers in the margins, and he also started to write notes that he inserted between his handwritten pages. By this time his handwriting was spiky and wayward, his syntax more and more unruly. Sometimes his additions concerned the text. He must write to Leatrice: she would have dates and details he needed. He must write to Edna for the same reason. He must write to Marianna, whom he had forgotten was now dead: he must know the year and the month she met Adolf, and how did they meet? Did Adolf advertise? And when she met him first did she know Adolf's wife was living away from Cabra Grove and residing with one of her daughters? If she did, was she put off by getting together with a married man? When she was with him did Adolf ever talk about Rita, or his children or his son? He burned to know this and a thousand if not ten thousand other facts from his receding past.

His additions to the manuscript sometimes concerned his life:

He must try to recover the money Jane stole (and these reminders about recovering his money contain many asides about Jane's avarice and infamy, notwithstanding all he had written about her glory and their love at the end, and which, it should be noted, he also continued to declare), or else had sent to her sister, Mavis (he wasn't sure which).

He must find his missing pension book ('Have final search for pension book before reporting it lost. Look under own mattress').

He must apply for money to the Irish Arts Council (who handed out an emolument to artists known as the *Cnuas*).

He must give Isolde, his sister Louise's daughter, who lived in the cottage he owned, the key to 92 Coliemore Road so she could get in and out.

He must turn off the gas.

He must check the gutters for leaves.

He must tidy the garden.

He must find his typing paper. ('Where is typing paper etc? Was on lower shelf of kitchen green shelves? I put it "away"?')

Et cetera, et cetera. He wrote thousands of reminder notes, which presumably he forgot about as soon as he had written them.

II

Though he was apt to forget what he had written, whether notes to self or notes for the Autobiog, what he had not forgotten was how he had planned to shape his material in order to make it tell the story that he wished people to believe was the story of the life he had led, and he wrote a mass of guidance notes on this subject for himself.

As he saw it, the corner stone of his blighted life was the marriage of Adolf and Rita. This was the context into which he was born, and in which he grew up.

Both parents were difficult individuals. His father was a selfish drunk, a bully and a curmudgeon, while his mother, towards whom his feelings were a little more generous, was a more complex figure. On the negative side, her life of toil and marital misery came at a cost. It made her bitter and brutal. It turned her into a disbeliever in self-improvement and a philistine. It made her into a harridan who when she lashed with her tongue inflicted terrible hurt. On the plus side, though, she was a woman with an unstinting capacity for hard work, who raised six children without resources or support, a miraculous feat.

This was how they were, as his notes freely acknowledge. For the Autobiog, though, the facts needed to be massaged. The poverty, all right, he would admit to that. Ditto his parents' endless squabbling and sparring with one another and the misery this engendered. But his father as a straightforward boor and his mother as the victim was not quite going to fit his purpose, which was to indict both. To do that, Adolf needed to be improved and Rita needed to be made worse – and so he planned. Yes, he was going to say, recalling the Adolf of his childhood, he drank recklessly (he couldn't magic that truth away), but also, weirdly, he was a grafter, who 'despite having a spiteful aging older woman for a wife and antagonized children who hate[d] him,' (with the exception of Ada, who was too old when the propaganda started), nonetheless soldiered on heroically, 'earning a living by playing music in cinemas, and thereby putting bread on the table, though he [got] no thanks' from anyone – not his wife, not his children, and certainly not his eldest son. In other words, Adolf, while far from being a paragon, did at least provide, while his mother, her nurturing discounted, was made far more responsible for the breakdown of the father–son relationship than was the case in practice.

III

As my father saw it, he suffered egregiously, and of all the wrongs he suffered the principal one that churned him up every day unfailingly and about which he wrote with monotonous regularity was his ignorance of things musical. He found it incredible and astounding that his father was a musical prodigy, yet he, the firstborn, who had an innate musical disposition (great pieces of classical music stirred him, 'dimming his eyes and suckering the breath'), could not play a note:

> *My professional musician clarinet player father [...] (sent by his father to the Prague Academy of Music (the Conservatoire) to take clarinet, fiddle and piano – from which he issued professional in all 3), never moved a finger to teach me a note of music or anything to do with it.*

How did this happen? How did that great crime occur? Why did his father fail to educate him? His answer to these questions was to form one of the storylines in his Autobiog, whose expression would offer him the satisfaction of having his say and venting his resentment.

There was bad timing, for a start. Ada was lucky enough to be born before the war, so she got two precious years with her father, in which they bonded. He, the second, arrived after the start of the war, by which time Adolf was gone. They did not bond because they could not because Adolf was away, in the camp.

351

It would be nearly five years before Adolf got back to his wife and children, and by then great changes had occurred.

Rita had now grown so old that Adolf didn't recognize her, which had a corrosive effect on their relationship, whilst Adolf, after so long away in the exclusive company of men in a hard labour camp, couldn't function properly in the domestic sphere. He had forgotten how to cross the road, how to eat with a knife and fork, how to handle money, how to behave around women, and how to do the hundred and one other things necessary to live successfully as a civilian.

In 1919, Rita should have been the one who re-educated Adolf, but his failing to recognize his wife produced, at the very least, a reticence, an awkwardness, a reserve on the part of both parties, and at worst, outright revulsion. This left a space, and into that space, in the place of his wife, stepped the daughter, Ada, with whom he'd formed a relationship before he went to the camp. Thus, when he came back, it was Ada who became his teacher, his translator, his entertainer and his helpmate. It was Ada who reintroduced Adolf to all that he had forgotten, and she did it with charm and wit and the most lovely grace. Adolf was grateful of course. Who wouldn't be? He was also hypnotized, transfixed and smitten. This was inevitable given the circumstances: after years of incarceration the tender attentions of his golden-haired child were intoxicating and beguiling.

However, their relationship as it developed post-camp also had a fatal consequence. As my five-year-old father saw it, following five years during which he and Adolf had had no contact, Adolf had re-entered the family, and by everything he said and did he had indicated that Ada was the child he preferred. My father's apprehension of this inequality had two consequences. It made him hate Adolf (on top of or in addition to the hatred Rita had already given him, assuming that is true), and it laid down the foundations of what would be his lifelong feelings of jealousy towards Ada.

And then, in this tragic story of a son denied his musical education such that he didn't learn to play anything, the other factor, which it was also his intention to have in his book's foundations, was the mother, Rita: 'Tiny, skinny, unlovely, ignorant of books, music and anything of that nature,' who filled him with an 'unfounded suspicion and dislike' of his father and got him so much on her side that in Adolf's eyes he appeared to be her creature entirely.

With these determinants in place, the history of musical education in the family ran thusly, and he intended to narrate it in this way too. Ada got music first. Obviously, she was the eldest. Adolf gave 'her piano lessons – shouted at her from various parts of the house, such as the lavatory' after he came home. It was not till my father was aged eight or nine that his turn to learn came, but it didn't happen. How could it?

> *how could a father* [like Adolf] *induce an Ernie* [a wayward, hostile child] *to sit down and learn and practice in a room alone? How could he when Ernie even at 8 or 9 looked at him with mute blame?*

And it could have been so different:

> *Instead of agitating from the kitchen in her usual way as if addressing the neighbours – always referring to Adolf as 'he',* [if only Rita] *had said to Adolf gently, 'I do hope, please, Adolf, you are going to start Ernie on* […] *the piano soon. You are such a very good teacher. I just know he would love it* […] *Oh please do.'*

Actually, as his notes showed, he did get lessons. He just didn't take to the fiddle. He just didn't have the powers of concentration, the interest or the fidelity to a regime of practice, and so he shrugged it off. But that truth was not part of the Autobiog's design. This was to be the tale of a lad whose lucky elder sister monopolized his father's attention, and so got music, and whose mother conditioned her son to hate his father, thereby ensuring that he did not get music. That was the story he intended to tell.

IV

Having survived his awful childhood (and a lot of it was awful, that was true, it just wasn't awful in exactly the way he planned to claim it was), he entered adolescence, and as he would have it – oh, bitter times, bitter days, bitter nights. His father, who 'gave his eldest, his firstborn son, nothing, not as much as where middle C was on the piano,' put him to work in 'a carbon arc [fume] filled "operating box", winding film and machine-minding all day for a few shillings a week.' It was horrible, vile, a desolating experience. Fifty years later he was still angry with his father for putting him to work like this, though he would also admit that given the circumstances, the Great Depression, mass unemployment and so on and so forth, his father thought that he was doing his son a favour. He would admit this, but would not pretend that his life as a projectionist had many virtues, though it did have two. One, it was so awful it put iron in his soul, it gave him something to kick against, to rebel against. Two, it gave him time to develop himself once he had determined, as he did, to make himself into something. At that point he knew he couldn't go the music route, which was unavailable due to his ignorance. But he had always told himself stories (that was one fact from his childhood he wouldn't have to change), and so he started to write. First, with enormous difficulty, he wrote journalism, followed by stories, and the socially enlightened first novel that did some business but got banned in Ireland. Then he wrote *The Plymouth Adventure*. He made money, a lot of money, as he had always intended, with the idea that with the money that he earned he would then write non-commercial high-end material.

Unfortunately, and this was the next part of the story, the money he made didn't liberate him and enable him to be a writer of authentic work as opposed to the hack work that was *The Plymouth Adventure*. On the contrary, the money led him into a disaster, the disaster that was Leatrice. (But then, what was it they said about the best laid plans?

They unravel, don't they? Always.) My father considered that in his case matters were actually worse than that: they didn't just unravel, they backfired, and the back blast badly scorched him.

Leatrice was attracted to his money. Well, obviously. She was American and female, and that was what American females looked for: men with money, men who would support them. And he, stupidly, was attracted to the American who was attracted to his money, and had failed to grasp that it was his money and not the man she wanted. Why did he fail to see that? Well, she had colossal erotic allure, obviously. But then that's men, or at least it was the man he was. He was stupid. He didn't see, he didn't understand, he couldn't think things through, read the runes, predict the future. He simply thought, well she likes me, and I have the money with which to buy her what she says she wants, and so I will buy her what she says she wants and then we will live together and we will be happy ever after.

That was the trouble with the book money. It allowed him to believe that he could give Leatrice what Leatrice wanted, and in return he would enjoy wifely devotion. Oh how different his life might have been if he hadn't had the money and hadn't taken the path he took. But he did. So the tragedy was set in motion by money. He married Leatrice and he bought Lake Park and they had their son, and then, because Leatrice was a typical American woman, self-serving, spoilt beyond redemption, she took their son and bolted (well, not exactly, but it felt like that), and he was left with a broken psyche, plus a house he couldn't afford and debts and chaos. Moreover, he never did get to write those pure true works of literature, not even after she went. No, he was too depressed, too atomized by the whole sorry mess. But there was one consolation, one comforting certainty that he pulled from the wreckage. He believed that a son would always want his true father and would never give up looking for him. That was the law of nature. Yes, one day his lost son would come and find him, he was sure of it.

V

After the divorce debacle (and the next stage in the story), there was another legal catastrophe. Once again the instigator was female, in this case his sister, Ada, who had been a continuous irritant ever since he transplanted to London and started to be successful. Back then she had demanded money, and when he wouldn't give it wrote to the BBC and denounced him as a communist, and now she pulled a new stroke, because, oh yes, she was the nightmare who just went on giving. This was what happened:

Rita died, Ada made her allegation that her mother had been poisoned in the last months when she had lived at Cabra Grove, and Adolf was interrogated. Simultaneously, Rita's corpse was cut open, the autopsy was performed, and then there was the terrible Coroner's Court, and although Adolf was exonerated, such was the damage done by the situation, which his oldest and once favourite child had initiated, that Adolf left Ireland (he had no alternative) and went to San Francisco, where he died, solitary (though he had Marianna, she didn't count according to my father), defeated, morose, broken, knowing that he had failed absolutely, both on a personal and a musical level. It was the bitterest of conclusions to a failed life, and my father proposed to lay the blame, at least for the awful way in which Adolf's life ended, on his firstborn daughter, his sometime helpmate, but latterly his insane avenging destroyer, Ada.

VI

But even while he wished to impugn his sister and to reveal Adolf as her victim, he also wanted to impugn his father.

One of his charges was that Adolf was mean. He looked after himself and his family, but he never bought my father a single article of clothing. Even when he made his first Holy Communion, he did so in a suit borrowed from his Aunt Bee rather than in a suit purchased specially for the occasion, which was the tradition. My father never forgave his father for that.

In later life, Adolf's meanness took the form of withholding praise. Adolf never mentioned that his son was a professional writer who published books to any of his musical associates, or anyone else for that matter, or so my father has it. What lay behind this was Adolf's failure to flourish musically. He had enough talent to be a very good orchestral musician, but he was not good enough to be a soloist. He resented this and felt that he deserved to be more than just an orchestral player, so when his son succeeded Adolf resented him because he had not enjoyed the same level of success, success commensurate with his talents, and that was why he never praised his son.

My father's other line of attack was to re-imagine his father's death as a futile event that sprung from hopelessness and weakness, and when he was working on his Autobiog he wrote up his account, which offered a completely different narrative to the facts as he knew them, several times. His version went as follows:

San Francisco, California, spring, 1963. Adolf buys three bottles of whiskey and smuggles these into the modest suburban house where he lives with Marianna. He hides these in readiness for what he has decided he would do.

Finally it comes, *the day he will do the deed*. Marianna announces that she has to go out. Will Adolf be all right? Yes, absolutely, he assures her. 'Go on, go on,' he says. She puts on her coat, she checks her handbag, she gives him a kiss. 'Go on, go on,' he repeats. She leaves.

Adolf hears the front door close. He does not move. He waits to allow a bit more time to pass so he can be sure, absolutely sure, that she will not return. He waits, perhaps for ten minutes, maybe longer. To be unmasked at this juncture would be a catastrophe.

Then, once he is sure, really sure, he gets the spirits from their hiding place. He opens the first bottle. He starts to drink, slowly, steadily, indefatigably....

And there the accounts all end. They were unfinished, but the meaning was obvious. Adolf's death was suicide catalysed by whiskey.

So why did my father write this version that so violated the fact that Adolf died in a hospital? The answer of course was that it was what he wanted to believe, and in human affairs, especially when there is bitterness and distrust and rage and grievance, wishes have a way of trumping facts.

His desire, bordering on the fanatical, to replace facts with poisonous fantasies was the mainspring of his Autobiog project.

VII

The Edna story, the most complex as well as the bitterest part of his tale, would be of all the episodes comprising his life the one where his version would most flagrantly trump the facts, and therefore was the part that was going to require the most reconfiguring.

They met post Leatrice. The dawn of their relationship was bliss. She reconnected him to his lost paradisiacal childhood. That was why he fell in love: it was what she gave him access to and what she helped him to recover that was what did it for him.

They married. He started a second family. It should have been enough. It was for him, but not for his young wife, at least as he saw it. She wanted to write, was desperate to write. He decided to help her 'by writing her books, but in such a way she will think at the end they are hers.'

I started with a little sketch of a plot for a light novella. Gave it to her to read. Pretended to put things into plot that she thought she had said. My ideas very soon became hers [...] I sketched out a rough first chapter [...] and started her off with a few pages in a very simple style. She got the style all right [...] I took this and typed it but in the process heavily corrected and rewrote what she had written. She retyped it – again and again – and in the process it came to be hers totally – which I had hoped would happen.

How did she then reward him? First she abandoned him, and then she poisoned the minds of their children so they opted to live with her and not with him:

She had made it plain to them on their frequent visits [to her house in Putney] that they would have freedom to stay up at night, miss school, neglect to wash themselves, and eat as [many] sugary cakes and [drink as many] fizzy drinks while goggling at TV as they wished.

The result of that, inevitably, was that:

They opted to live wholly with their mother at age 11-12, and have since then never shown any need or curiosity [to] spend any time with their one and only father.

And again:

Carlo and Sash – yes, Edna saw to it that I would see precious little of 'my sons' after the time she lured them away. ('Don't let father hear you laughing with me – he won't like that.') She saw to it by bending their very bendable peasant minds – sweets under the pillow at night when they were with her, etc. I had to do the necessary like making them go to school. And when they elected to go to her she instantly packed them off to a boarding school with money earned by the books I wrote for her! I shouldn't have been let out, as Tom O'Brien [the publisher] said.

The trouble with this was that he did not write my mother's books, and my brother and I weren't lured away: we wanted to leave. But these facts would not be allowed to intrude into his version because that would compromise his case.

VIII

His story had many elements, but one primary, overarching theme: the damage mothers and wives did to their sons by separating them from their fathers, of which there were many examples in his life. His mother made him her creature and turned him against Adolf. Leatrice literally stole his son then brainwashed him into thinking her fifth husband was his father. Finally, his second wife, Edna, seduced his sons, lied to them about his cruelty and bribed them, and that way she got them on her side. And there he had it, there was the pattern: his had been a life destroyed by finagling, malignant mothers and wives who had systematically destroyed all his relationships, including his relationship with his father and his relationships with his sons.

Oh what a terrible story, but it wasn't over yet. To round it off there was one final blow, or the last in a succession of blows, the icing on the cake. Jane, the woman on whom he had showered gold and treasure, showed herself not to be loving, kindly, amorous Jane, but avaricious, treacherous, scheming Jane when, without a word of warning, she ransacked their joint account and disappeared to England with his money. That was how he proposed to tell it, with a coda tacked on to the effect that she returned, love and amity triumphed, and then she died, the one true love of his life plucked by the cruel Gods from him forever. This part of the story could definitely go under the 'having your cake and eating it' heading, and of course it was only possible to sustain the conceit of Jane as both monster and love of his life because his mind could no longer see a contradiction between these two positions.

IX

So … you couldn't make it up, this story of his, and he hadn't either – or so he wanted readers to believe. This was it, the life of Ernest, the deceived but doughty victim of a succession of women: Rita, Ada, Leatrice, Edna, Jane, though at the very end she came right.

And what a story. What sweep. What power. And he knew it so well, this story. He had it there within his grasp. Of course he knew that his material, his Autobiog as it currently existed, had no shape. It was just hundreds of pages of notes and letters that had to be assembled and burnished and turned into the book he had worked out in his head. Only as he struggled to marshal his material he found that he couldn't arrange it: no matter how hard he tried, he just couldn't get it to coalesce because he had lost the ability to fashion it into a coherent entity. The thing that was happening in his head (named Alzheimer's), which had been one of the prompts that had had got him to start his Autobiog in the first place, was now preventing him from advancing and finishing it.

X

This was how I imagine it was during the time he was trying but failing to write his version, with all its deceits and feints, untruths and misdirections.

Every day he woke alone knowing that he wanted to write his Autobiog. He knew that in order to do this he would have to shape the material, changing this and suppressing that, and hey presto he would have the narrative that told the story he wanted the world to believe was the story of his life. He hadn't forgotten this.

So he would then go to his desk, and every time he did he was confronted by the evidence of continuing work, and once more he endeavoured to go forwards. But as he struggled to craft his material into the shape he wanted it to have, he discovered it had gone. He had lost it. He had lost that ability to bend words to his will, to make language sing as he wanted it to sing, so that it bore the burden he wanted it to bear and carried the message he wanted it to carry out into the world and into the minds of his readers. He knew that he had once had this talent: he knew that he had published novels and told stories. He had been a writer once, but that capacity had now perished.

What he couldn't remember, however, was that this experience of finding that he couldn't marshal his materials was one that he had struggled with the day before, and the day before that, and so on. In other words, he could no longer remember in the long term that he had lost the ability to control words, but had to endure the rediscovery of what was lost every working day anew.

And unfortunately, what he had not forgotten was that there was a book he must write. That impulse was still there, and the part of his brain that remembered facts and scraps of dialogue hadn't gone yet either. So in lieu of writing the book he wanted to write but couldn't, he found himself, as he sat at his desk, writing the things he was still able to write: things he remembered, fragments, bits of dialogue, notes, along with admonishments, research directives and other notes to self.

He would then leave his desk, and when he next returned to it to start anew the struggle to write this book, all he could manage was to scribble a few more notes and a few more admonishments. On and on it went, this cycle of failing and scribbling, scribbling and failing, throughout which he knew he had a story, as far as he was concerned an utterly plausible and necessary story, that he wanted and needed and yearned to put over, and he knew that he must convey this story before he died, but no matter how hard he struggled he could not accomplish the task. It was hellish.

XI

The atrophy of his brain was one long, unceasing, terrible process, and then something happened that impeded his access to the well where his memories, both real and imagined, were stored as narratives – narratives that made sense, at least to him. And once access was choked off, all those events about which he was once certain (and wrote about over and over during the course of his work on his Autobiog) were gone, or else were reduced to incomplete narrative slivers that no longer made sense.

He remembered, for example, from the dark days after Rita's death, the two detectives who came to Cabra Grove. He remembered ordering them out, but the rest was gone. He could not remember why they had come to the house. He could not remember Rita's death or the Coroner's Court. All such narrative details were gone, and all he had left, bright and clear before his mind's eye, were those two detectives in Cabra Grove. He knew that they must have come for some reason (his wits were still working to that extent), and so, since he couldn't remember, he now came up with an explanation that explained why two policemen might have come to Cabra Grove: 'Were we (me) members of an unauthorized party – meaning the IRA?'

And then, from being unable to remember what he once remembered, he started remembering what never happened. No doubt these fantasies were always there in his psyche, only when he was younger he was able ruthlessly to repress them. Now that his brain was fraying he couldn't control these materials, and so up they bubbled.

He remembered, for example, a dark summer's day sometime during his childhood. He was a boy. He was on the beach at Tramore facing the sea, Adolf was nearby, and he was playing melodies from *Tosca* on the clarinet. The music was soft and melancholy. As he listened he thought of his father as an exile estranged from the pre-war concert halls and opera houses of Europe, now trapped in careless Ireland and doing his best to rear his family and live without angering the acidic, aging woman that he had awakened one day, and to whom he found himself inexplicably married. This was an adult thought, but he imagined that the boy on the beach had thought it.

And then, thanks to the magic of imagination, he was sitting by his father, only now, he, my father, was an adult.

'When you play,' he asked, 'are you playing for yourself? Are you listening to what you play?'

'Yes, it's like someone else is playing for you,' said Adolf. Then he added: 'I'm sorry I didn't give it on to you. It was the worst thing I ever did in my life – not giving you music.'

'Oh, you did,' he replied. 'Listening to you as a child, you gave it to me all right.'

XII

Now that his mind was in full spate, the letters started to pour out of him. Some were partly addressed to his second wife, my mother and partly to himself.

My dear Edna – why have you not told me where you are staying in Dublin – so that I might ring you up if need be – ? You can have a room here.

Ask hotels = have you an Edna O'Brien staying?

Dear Edna – I could not imagine myself visiting London and not seeing you. Nor, as you did here – keeping your address while here secret.

And then there was this, one of dozens never sent.

20 November 1989

My dear Edna,
    […]
    Yes, as the time draws near I get more impatient to be with you.
    Anyhow, keep me informed as to how near or far we are from the happy day?
    Lovely soft autumn weather. Great drifts of leaves around the road gates – many quite big trees now in the front garden. Warm

rain now and then at night – and that delicious silence stretching across the bay to Howth.

After a few days in this lovely windy mild weather you should be able to settle down to arranging yourself and deciding – if you have nothing in hand, what you are going to work at on the blank page.

Remember, you're not leaving London forever – it's just a plane hop away. Think it would be best to meet you at Bus Aras, the Dublin Bus Terminus […] nearer place. Less confusing. Let me know flight and arrival time.

I am looking forward to taking you out and about this splendid coast […] Around Dalkey village is now one of the sought after places to live. Property prices are sky high.

Come on love, get a move on.
Ernie.

XIII

He had left the world he knew, and gone to an alternative world where everything that had gone wrong could now be put right.

68.

Decline

I

In Ackerley's *My Father and Myself*, one of the most searing passages concerns the documentary glories he squandered. Immediately after his father's death, and having discovered that his father had a second family, Ackerley visited his father's office to meet his father's unhelpful business partner, Arthur Stockley, who suggested that his father's desk and the trove of papers it doubtless contained, should be taken away and burnt without Ackerley *fils* even taking a look. Ackerley, who says of himself that his was the kind of pliant personality that blowhards like Stockley could always prevail upon, sanctioned this idiotic act of destruction. Naturally, as he ruefully adds, 'This was a decision I was to regret in later life more than anything else.'[19] At the very least, his decision made *My Father and Myself* much harder to write.

---

19 Ackerley, J. R., *My Father and Myself* (The New York Review of Books, 1999) p. 207. It was first published in Great Britain by The Bodley Head in 1968.

I, on the other hand, enjoyed the reverse of Ackerley's experience. I was the beneficiary of documentary plenitude. Now had Jane lived I doubt I'd have got anything, But despite being younger she predeceased him, which for me was incredibly fortuitous. Oh yes, I was so lucky.

II

In 1991, alone, forgetful, baffled, troubled and disorganized, my father tumbled at his home and cut his cheek on the corner of an electric fire. He was taken to hospital in Dun Laoghaire, where tests were run. A few days later I was summoned to this hospital, where I saw first a gerontologist, who told me that my father had Alzheimer's and would have to go into a nursing home, and second a social worker, who told me that I must clear his house of his effects so it could be sold to pay for his care. Then she said my father was a drain on the Irish state and the sooner that stopped the better. So I was left in doubt: what I had to do I had to do quickly.

III

A few days later, my wife, the children and I went to *Cnoc Aluin* to begin the clear-out. The house we entered was a dark cave of papery glories. My wife and I agreed that we would clear different rooms. I bagged his study, a small square room at the back with a high ceiling and a single casement window.

I went into this room. It was crammed with papers piled higgledy-piggledy on the shelves and in the open drawers of his desk and all over the floor. I looked about, and pretty quickly I located the red and blue desk diaries I remembered from my childhood. I was anxious to get hold of them. I flicked through a few. As I expected they were full of stuff about what I was doing during the early sixties when we lived together. This was calendrical gold.

I turned then to the papers piled around. The papers were of many kinds. There was typewriter paper. There were lined pages torn from school jotters. There were ancient bank statements. There were tea cartons that had been flattened out. There were brown paper bags that had been cut open. And then, scrawled all over these different papers, mostly in Biro, sometimes in pencil, occasionally in ink, were words. I knew them to be his words because they were in his characteristic spiky handwriting, his scrawl seeming to mirror his angry, pugnacious temperament, which I recognized, or to be more accurate, which I knew from childhood and had never forgotten. I assumed that these were notes he had drafted when writing his books and plays and letters. I was right, partially. A lot were, but not all – there was also something else here that until this moment I'd never known existed, and it ran to hundreds of pages. The pages were stuffed inside two bulging lever arch files and three document folders, and together all these pages comprised the notes he had written towards what he called his Autobiog, the book that he hoped would crown his literary life, and from the dates scribbled on the pages I could tell that he had been working on these notes for the last few years, right up until his fall.

My heart soared. Here, I imagined, was an intimate account, by a man with whom I had almost no relationship, of the life he lived, which was a life about which I knew almost nothing, but wanted to know everything.

I turned a few pages. My heart sank. Very quickly I could see that this material was exactly what I imagined someone assailed by Alzheimer's would produce. It was prolix, confused, wayward, repetitive and contradictory. And it was just bits, short notes, odd lines of dialogue, fragments of memory, scraps of story, a whole lifetime's experience jumbled up over hundreds of pages. One of the document folders had 'Out of Order' painted on the front, and that was exactly how and what the material was. It was out of order.

I threw everything unsorted into trunks, and I brought it north, to Enniskillen, where I lived, and I stored it away.

69.

My Diary

I

Monday 25 September 1995.

A taxi came to collect me very early to take me to the bus station in Enniskillen. Jack (eight years old) was up when I was leaving the house, and instead of waving from the window like he usually does he came out and gave me a kiss and closed the taxi door. He was not a child at that moment, but older than his years and solicitous.

As I drove away down the lane I looked out at the wet, rolling landscape and I was filled by this extraordinary certainty about my father. He did not love me, I thought, and this was a complete and distinct thought. It was also unemotional, and I did not find it troubling. It was just a frank admission to myself of something. He didn't love me: there it was, and I could see it and accept it. It was like the moment in *The Secret Orchard of Roger Ackerley* where the narrator, Diana Petre, is on the bus travelling around Hyde Park Corner and suddenly she realizes that her depression is lifting and that the crippling neurotic pain that has afflicted her all her life is finally on its way out. My experience in the taxi was a moment of simplicity and certainty and completion. I saw, I really *saw*, and I accepted.

I wonder now, as I write, why this came when it did. Perhaps it was my son Jack's autonomous demonstration of affection that produced the conditions that not only allowed me to see what I saw, but to accept it.

II

Monday 20 November 1995.

Train to Dublin and out to Killiney to the Grove Nursing Home. My father was in his new bedroom – it was downstairs – one sock on, one sock off, wearing a stained pair of grey tracksuit bottoms and a dirty jumper.

'Put your sock and shoes on, Ernie,' the care assistant said, and as she dressed him she said: 'Will you get him some new trainers or runners like these? Any kind will do, just so long as we can wash 'em.'

'Does he soil them?' I asked.

'Oh yes, he's got no control any more. He wears a pad now.' She then added, cheerfully, 'Don't you, Ernie?' as if she were addressing a child.

The shoes and sock on, she led him along the corridor towards the sitting room. He was bent over and moved like someone about to break in two.

'Will you stand up straight, Ernie, stand up?' she urged him, but he wouldn't.

'It's all show,' she said, 'he can walk perfectly normally, you know.'

She brought tea – he got a beaker and I got a cup – and we had the usual halting conversation that we always have (tedious, infuriating, mind-numbing).

'Do you know who I am?'
'No.'

'I'm Carlo.'

'Oh yes.'

'Do you know who I am?'

'I can't quite put a name to you.'

'I'm your son.'

'Really?'

'You've got three sons. You've got me and you've got Sasha and you've got your American son by Leatrice, and you've got four grandchildren in Enniskillen – India and Jack and Finn and Georgia. Do you remember that?'

'No.'

'Do you remember Adolf?'

'Who?'

'Your father, Adolf?'

'No, Adolf definitely wasn't my father. He's gone away.'

When I asked him if he wanted anything he stared out at Bray Head and finally said, very slowly, 'Yes, I need some horse manure,' and he pointed at the garden of the nursing home, which stretched beyond the window.

III

Thursday 21 March 1996.

I drove to Dublin with Jack and Finn. We meet John, my half-brother, at the Killiney Dart station. (John, as he now is known, my father's son by Leatrice, having discovered who his father is, has left California and moved to Ireland so he can be with him). We bought sandwiches and ate them sitting on a miserable patch of grass overlooking what I thought was Killiney Strand. There was a big notice that said 'No dogs', and everywhere people were walking their dogs.

After we finished our food we went up to the nursing home. In the front hall I noticed that the stuffed fox in the glass display case had big black stitches on the shoulder that faced outwards. What was the taxidermist thinking? I wondered. Then I noticed the smell, a mix of fish fingers and pee. The residents ate a lot of fish (whenever I visited, that's what they were usually eating), and they peed a lot, so that explained that, I thought.

My father was in the day room, bespectacled. His grey hair stuck up like the bristles of a toothbrush. He reminded me of a bald child.

'Look, he's got my glasses,' said John, pointing to the spectacles, which I now recognized were once his spectacles.

John explained: 'Last time I was here Ernie's eyes were red from rubbing because he couldn't see, so I gave him my glasses and the red went almost straight away.'

I noticed that John had written my father's name on a piece of paper and stuck it with Sellotape to the frame.

John sat beside him, where he could touch him. I sat opposite my father, where I could see him and he could see me. Every time my father looked at me and I looked back, I saw anger, hatred, resentment, him for me: and he saw my feelings of antagonism, I suspected. Or perhaps this was all my imagination.

Whatever the case, as this conflict (as in an Ingmar Bergman film) between a senile old man and his son was conducted entirely in stares, my half-brother clowned with him, offered to shadow-box, and produced bananas, oranges and monkey nuts from his knapsack, all of which my father wolfed down. John said that he thought he was thin and that the nursing home wasn't feeding him. (He never passes over an opportunity to criticize the home.) I explained that our father was always thin.

John produced an envelope and wrote our two names and tried to get my father's reactions to the names. Then John described himself to my father as the idiot son from America. I was the clever one, he said, the writer. When he had seen my father earlier in the year, John said to me, and had written out his name, John, just like now, my father had spoken of having had an early son called John. Alas (for him), today's repeat of the exercise with the names produced nothing so startling. My father simply looked at the envelope with our names written on it, and then pronounced the names, although it was impossible to tell whether from memory or because he was reading them. There certainly didn't seem to be any recognition. Not a flicker.

Jack and Finn (yes, Jack and Finn had been sitting watching the whole time) now got their grandfather to write his own name by guiding his hand. He was patient and unselfconscious as only children can be.

We manoeuvred my father into the car for a drive.

'Look at how he listens to the engine,' said John as we drove off. We took him to see his old house, *Cnoc Aluin*, but he seemed not to notice where he was.

'Last time I brought him here,' said John, 'he said, "Are we going in?" '

We stopped on Vico Road and picked blackberries with the trains rumbling along the coast below. Jack and Finn put berries into their grandfather's crooked hand. My father ate a couple and made a face.

'Not sweet enough,' said John.

'All his life he was an implacable enemy of white sugar,' I said, 'and now, in old age, he only wants sweet things.'

Back in the home the sitting room was full, but a woman saw us looking for a table, stood up and waved us over.

'I'm trying to escape from that horrible film about the *Titanic* that's on next door,' she said. 'Have my table.'

She went, we sat, and in the next room I could indeed hear the film.

As we had tea John smiled at my father as he talked away to me. Every now and again he wiped the drool away from my father's mouth. John was tender and delicate with his father, for as far as he, John, was concerned, here was a sweet old man whom he could love, and who probably would have loved him, John, if Leatrice hadn't cruelly separated them. That's what he believed, and I wasn't going to disabuse him.

Sunk in the chair opposite my father, I was guarded, careful, suspicious. I couldn't be light or happy or affectionate. I could not be loving. I could not be forgiving. Unlike John, all I saw was the man – or the remnants of the man – who presided over an unhappy childhood throughout which I was controlled and restricted, endlessly criticized and denigrated for being the imbecile offspring of my mother.

As I sat there, an appalling thought then struck me. When I was a child I was closed off and had no capacity for spontaneous joy. That came from my father. He'd moulded me into that cussed thing. Then I grew up. I had been able to elude my nature, but I had never been able to outrun my nature. It had always been there, behind me or inside me, and now, because of being a writer and working alone, these characteristics were in the ascendant, and there was now the danger that I would become my father's creature completely as I grow older. All the psychoanalysis in the world could not change the basic life experience that made me what I was. All it did or would do was lay bare the workings of my mind. Understanding changed nothing.

When I saw this, I saw why I had so not wanted to come today (which I hadn't). It was because I knew that I would have these thoughts and I did not want to run into them. Yet nothing is ever exactly as one fears it is going to be. Yes, the visit had filled me with fears – basically that I was going to become like my father, and I was right to anticipate that this would happen, and indeed it did. Yet when the time came to leave, which I had not anticipated, I was flushed with pride at my own two sons' impeccable behaviour. They had turned out to be such thoughtful, delicate, kind children.

We drove home, northwards. John was with us. He was coming up for the weekend. John said, 'You know, I've seen what a grump Ernie could be. He just looks at me sometimes and I see this grumpy old guy who doesn't like noisy children and who just wants quiet.'

IV

Friday 18 November 1996.

John was with us, again, in Enniskillen. We had been combing through some of the papers I brought up from Dublin when I cleared my father's house.

There had always been the tiny hope in my heart that my father would make his will out in favour of my brother and me, thereby giving us, me, the assurance that in some way he liked us, or at least wanted to do the normal thing, wanted to pass on what he had to his children. If this wasn't going to happen, then my hope was that he would make out no will, dying intestate. That wouldn't be as good as a will made out in our favour, but it wouldn't be as bad as a will made out in someone else's favour. If he died intestate, I could always (my thinking went) console myself with the belief that he didn't hate us enough to make it out in someone else's favour at least.

However, it turned out that his wish (whether he had effected it or not I didn't know) was to make his will out in someone else's favour and supply us with a letter explaining why we were getting nothing.

I know this for sure because in the course of going through some of the papers John turned up an envelope on which my father had written a note to remind himself (this was just after Jane's death) to change the will (he was leaving everything to Isolde) and to include a letter for the boys (Sasha and me) to explain why we were getting nothing.

Despite my hopes, I had also always known that he would disinherit us. However, I had managed to stop myself knowing that I knew this, until this moment with the envelope with the message on the back, which John found, which I had never seen before.

V

Saturday 19 November 1996.

I woke up feeling wretched and I stayed feeling wretched all day, and I found it very hard to write. I made myself write – I can always do that – but it wasn't very good. And the source of that wretchedness was that the very last little bit of hope that I had always had about inheriting had been taken away by that miserable message on the back of that miserable envelope. I'd always known, but now I really knew with a vengeance, he didn't love, he wouldn't love, he'd never loved me.

VI

Monday 18 November 1997.

Tyga woke up as I came to bed to tell me that the Grove Nursing Home had been on the phone to say that my father was in hospital.

VII

Tuesday 19 November 1997.

I rang the hospital in Loughlinstown. My father was ill, a bit disorientated. I received the news with a curious feeling of detachment.

VIII

Saturday 24 January 1998.

Fiona, a nurse at the Grove Nursing Home, rang to say that my father was dying. John and Isolde (my cousin Louise's daughter) had both been told this on Friday, but amazingly had not telephoned me, although they had both told Fiona that they would. Isolde may not have wanted to talk to me because she challenged my application to make my father a ward of the court. In the case of John, I presumed he didn't call because he wanted to have an exclusive relationship with Ernie. He wanted to be the good son to the man who had lately been revealed as his real father, and he justified his actions by telling himself that Sash and I had such a bad relationship with Ernie we wouldn't be able to care for him as John did, or wouldn't want to care for him as John did, or something. As John saw it there was bad blood between us and our father, whereas he was free from rancour. I was furious: our relationship was none of his business. Later, of course, I was struck by the strangeness of my reaction: why such proprietorial feelings about a man with whom I'd had such a calamitous relationship? Strange. But I did, and there it was.

Sasha was in Donegal sorting the planning permission for my mother's house. (Typically, he can't see the Planning Officer, as Mrs Planning Officer had just had a baby and therefore no planning decisions were being made in Donegal.)

Sash came with his new girlfriend, a Filipina girl, Joyce, an IT student. Joyce was sweet, but terribly young and shy.

IX

Sunday 25 January 1998.

Drove to Dublin in convoy with Sasha and Joyce. I had India and Georgia with me. In the Grove Nursing Home we found Ernie asleep in his bedroom, snuffling under the covers, flannel pyjamas, hand outstretched, fingers curled, head bald, hair short and sticking up, also strange marks on the pate, like stretch marks on a woman's belly. I wondered if these were made by forceps at his birth.

'Grandpa's sleeping, don't wake him,' Georgia whispered.

Sasha suggested a photograph. Georgia immediately puts herself beside the sleeping figure and adopted her winning 'photograph' smile.

'Hold Ernie's hand,' said my brother, and she reached shyly forward and took hold of one of the fingers of Ernie's outstretched hand.

At this moment India spotted the huge incontinence nappies (a particularly awful shade of fern green) and the industrial tubs of Sudocrem on the bedside locker.

'What are these?' she asked, and when I explained she looked disgusted and began to cry and ran from the room.

'This is probably the last time we'll see him alive,' said my brother.

Later, in the car park outside the Grove, the subject of Ernie's funeral and John comes up. I told Sasha that I had instructed the Grove that I must be the first to be telephoned in the event of Ernie's death and that I would make the funeral arrangements.

'John will want to do it,' I said, 'because he believes we don't love Ernie, and won't do it properly, whereas he loves Ernie and therefore will do it better.'

'What does he know about us and Ernie?' asked my brother.

'He thinks we don't love him.'

'We never had a relationship with the man, what is he talking about?'

X

Monday 26 January 1998.

At Laura's (her childminder's), Georgia announced that she needed a dress to wear when she went to see her mother, Tyga, in the hospital after Tyga had her Caesarean section. I rushed home, got a selection of dresses and dropped these back to Laura's. Then I went to the hospital where Tyga, pregnant with our fifth child, was about to have a Caesarean. I found her in her room.

'They've made me take off my nail varnish,' she said. (She'd painted her nails the previous day, 'ready' for surgery.)

She gave me all her jewellery. That had to come off too. She was wheeled off to a different room. I followed. I gave her Jack's Discman. Several nurses came to check Tyga's details (name, et cetera).

Just before two, we wheeled Tyga in her bed towards surgery. Tyga listened to Victoria de los Ángeles on the Discman. Her face was very pale and small, and I felt extremely anxious.

I followed the bed with Tyga lying in it through the swing doors and into the vestibule of the operating theatre. I watched a nurse pull on a pair of disposable pampooties, shoes made of untanned folded cowhide. Someone carried a chair into the corridor so I could sit outside the swing doors and wait. I kissed Tyga goodbye. She vanished.

I sat on the chair for a bit, then I had to leave. I went outside the hospital and had a cigarette. The day was grey and cold. It was winter, not spring. I stared at the yellow straw-coloured reeds sticking up out of the sluggish, dark waters of the River Erne.

I went back in and sat in my chair in the corridor. I read the *Guardian*. Several articles on Monica Lewinsky's alleged affair with Bill Clinton. Tensions between Israelis and Palestinians and Saddam's refusal to allow UN weapons inspectors in to his presidential palaces were as nothing compared to the fact that the president ejaculated in an intern's mouth. What sort of a world was this?

A black nurse with a beautiful smile came out and said, 'It's a beautiful boy.'

The midwife followed with a black-haired boy, his skin covered with waxy vernix.

We all went to the recovery room. The midwife weighed him, (eight pounds three ounces) and measured him (fifty centimetres), then I held him in my arms. *Blankety Blank* on the television. He wanted to open his eyes. This was hard; the lids were stuck with vernix. Eventually he got one lid up and then the other. The pupils were very black. He stared at the world, and I wondered what he was seeing.

Tyga was wheeled in, groggy, and even smaller (it seemed to me) than when she was wheeled into the theatre.

The baby (no name yet – Euan? Erskine? Cameron?) made a noise. (He'd been agitating for a feed for some time.) Tyga woke up at once.

'I want to see him,' she said, but she couldn't sit up to do this. She was in a lot of pain.

The midwife put the baby on her breast. He found a brown nipple – it was as big as a thimble – and began to feed.

Time drifted slowly. India came with white tulips, a hat for the newborn and a Milkybar for Georgia. Tyga was hurting but happy. I went to fetch Georgia just before five. She hid from me in the corner of the childminder's house. She had on her blue dress and her patent black shoes. I took her to the hospital. She insisted on being photographed with her new brother. Our friend Maeve brought the boys, Jack and Finn. We left at seven. We got home. The phone rang. India answered.

'It's the Grove, Dad,' said India with a long face. 'I think, probably …'. I took the phone.

'This is the duty nurse from the Grove Nursing Home, and I'm sorry to have to tell you that Ernest died at 7.40 p.m.'

It was entirely expected, and so entirely unshocking. But of course the baby's birthday and Ernie's death would forever be entwined.

My brother was upset and tearful, I thought, when he spoke a few minutes later. He had no one, no family, no wife. He was alone. Ernie's death would hit him harder.

The woman from the Grove said that she would ring me at 9.30 to know what arrangements I had made regarding the funeral. After dinner I got on the phone. I got through to Kirwan's, the undertakers (recommended by my Dublin friend Greg).

'I want the cheapest coffin,' I said.

The man at the other end took a deep breath. 'A chipboard veneered coffin is 350,' he said.

As he ran through the costs, urn, removal of remains, embalming, etc., I felt strangely blithe and pragmatic.

70.

A Resolution

I

After my father's cremation, all the mourners went to the Shelbourne Hotel. Our table was covered with a starched white cloth. The cutlery was solid and heavy. The plates and glasses were bright and gleaming. After the funeral it was salutary to be with these objects. Food was now eaten. Wine was drunk. My wife, Tyga, and my brother, Sasha, talked. The subject was my father and the subjectivity of one's memories. My memories of my father were threadbare and mostly miserable; my brother's were not. But that was so often the way, wasn't it, my wife said. One child could be happy while another was unhappy, though they lived in the same house at the same time with the same people. She didn't add that this was what makes the whole business of family truth so slippery, but the implication was there in her words.

II

My father now dead and our life together more vivid in my mind than ever precisely because *he had died*, I decided, because I finally felt free, to put into practice what I'd always had at the back of my mind to do, which was to write a book about him and me, a book that would tell our story. Inevitably, Ackerley's book *My Father and Myself* having remained with me, the first thing I did in order to prepare for the task was to reread it.

As a model, it wasn't useful. Ackerley's chronology was explicitly wayward ('I have disregarded chronology and adopted the method of ploughing to and fro over my father's life and my own,'[20] as he put it in the foreword), whereas I knew instinctively that what I was going to write would have to have everything in the exact order in which it happened.

However, as a warning against my tendency to over-describe and overcomplicate, and as a reminder that I must stick to the point and just tell the truth, Ackerley's memoir was nothing short of inspirational. Here was a text to catalyse writing that is as plain and simple as a shaker chair.

III

I got out the trunks containing all the papery materials I had brought up from Dublin and I disinterred everything. I separated out the desk diaries, the photographs and the letters, and then I turned to his Autobiog notes. I had only looked at them cursorily when I was clearing his house, but I now spent a few hours leafing through them. It was a desolating experience.

An autobiography is the creation of a mind remembering, but my father's material was the creation of a mind that, as it was writing and as time ran forwards, was gradually forgetting not only the subject, the story of his past, but also his present, his writing down the story of his past. This meant that when he returned to his pages he had often forgotten what he had written, and so he would write it again, or he

---

20 *Ibid*, Foreword by J. R. Ackerley, p. 9.

would look at what he had written and feel confused because what once made sense no longer did. Of course he knew that his mind was not functioning as it had once functioned, but he didn't know what was happening. So he was left with just his panic (he knew he was losing his grip) and a sickening apprehension of an atomizing but unnamed catastrophe gradually closing in and closing him down. All he could do in the face of the impending catastrophe was struggle. And he struggled. Indefatigably. Ceaselessly. The signs of that struggle were in the margins of his notes and on paper scraps interleaved between his pages, and they were often written in red Biro, the innumerable notes to himself that he penned. Sometimes these expressed straightforward doubt and uncertainty: 'Did this happen?' was a note that appeared regularly. And sometimes what he wrote were reminders to remind himself to find out things he knew he once knew but now no longer remembered:

Is Rudy dead? Find out.

Write Mike (J. P.) Donleavy for dates […] right from Trinity days. Do it now — don't forget.

When did I meet Edna? Find out?

As far as I could tell from my survey of his pages, he never acted on the notes he wrote. Well, of course not. How could he when he couldn't remember writing these reminders?

After a few hours, I made a decision. These autobiographical notes were too hard to decipher and too truculent to work with. They would not help me with the book I wanted to write. I would eschew them. The desk diaries, on the other hand, were lovely and clear, and they told me where I was when I was a child on a day-by-day, week-by-week, month-by-month and year-by-year basis, and they were all I needed, along with some letters and photographs and some documents (birth certificates, passports) to write my book.

IV

Father & I, that book about us, was published in 2000. I was forty-six. Mortal thoughts had never bothered me before, but after that book was done there crept up on me the thought, catalysed by the book I believe, that I'd passed the halfway mark. I'd lived more years than I'd years left to live. I was going to die. This isn't to say that I hadn't known about mortality before; I had. But when I was young I'd believed I'd plenty of time, so I'd dodged the issue, but now I was two-thirds or so done, and I knew it. I couldn't dodge the fact any longer.

That in turn got me thinking about what I never thought I'd think about again: it made me think about him. I might have explored the life I lived with him, but he had had a whole other life – the life he lived outside my experience. When I was writing *Father & I*, with its obsessive focus on my own preoccupations, I'd paid his life, the one he lived outside me, scant attention. All I cared about was our narrative, and that's what got the lion's share of the words. It now occurred to me that I was not yet finished with us, but I didn't follow the thought through; I didn't act on it.

V

Time passed. One evening, I found myself in the bar of the Shelbourne Hotel talking to the writer Anthony Cronin about literary Dublin after the war, and my father, whom he knew.

'Your father was an ambitious man,' Tony said, 'a very ambitious man, in those days possibly Dublin's *most* ambitious man of letters.'

This was news to me. I'd never heard this said of him, and it was a shock, a genuine shock to hear what I had never heard said before.

Later, turning the conversation over in my mind, I realized that this was precisely the sort of information that I was bound not to know because of how I'd set about *Father & I,* and then, immediately following on from this, I was gripped by the conviction (most unexpected, this) that I should make amends and get that unknown narrative into print. Partly it was the child in me who felt that here was something I could and should do for a parent, even though our relationship had been a catastrophe. Perhaps I wanted to balance *Father & I*, or at least to enrich the portrait, add more detail and so on. Partly it was the writer in me, who felt that not only was there a story to tell, but the means were to hand just waiting to be used, and they were fabulous. Oh yes, all those Autobiog papers that I hadn't used, what a rich seam for biographical excavation they were. All I had to do was knuckle down and read them properly.

I started. The deficiencies in orthography combined with the confused and wayward nature of the material (the chronology was askew, it was contradictory, and there were huge lacunas) made them exceptionally difficult to absorb. I could only manage a few pages and then I had to stop, irritated and befuddled. A month later I tried again. Same story. I set them aside. More time passed. I decided I would have another go, but it led only to more irritation and befuddlement, and I gave up again. More time passed. I had another try. I failed once more. I shilly-shallied like this for years actually. I just couldn't get through them. Then it occurred to me – and why it took me so long to think this I have no idea – that the thing to do was to have it all typed up. Yes, it would be horrible to do, but once done at least the words would be clear, and there would only be the insanity of the sequencing to struggle with, and I would have a better chance of getting through and making sense of what he wrote.

A start on the typing was made. The process was long and fiendish, owing to the illegibility of his handwriting, his wayward grammar, and the difficult-to-decipher proper nouns and the contradictory dates. Also, as the material was out of order, completely out of order, the 'one thing leading to the next' impetus that carries one forward when typing wasn't there to carry one along, so it took months to type up and it was hard work, but then it was done. It amounted to over a 123,000 words.

And it was worth it. In typescript the material was readable – confusing, yes, but readable. And I read it. The reading experience produced a mix of elation and despair.

The elation was provoked by the biographical and narrative content, the descriptions of things he did and that happened, the stuff of his story. Of course I already had a rudimentary idea of the shape of his life when I began, but what I found on his pages was nearly all new to me. This was mostly stuff I didn't know before, and by the time I finished reading I felt like an archaeologist who, on finally getting around to the site he had always known about but had never properly explored (this was the site at the bottom of his garden so to speak), turned up an even greater hoard of treasure than he had expected.

The despair was provoked by the editorializing material, the passages heavy with opinion and malice, the heavy-handed sections where he deliberately sought to impugn and besmirch those he disliked. The list of targets was long, and included his parents, all his sisters with the exception of the youngest, Irene, all the women with whom he had relationships (the only exception was his first love, Sally Travers), his sons (my brother and me), plus numerous editors, publishers, critics, fellow writers and many others encountered on the journey through life.

The balance between the two types of material was probably 75 to 25 per cent: 75 per cent narrative, rich, specific and interesting, to 25 per cent vitriol. I was relieved by these proportions. There was deep and worthwhile material here, and augmented with letters and photographs and all the other materials I had, plus what I knew, the riches of family lore, I could make a book that did the reverse of *Father & I*, giving, rather than our story, his.

VI

But then the doubts came: The details seemed to fit with what I knew, but since I knew so very little about his life, having had no real relationship with him, how could I be sure? It could all be nonsense or invented, and my ignorance made judgement very difficult. Also, I could not discount the possibility that I found his 'facts' so persuasive because I *wanted* to believe them. They filled a story-shaped gap in my knowledge, offering me a complete narrative that I had never had before, and I relished them, perhaps to the point of being blind to their deficiencies.

There was only way to sort this out, and that was to run a sort of simple truth test. I would take a bit of his text with lots of detail, compare it with the reality, and see if they matched, or not.

Topography, it occurred to me, might serve my purpose nicely. I could take his description of a place, I thought, and then go to that place and compare what he had written with the place as it now was, and providing the place had not changed much I would be able to test how accurate his account was. And I thought I might know just the place – Jimmy O'Grady's cottage at Ballybrew, where Rudy and Bunny and their children spent their summers and where my father stayed many times during the forties.

VII

I tracked down Rudy's son, Karl, and telephoned him. He confirmed that yes, his parents did rent a labourer's cottage from Jimmy O'Grady in the townland of Ballybrew during the 1940s (the cottage was in the Wicklow mountains above Enniskerry), and yes, Jimmy O'Grady stayed in the cottage with them when they were there (he slept on a settle bed in the vestibule), and yes, though he was a young child, he remembered my father being a frequent visitor.

Karl told me how to find the cottage at Ballybrew. I was to go to a pub above Enniskerry, proceed down Military Road, also known as the Devil's Elbow, cross the Cookstown River and, hey presto, the Ballybrew cottage would appear on my left below the level of the road.

VIII

It was early August, rain and sun, clouds and silvered puddles: an Irish summer's day, muggy and intoxicating. My friends Philip and Laura drove me up into the Wicklow Mountains. We found the Devil's Elbow easily enough and set off along it. It wound fiendishly. We drove for ages, or what seemed like ages. We ought to be at the Cookstown River by now, we all agreed – had we missed it? Was this the wrong road? We agreed that we would have to ask someone. The decision was no sooner made than we came on a man at the side of the road pinning a piece of wayward barbed wire to a telegraph pole.

'I'll ask him,' I said.

We stopped. I got out and went up to the man. The usual courtesies were exchanged, then I explained that I was trying to find a cottage in somewhere called Ballybrew, which was once owned by someone called Jimmy O'Grady but was rented by a family called Jones, and that my father often stayed there in the 1940s. 'He wrote a lot about it,' I explained, 'and I'm curious to see how accurate he was.'

'Oh,' the man said, 'well, that's my house.'

I couldn't have stumbled on my quest this easily, I thought. 'Really?'

'Oh yes,' he said, 'I live in Jimmy O'Grady's cottage now,' and he confirmed that indeed it stood in the townland of Ballybrew. 'I'll bring you down when I'm done here.'

The man finished and got into his car. We followed him down the road. It twisted and turned, and then it crossed a bridge over what I assumed was the Cookstown River, and then, on the left, I saw the roof of a building that stood well below the level of the road. Our guide parked, and we followed suit. We all clambered out, slipped through a gate, descended a precipitous path and reached our destination.

'It's been modernized and extended,' said our host, pointing at his house, 'but you can still see the original cottage, Jimmy O'Grady's cottage as it's known.'

And one could, for there in the building's centre, tucked between the various additions added in the late twentieth century, I could see a classic Irish three-roomed cottage, Jimmy O'Grady's cottage.

'Come in,' said our host. We followed him in. He showed us around the cottage part. Despite small changes, the internal space was still recognizable as being the same space my father described with its kitchen, two bedrooms, and vestibule, where Jimmy O'Grady slept.

I was impressed, but I had a question, the answering of which, I believed, would help me the most. In his 1979 diary on 7 November under the heading 'Jimmy O'Grady's cottage at Ballybrew' there was a tantalizing reference to a sloping one-acre field that Jimmy O'Grady's forebears had 'laboriously made on the hillside' by the cottage, clearing the stones and adding materials that rotted into earth, and how then, one spring:

The whole sloping acre of O'Grady's field, the top surface of it for a foot deep, down to the marl & stones, the bare underneath, disappeared into the river below.

It was quite a sight, and could be seen from two miles away, the acre of yellow crumbling marl sloping down to the river that had once been a field. I reprised my father's account and asked our host if he had ever heard this story. 'Oh yes,' he said. It was before his day, back in the forties probably, but yes, he had. He led us back outside and brought us over to a fence at the side of his garden. 'That's where the field was I'd say.'

On the other side I saw an enormous hole, which might have been made by a mythical giant who had scooped the earth away with his vast hands. It was an inverted bell, steeply sided, about fifty feet deep and sixty feet wide. The floor was littered with debris and criss-crossed by dry water channels that our host assured us would be full of fast-flowing water once the winter rains began.

'All the fields around here,' said our host, 'have springs and water channels deep under the surface.' He indicated other small fields. 'You can hear them sometimes.' He pointed at the inverted bell, 'The field that was once here was no different: it also had a spring, or springs more likely, underneath.'

He then explained how over decades, or even centuries, the underground waters ate the soil away and carried it into the Cookstown River as sediment. A vast cavern was gradually hollowed out underneath the crust of topsoil. One day, the eggshell of topsoil, made heavy by torrential rain and, unable to support its own weight, collapsed with a thunderous roar, disappeared into the river and left behind the hole into which I was staring.

I did a little tally in my head. The proper nouns in my father's notes: Ballybrew and Jimmy O'Grady, were correct. His account of the cottage layout was correct, and so, it transpired, was the story of the vanishing field, sort of. Yes, he omitted to mention that the collapse was caused by underground waterways eating the ground away, but perhaps he never knew about the underground springs to begin with, or had forgotten by the time he made his note about the field that vanished in 1979. His account didn't really communicate how epic the collapse was and how big a hole was left behind; he only said that it was a foot of soil that slipped away. But he was right in storytelling terms: the field did disappear into the river and it did get carried away, and for me that was good enough. Judging by what I had discovered at the cottage, my doubts about the material could be discounted. His 'facts', I decided, were probably true.

After the field trip I went home and looked back over the Autobiog material once again, as well as his diaries. I could see even more clearly how rich in incident and fact the material was: oh yes, there was the story of a life in here.

I now asked myself if the material, as currently constituted, with all the grammatical wrinkles ironed out and with everything rearranged into the right order, but left as it was in my father's voice, could work as a published text. I decided that the answer to this question was no. To make that work I would have to write a lot of extra words providing context and background. In other words, I would have to pass myself off as him. Whether I could do this I didn't know, but more importantly I felt sure that such a text would unsettle readers. They wouldn't know which words were his and which were mine. They wouldn't know where he ended and where I began. It would be confusing. It could even seem dishonest.

In which case, if I wanted to make something out of this, I thought, I would do the following. I would treat it as raw data, like an interview for instance, and I would comb the material through, identify the best facts, lift these out and organize them into something chronologically coherent. I would then augment what I had with passages of context and background, drawn from my store of family lore. Would I get things wrong? Of course. But this would not be because I wanted to. My ambition would be to make something true to the spirit of the raw material. I would not set out to distort or alter for my own purposes. But I am fallible. There was always a chance I would get things wrong. The great virtue of doing it this way was that the nature of the artefact would be clear to the reader at all times. The facts might be his, but the artefact was mine. This was very much a version, my version.

So, I had a plan. I went to the desk. I opened a file on my computer. I was ready to go. I began to type.

Acknowledgements

I would like to thank my daughter, Georgia Gébler, for transcribing the chaotic materials on which this book is based; Teresa Maginess and the members of the 'Journeys around Memory' seminar at Queen's University, Belfast who prompted the creation of the first draft from which the text emerged; the Arts Council of Northern Ireland for their financial support; Stephanie Calman for both the title and the idea that a book such as this could be written; Gerald Dawe, my first reader; Anne Fogarty, Éilís Ní Dhuibhne and Eibhear Walshe, the editors of *Imagination in the Classroom* (Four Courts Press, Dublin, 2013) for permission to use part of my essay, 'The Helmet that Never Was'; and finally, I thank the following people for providing information: Dermot Bolger, John Bowman, Anthony Dack, Roger Doyle, Jason Hartcup, Emer O'Kelly, Helen Quinn, Marian Richardson, Karl Ross, Philip St John, Richard Pine and Shaun Whiteside. All mistakes are my own.

– Carlo Gébler